I0729636

Guy Tal

The Interior Landscape
The Landscape on Both Sides of the Camera

Reflections on Art, Creativity, Expression,
and a Life in Photography

rockynook

The Interior Landscape
Guy Tal (guytal.com)

Editor: Jocelyn Howell
Project manager: Lisa Brazieal
Marketing coordinator: Katie Walker
Layout and type: Hespenheide Design
Front cover design: Gary Hespenheide
Cover production: Hespenheide Design

ISBN: 978-1-68198-891-7
(1st printing, December 2022)
© 2023 Guy Tal

Rocky Nook Inc.
1010 B Street, Suite 350
San Rafael, CA 94901
USA

Distributed in the UK and Europe by Publishers Group UK
Distributed in the U.S. and all other territories by Ingram Publisher Services

Library of Congress Control Number: 2022941804

This book is printed on acid-free paper.

Printed in Korea

The few photographs I'm try-

ing to make show my interior

against the landscape I'm in.

—Robert Frank

Table of Contents

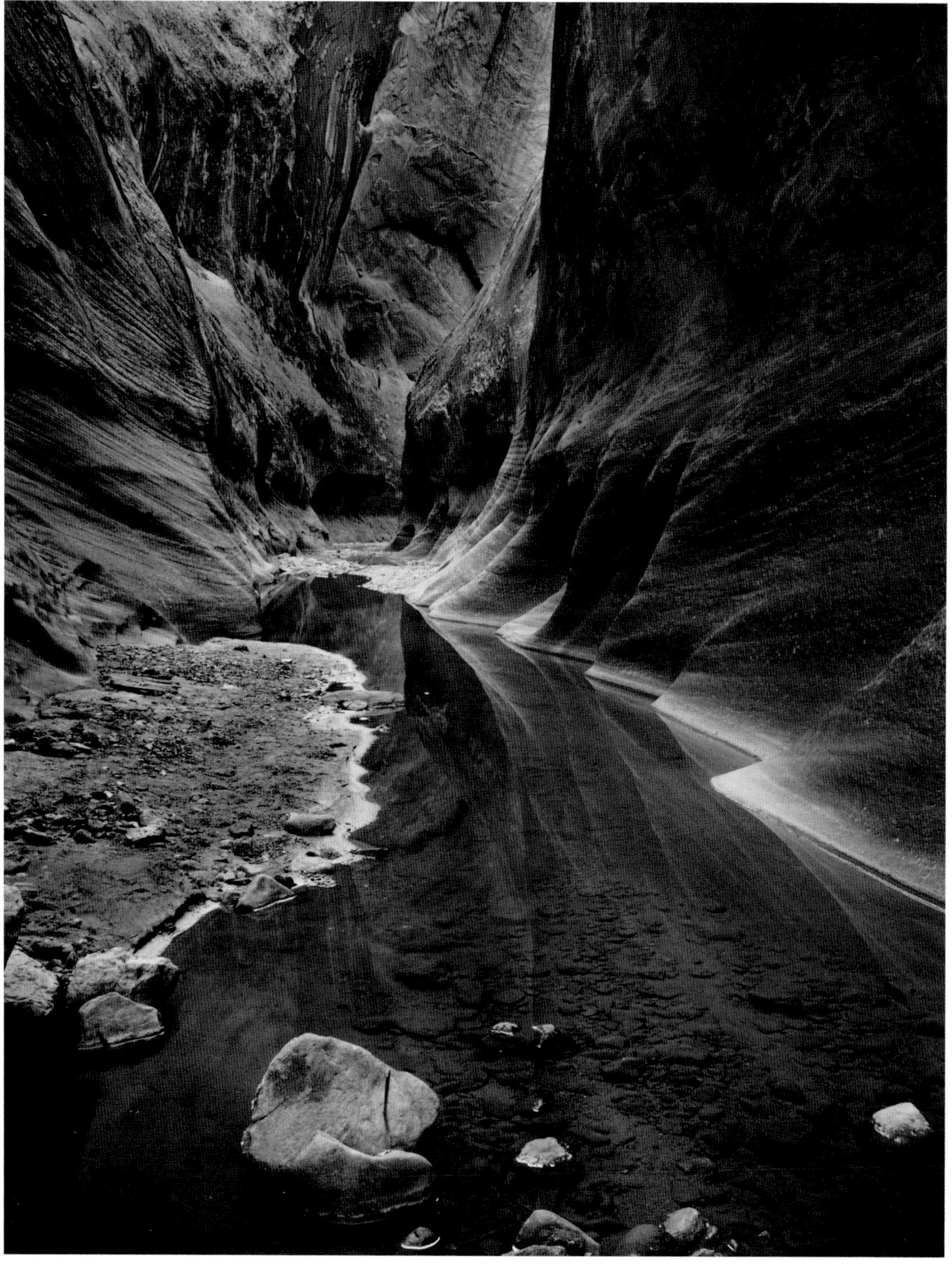

Introduction

In his book *Crossing Open Ground*, the late writer Barry Lopez distinguished between two landscapes: the exterior landscape, which he described as "the one we see," and the interior landscape, which he described as "a kind of projection within a person of a part of the exterior landscape." Each landscape has its own elements and relationships, but the two also interrelate. Lopez explained: "The interior landscape responds to the character and subtlety of an exterior landscape; the shape of the individual mind is affected by land as it is by genes."

The term "landscape photography" may be used to describe photographs of the exterior landscape—the one we see. The term may also be used to describe expressive photographs reflecting the interior landscape—the one each of us carries within.

Each person's interior landscape is unique and largely invisible to the eye. Still, if we know something about the ways one's interior landscape may be affected by elements of the exterior landscape, we may use these elements to express our own interior landscapes and to affect other people's interior landscapes. Such is the purpose of landscape photography practiced as expressive art.

Photographic artists aiming to express subjective notions—aspects of their interior landscape—in their work often find themselves at odds with those who, despite overwhelming evidence to the contrary, still believe that "true" photography consists only of objective representations of the exterior landscape.

"What is truth?" asked Friedrich Nietzsche; he then answered his own question: "a sum of human relations which have been poetically and rhetorically intensified, transferred, and embellished, and which, after long usage, seem to a people to be fixed, canonical, and binding. Truths are illusions which we have forgotten are illusions."

Truthfulness is not a quality imposed by any medium; it is a quality of information relative to context. Just as information exists in many forms and may assume different meanings in different contexts, so too does truth come in many varieties. There is objective truth and subjective truth. There is truth to appearances and truth to feelings. There is literal truth and metaphorical truth.

The truth of art is not necessarily the truth of nature, just as the truth of a metaphor is not necessarily the truth of its words taken literally. Being literal or metaphorical, in turn, is not a measure of the value or greatness of the truth expressed. However, failing to account for the distinction—treating literal truth as metaphor, or metaphorical truth as literal—may lead to great errors and misunderstanding. This is what Johann Wolfgang von Goethe meant when he wrote, "The genuine law-giving artist strives for the truth of art, the lawless artist who follows a blind impulse strives for the reality of Nature; through the former, art reaches its highest summit, through the latter its lowest stage."

As an avid naturalist and outdoorsman, I began my journey in photography more than three decades ago, striving to document the exterior landscape—the truth of nature—believing that no form of beauty can improve upon natural aesthetics. Today, I am an expressive artist striving to express my own internal landscape—the truth of art. I still believe that natural aesthetics cannot be improved upon.

What I was lacking in my earlier years—the linchpin connecting my love of natural beauty with qualities of my inner experiences—was an understanding of art, and an understanding that the truth of art is not in contradiction with the truth of nature. "Art," wrote Paul Cézanne, "is a harmony parallel to nature."

László Moholy-Nagy proclaimed, "The illiterate of the future will be the person ignorant of the use of the camera as well as the pen." To be photographically literate means, among other things, to recognize that some photographs are intended as reportage, others as art. Some photographs are meant as objective illustrations, others as subjective expressions. Some photographs are best understood literally, others metaphorically. Some photographs aim to portray the truth of the exterior landscape, others the truth of the photographer's interior landscape.

In this collection of essays, I hope to help readers consider landscape photography as art: as expressions of a photographer's interior landscape, distinct from landscape photography as objective representations of the exterior landscape.

Guy Tal
Torrey, Utah
April, 2022

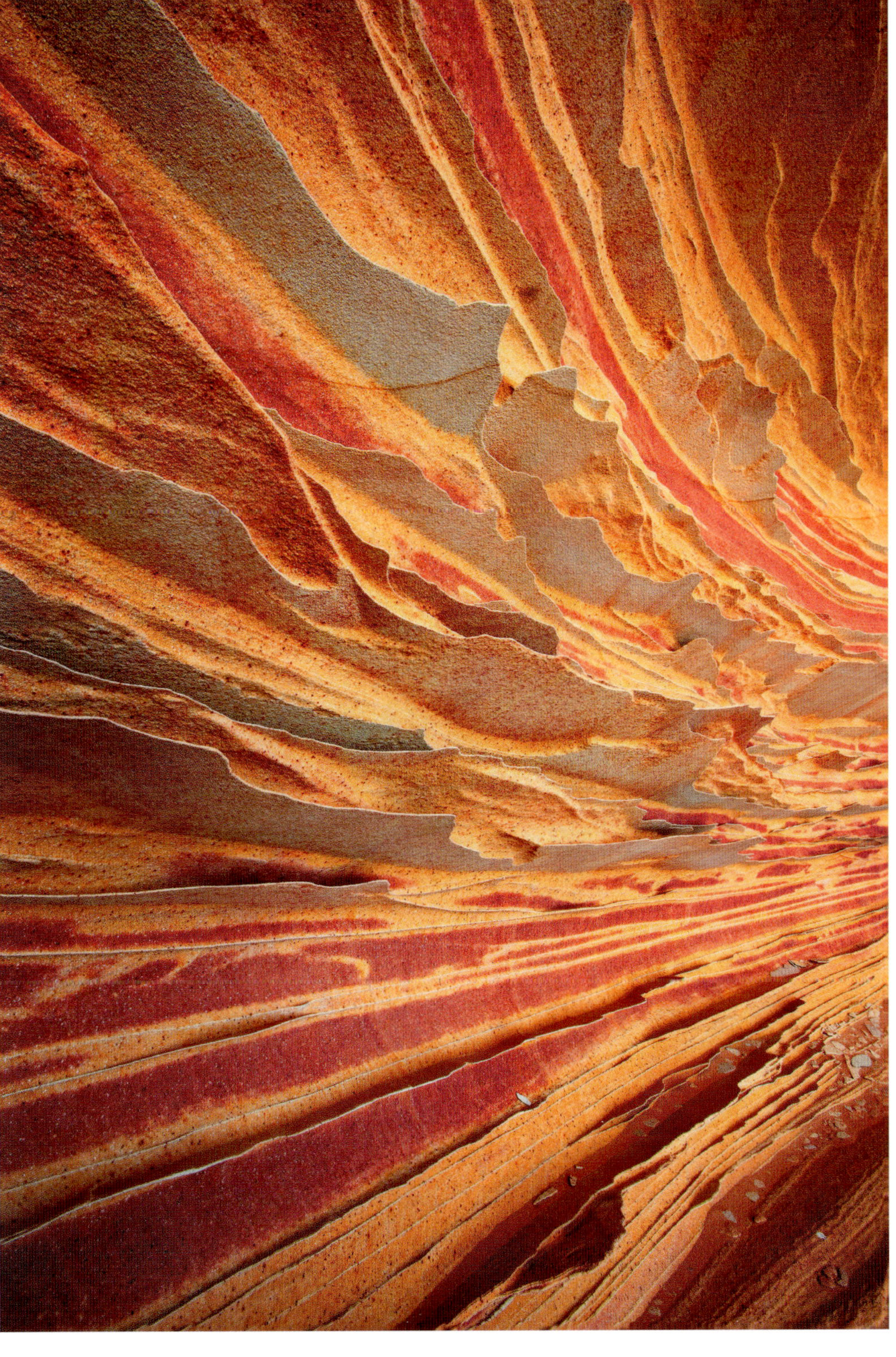

PART I • INSPIRED BY REALITY

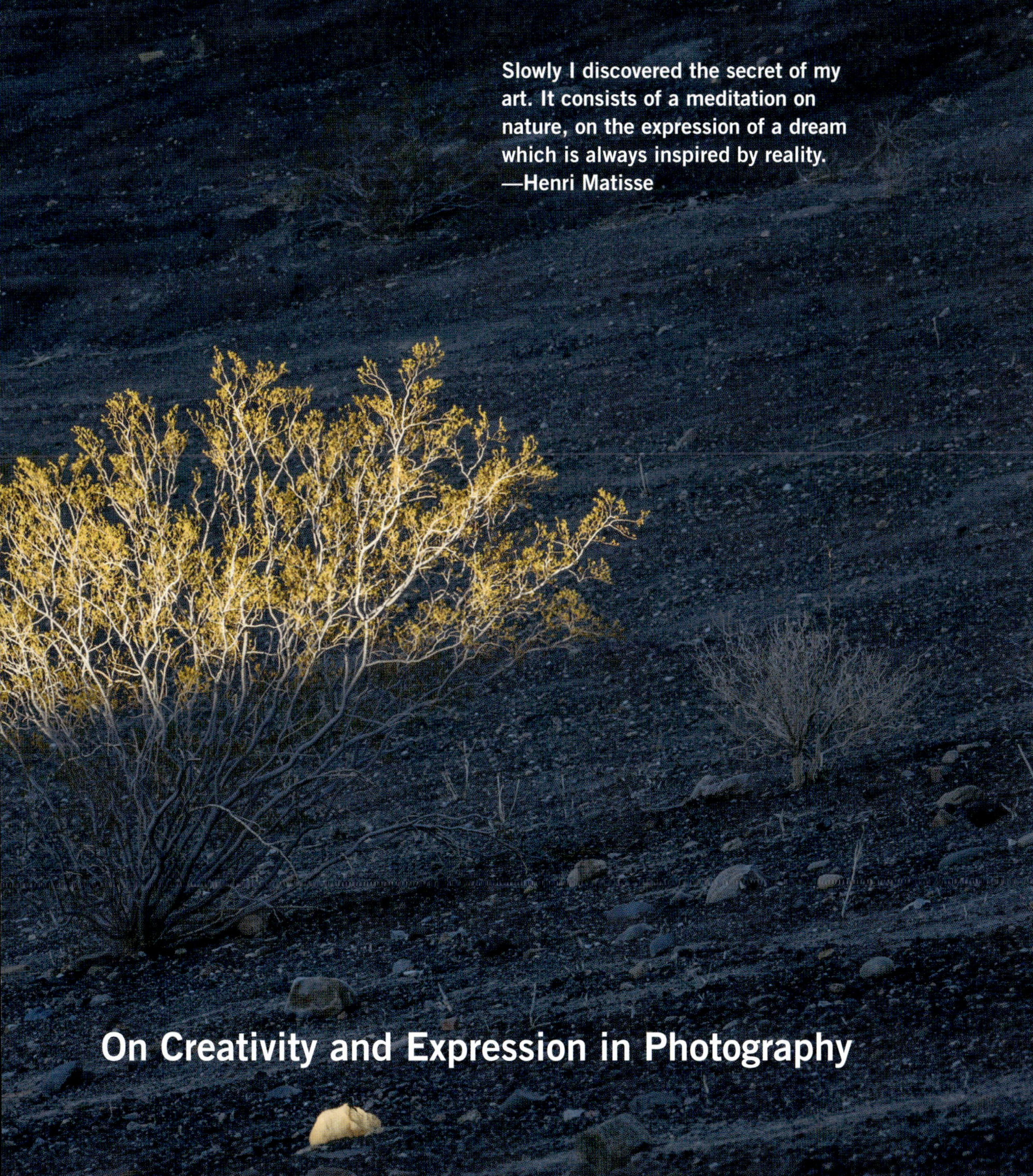

On Creativity and Expression in Photography

1 Poetic Odds

Photography's potential as a great image-maker and communicator is really no different from the same potential in the best poetry where familiar, everyday words, placed within a special context, can soar above the intellect and touch subtle reality in a unique way.
—Paul Caponigro

Many artists, including photographers, often refer to poetry when describing their work and philosophy. The correlation is easy to understand when we consider that "poetry" derives from a Greek word meaning "to create" or to bring something into being. This definition is close to that of the word "art," derived from a Latin word referring also to items brought into being by human skill (as opposed to things occurring naturally or randomly).

The distinction between prose and poetry in writing is analogous to the distinction between representation and artistic expression in photography. In both cases, the difference comes down to how one expresses meaning: literally or metaphorically, objectively or subjectively, decisively or ambiguously, descriptively or implicitly.

One glaring difference between writing and photography, however, is this: Among writers, neither poets nor journalists try to assert their own form of writing as the only valid form of writing or to demonize other forms. In contrast, in photography, expressing meaning poetically, departing from objective representation when it serves no useful purpose (or even distracts), is often met with ire. In writing, no journalist is concerned that the existence of poetry may diminish the importance or credulity of reportage, and no poet worries that readers may feel deceived if they realize that poetic verses are often not meant as literal statements of fact. In this

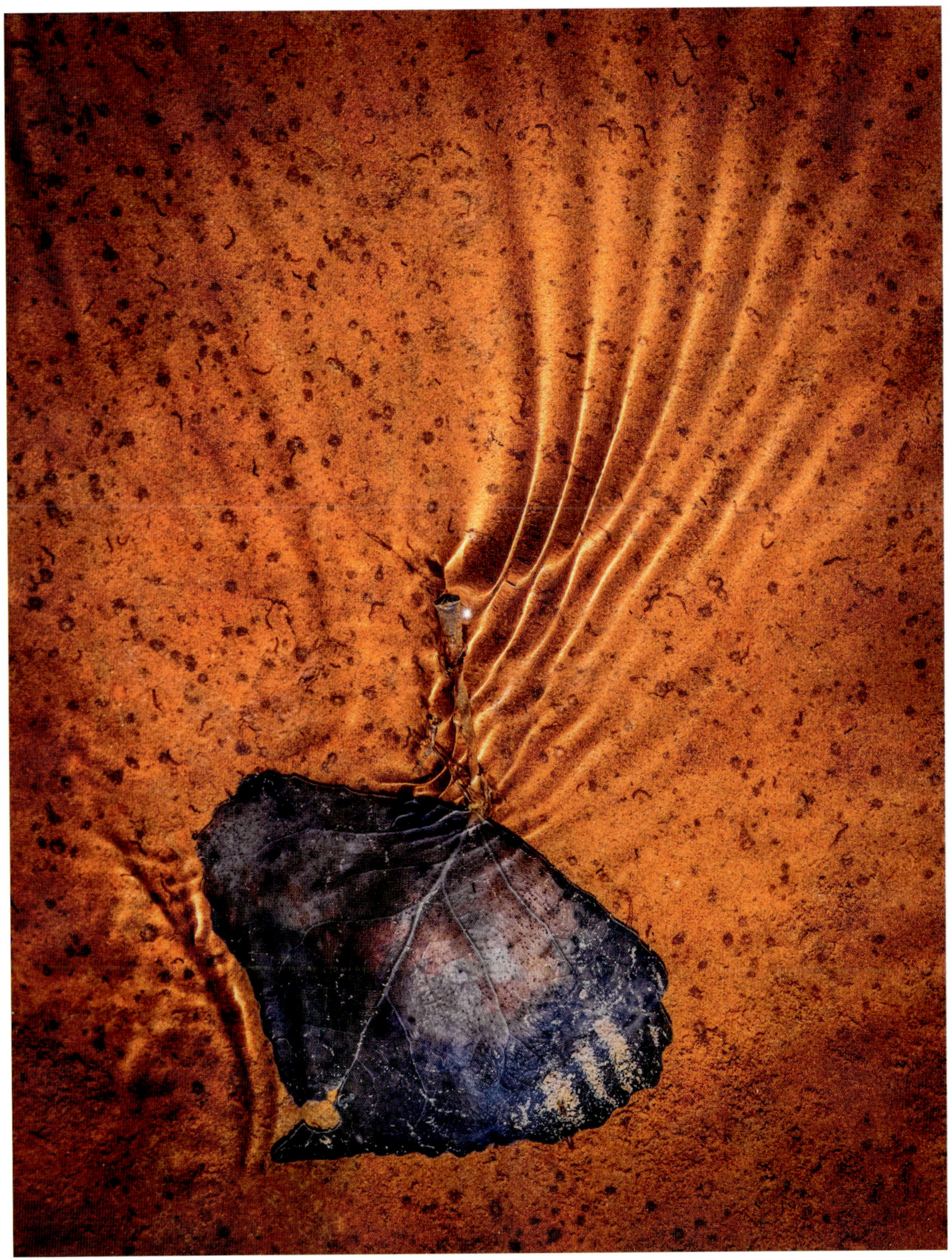

sense, the analogy also makes it plain how far photography still has to go as an art medium, if only just to catch up to where other media already are.

Pondering the challenge facing photographers aspiring to creative expression, W. Eugene Smith wrote, "I am constantly torn between the attitude of the conscientious journalist who is a recorder and interpreter of the facts and of the creative artist who often is necessarily at poetic odds with the literal facts." It seems unfortunate to me that any photographer should feel torn between these two intents, as both are squarely within the capacities of the photographic medium. They are only in contention because of misinformed assumptions about nonexistent limitations people assume are inherent in the photographic medium. There is no practical reason, not even in terms of photographic purity (however one chooses to define it), why photographs can't serve both purposes without diminishing either.

Among photographers who pondered photography as it relates to poetry, Minor White (who was a poet as well as a photographer) wrote:

> *My pity for the pure photographer*
> *My pity for the pure poet*
> *Is tempered by the responsibility*
> *I have to three media*
> *Whereas they to only one.*

Ernst Haas, former president of Magnum Photos, wrote, "We are on the way to speaking our very own language. With it we will have to create our own literature. You will have to decide for yourself what kind of works you want to create. Reports of facts, essays, poems—do you want to speak or to sing?" Henri Cartier-Bresson wrote, "I'm not responsible for my photographs. Photography is not documentary, but intuition, a poetic experience."

Despite such historical figures acknowledging the artistic, poetic potential of photography, many photographers today still wish to clip photography's expressive wings—to renounce photography's ability to serve as a medium for visual poetry, distinct from but equal in importance to its ability to serve as a medium for factual representation. This is not to say that a photograph can't be both factually representational and poetic in meaning, only that there is no tenable argument for why the former should be required for the latter.

Perhaps a stronger argument in favor of acceptance of photography as a means for (metaphorical, nonrepresentational) creative expression is that, regardless of opinion, poetic photographs—many decidedly not representational—already make up a great proportion of photographs one is likely to encounter in public media. This accords with the general trend in art—away from literal representation and toward greater abstraction, subjectivity, symbolism, and ambiguity.

Much of today's art, loosely referred to as "postmodern," is no longer about adherence to recognizable styles or purity of process. It is about the expression of ideas and about exploring the role of art itself, by whatever means the artist sees fit. This rift between art's evolutionary course and the opinions of some conservative photographic purists may force some to choose their allegiances and priorities. It's inevitable that for many artists, art in the larger sense is more important than any conflict plaguing one medium or another. As Jerry Uelsmann expressed it, "Much of the experimental photography that we revere today has been done by individuals whose commitment to photography is but one aspect of their commitment to art."

Photographer David Ward, discussing the importance of realism in artistic photography, commented, "Nobody gives any objection at all to the fact that paintings aren't real." This may seem obvious to us today, but it was not always the case. Until the late 19th century, fidelity to nature was considered in many venues (notably in France, which was the hub of Western art at the time) as the highest aspiration for art. Works that departed from realistic appearances, such as those by the early impressionists, were shunned, sometimes even ridiculed, and excluded from the most prestigious art exhibition of the day, the Paris Salon. In response, the early impressionists started a salon of their own and prompted a revolution in the arts. As painter Robert Henri put it, "History proves that juries in art have been generally wrong."

The invention of photography, portending a future in which the photographic medium could surpass painting in its ability to portray natural, realistic appearances, was seen by some critics as potentially ruinous to art. Charles Baudelaire, a distinguished poet and art critic, wrote a scathing rebuke of photography in an essay about the Paris Salon of 1859—just three decades after the invention of photography. In his critique, Baudelaire wrote this:

> In matters of painting and sculpture, the present-day Credo of the sophisticated, above all in France (and I do not think that anyone at all would dare to state the contrary), is this: "I believe in Nature, and I believe only in Nature (there are good reasons for that). I believe that Art is, and cannot be other than, the exact reproduction of Nature . . . Thus an industry that could give us a result identical to Nature would be the absolute of Art." A revengeful God has given ear to the prayers of this multitude. Daguerre[1]

---

[1] Louis Daguerre, inventor of the popular daguerreotype process.

*was his Messiah. And now the faithful says to himself: "Since photography
gives us every guarantee of exactitude that we could desire (they really
believe that, the mad fools!), then photography and Art are the same thing"
. . . this industry [photography], by invading the territories of art, has
become art's most mortal enemy.*

The infamous satirical critic Louis Leroy, upon seeing Claude Monet's painting *Impression, soleil levant (Impression, sunrise)*, commented, "I was just telling myself that, since I was impressed, there had to be some impression in it . . . and what freedom, what ease of workmanship! Wallpaper in its embryonic state is more finished than that seascape." Prompted by Leroy's mocking critique, the early impressionists adopted the term "impressionism" for their movement, rendering Leroy a historic laughingstock.

I mention the impressionists not only as an example of art evolving by revolutionary leaps (rather than by gradual transitions)—toward subjective expression and away from objective realism. Impressionism also holds another important (if not as widely acknowledged) lesson that is relevant to photographers who care about fidelity to an artist's genuine experience (which, in the case of poetic expression, does not necessarily imply fidelity to real appearances). The lesson is this: although impressionism became a roaring success as an art movement, in time it had lost its connection with real experience (read: subjective impressions) and came to be regarded primarily as a formal aesthetic style. This trend also is evident in photography, where many are content copying the styles (if not the exact compositions) of others, giving no mind to the fact that what such photographs ostensibly express often is incongruous with the photographer's real experience.

Monet famously credited the success of his works to the emotions he felt when working out in nature, rather than to the distinctive style of impressionism. Many other impressionists, despite lumping their work into the same category as Monet's, produced works of similar effect but without the experience of working in (and from) nature. As Monet himself put it, "My only merit lies in having painted directly in front of nature, seeking to render my impressions of the most fleeting effects, and I still very much regret having caused the naming of a group whose majority had nothing impressionist about it." This should serve as a warning to those interested in poetic expression in photography. Stylistic departures from realistic appearances are not enough (indeed, not even required) for an image to be poetic, but fidelity to true experience is required if one aspires to live a poetic life.

Authenticity and truthfulness are not so simplistic as to be reduced to objective representation alone. Some truths may be conveyed more powerfully by use of metaphor, rather than by literal statements of fact. Some truths stand to gain greater impact and acceptance if conveyed in poetry than in reportage. If this were not the case, there would be no need for art, poetry or other. Those who seek to deny photography the same evolutionary progression that propels all other arts may do so by some seemingly noble convictions, but such was the case for any historical movement seeking to repress progress. Whatever short-term benefits such attitudes may yield for some segment of the population, we must remember that they come at the risk of photography remaining mired in obsolete traditions and not considered a serious medium for art.

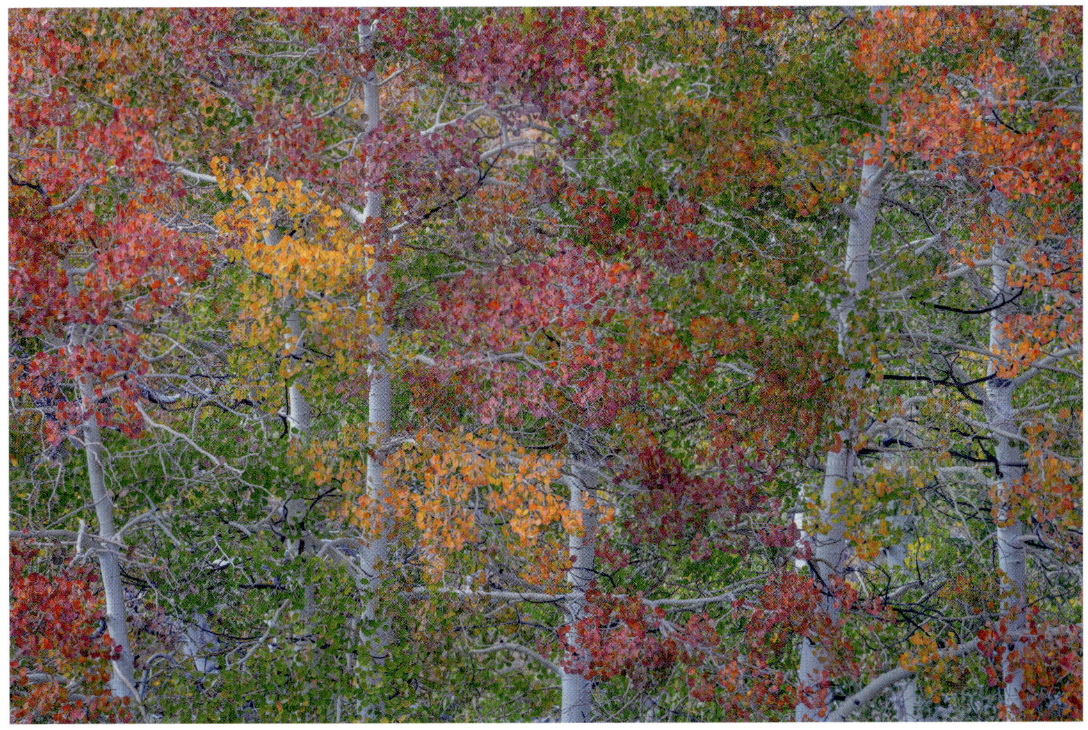

2 Creativity, Success, and Personality

One of those behind-the-scenes realities associated with the pursuit of art is the fact that—when it comes to successful work output—artistic failures nearly always outnumber artistic successes, by a considerable margin. Of course, this stands to reason. If every photograph produced was a clear and unambiguous winner, the pursuit, itself, would quickly lose its appeal.
—Huntington Witherill

When asked what advice I have for beginners, I generally quote the words of Edward Weston: "If I have any 'message' worth giving to a beginner, it is that there are no short cuts in photography." I then qualify that there are, in fact, a great many shortcuts in photography if one's primary interest is making popular or salable photographs. Weston's advice holds true only in the sense that there are no shortcuts in *creative* and *expressive* photography—the kind of photography I strive to make and find most rewarding. These qualities—creativity and expression—are also what I admire most when viewing other people's photographs. To be sure, photographers who are committed to creativity and expression are not common because these qualities are difficult to accomplish. Then again, that is exactly why I revere them and aspire to them in my own work. As Ralph Waldo Emerson put it, "The heroic cannot be the common, nor the common the heroic."

So much writing about photography today is dedicated to things you can buy and to recipes you can follow to make "successful" photographs, implicitly defining success in terms of popularity, recognition, or profitability. For the sake of this discussion, I will also use this narrow characterization of "success," even though I think there are other ways to define it that may be more useful in some circumstances. Specifically, I wish to distinguish success as a goal from creativity as a goal.

I think it's important for photographers to give thought and to acknowledge clearly whether their primary motivation is success or creativity. Although success and creativity are not mutually exclusive, when one or the other is considered as the primary driver behind a photographer's work, each comes with risks and rewards that the other does not. Considering these differences should guide photographers in choosing decisively which approach best fits their temperament and aspirations. Since the pursuit of success and the pursuit of creativity require different mind-sets and strategies, what may constitute good advice for a photographer motivated primarily by success may be poor advice for a photographer motivated primarily by creativity, and vice versa.

Consider, for example, the plethora of photographic tutorials—books, work-shops, articles, and videos—attempting to reduce such things as visual composition or what makes a "good" photograph into templates, rules, formulas, quantifiable metrics, or even stepwise recipes. These tutorials may undoubtedly increase one's odds of making successful photographs (to wit, many authors of such tutorials fol-low their own formulaic advice with proven success, despite this success ensuing from decidedly uncreative work). However, to pursue too closely such templates or modes of thinking will almost certainly hinder your odds of making truly creative work. More important, to pursue such advice will almost certainly prevent you from experiencing some rewards of creative living and artistic expression, which are not quantifiable or measurable by such things as sales, awards, or number of followers, yet may still enrich your life in pervasive and profound ways.

In contrast to so many how-to teachings, consider those resources promoting the value of things like mindfulness, exploration, trial and error, divergent think-ing, original creation, experiencing and expressing powerful emotions in your work. Such resources may be a boon to a creative person but may lead to frustration and dissatisfaction among those who prioritize success above creativity. Those driven primarily by success may, for example, return from even the most sublime of places feeling disappointed if their experience did not yield popular or sellable photo-graphs. Oftentimes, the disappointment may be further compounded by guilt for feeling disappointment—for having failed to appreciate your experience as others suggest you "should have."

In terms of reward, perhaps the most important distinction between creativity and success is this: Creativity is most rewarding not as something to practice ad hoc when making a photograph but as a general attitude toward life. A creative attitude

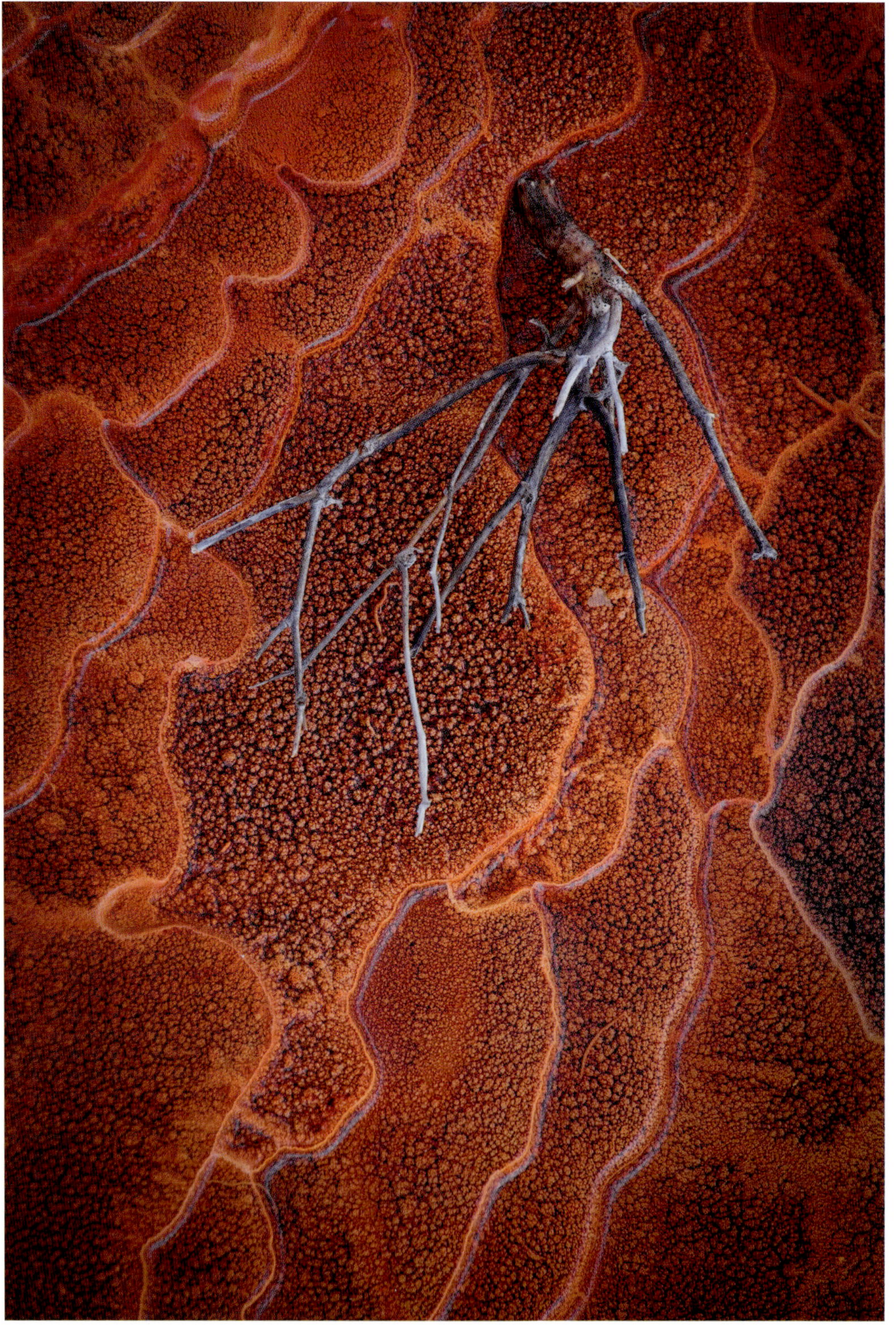

may lead to the experience of flow, to occasional grand discoveries and meaningful breakthroughs, which is not the case when you follow familiar (convergent) recipes and templates aiming to produce predictable, preconceived outcomes. Put another way, the rewards of prioritizing creativity over success are ongoing and sustained. They grow cumulatively over time and may on occasion yield immense and unexpected rewards, even the possibility of enriching your life with new meaning. Conversely, the rewards of prioritizing success over creativity, while not in doubt, tend to be anecdotal and short-lived. After each success, you will likely return to the same baseline you started from until the next "hit." This self-defeating cycle is known as *the hedonic treadmill*.

In terms of risk, a creative attitude never guarantees that any photograph you make will be "good" or "better" by any objective measure. In fact, a creative attitude relies on experimentation and on-the-spot (divergent) decision-making, which in many cases may lead to failure and to overall reduced productivity. Creativity is also not guaranteed to ensue from applying any formulas or following any set of directions. You can't force creativity; you can only invite it in and hope it accepts your invitation. This means by necessity that one who prioritizes the rewards of creativity above those of success must accept the possibilities of failure, of prolonged unproductive periods, and of potentially little material return relative to invested time and effort. The pursuit of creativity therefore demands greater courage, grit, and self-confidence than the pursuit of success. Indeed, some of the most creative works in history were originally met with doubt and criticism, even scathing reviews impacting some artists' reputations and livelihoods. Some creative geniuses even went to their graves before their works ever received recognition, let alone were considered important or valuable.

To prioritize creativity above success is to seek reward first in the *process* of making art—in thinking about art, in experimenting and exploring, in being mindful and receptive to new possibilities—and only second in any *product* of art. This may seem unintuitive, but studies show that this approach, favoring creativity over success, in fact, has the power to enrich an artist's life more than the pursuit of finished products. As Scott Barry Kaufman and Carolyn Gregoire put it in their book, *Wired to Create*:

> *Those who are more motivated to develop a final product (agreeing with statements like, "I work most creatively when I have deadlines," "If I don't have something to show for myself, then I feel I've failed") tend to score lower in creative potential and intrinsic motivation and higher in stress*

*and extrinsic (reward-oriented) motivation. Those who derive enjoyment
from the act of creating and feel in control of their creative process tend
to show greater creativity than those who are focused exclusively on the
outcome of their work.*

To be clear, I am not proposing that prioritizing creativity above success is necessarily the right approach for everyone. In fact, it may be the wrong approach for many. To know whether creativity or success should be *your* top priority, I recommend taking one of many freely available online personality tests, particularly those measuring the so-called "Big Five" personality traits of the Five-Factor Model of personality (FFM): extraversion, openness, conscientiousness, neuroticism, and agreeableness.

Material considerations (e.g., earning income) aside, those who stand to benefit most from prioritizing creativity above success are those who score higher than average in openness to new experiences and those who score below average in conscientiousness—the quality of being motivated by achievement and having the discipline to turn ideas into products. Those who score higher than average in conscientiousness likely will benefit more from making success their primary priority. Such people in fact may drive themselves to ongoing frustration and dissatisfaction if their efforts to make creative work are unsuccessful.

To give you a sense of where creative artists tend to fall relative to Big Five personality traits, a 2006 study by Mark Batey and Adrian Furnham concluded (according to an article by Furnham[2]) this:

> *Artists are significantly higher on Neuroticism than nonartists; lower on
> Extraversion than nonartists; higher on Openness than nonartists; lower
> on Agreeableness than nonartists; lower on Conscientiousness than non-
> artists, and higher on Psychoticism than nonartists.*

When it comes to deciding whether your living experience will be richer by prioritizing creativity over success or the other way around, the perennial advice holds: know thyself.

---

[2]Adrian Furnham, "Progress and Problems in Creativity Research." *The Nature of Human Creativity*, edited by Robert J. Sternberg and James C. Kaufman, Cambridge University Press, Cambridge, United Kingdom, 2018.

The Clearest and Strongest Way of Seeing 3

Science and Intuition

I don't know a thing about the rules of composition. I make my own. The subject is very difficult to write about, and perhaps can never be explained in words, since it is so involved in personal experience and growth. Words, "art criticism," and explanations are the curse of today so far as art is concerned. To me, composition is the clearest and strongest way of seeing a subject.
—Edward Weston

If you are a photographer who aspires to be creative and expressive in your work, my first bit of advice for you is this: once you become proficient enough in operating your camera and using your processing software to produce acceptably good photographs, shift your attention to composition. Certainly, you may still gain from learning and improving your technical skills, but this should become a secondary concern. Once you understand technical basics—proper exposure, depth of field, how to adjust color and contrast in your images to your liking—you already have most of what you need to express yourself visually. Further improvement in technical skills beyond this point will come inevitably from practice and experimentation, from learning as you go, from encountering specific problems and looking up solutions for them.

If you spend too much time striving for technical mastery before shifting your attention to creative expression (by way of visual compositions) you may unwittingly cheat yourself out of opportunities to engage with the world with an artistic mindset, in conscious and deliberate pursuit of elevated experiences worthy of artistic expression. The accounting is simple: Such elevated experiences, even if on occasion they don't result in photographs, are considerably more rewarding than any quantifiable measure of technical quality you may accomplish in your photographs. Don't confuse means with ends.

Gaining technical proficiency, to an artist, to put it plainly, is not the goal; it is a necessary precondition—an imposition you'll want to get out of the way as early as possible so you can move on to making art. Think of acquiring technical skills as the tilling and weeding of your expressive garden—the grunt work you have to put in so you may later enjoy, as early as possible, the bounty of fruit, the delicacy of herbal fragrances, the beauty of flowers, the joys of tending to living plants, seeing them thriving in gratitude for your efforts.

Photographers wishing to learn about visual composition unfortunately often find themselves in a labyrinth of confusing, contradicting, and plain wrong advice. Such advice sometimes comes in the form of "rules" of composition, tips for "better" compositions, compositional templates, or pseudo-scientific claims about some "golden" this or "magic" that. In this multipart essay, I hope to help you navigate your way through the chaos of information and misinformation about photographic composition, and to dispel some myths that may lead you astray.

If you have made the choice to pursue composition seriously, my second bit of advice for you is this: When you come upon any resources suggesting that photographic composition can be reduced to rules, tips, or formulas, examine them for signs of danger and proceed carefully. Better yet, avoid them altogether. Most often, such advice is not just futile but outright harmful in the sense that it may hinder your creativity and limit your expressive vocabulary for no good reason. To accept such advice as gospel may also rob you of profoundly satisfying states of mind such as flow and discovery. Flow doesn't come from taking shortcuts and applying easy solutions. Flow requires investing prolonged time paying focused attention to a challenging task. Likewise, the satisfaction of making meaningful discoveries requires trial and error, mystery, and risk. To experience a sense of discovery requires that you arrive at solutions by exploration and imaginative thinking, not by following directions. Preconception—following directions to a known-in-advance destination—is the antithesis of discovery.

No doubt, following rules, directions, or easy formulas may gain you some beautiful trophies. But consider the difference between earning a trophy as reward for some difficult endeavor versus purchasing someone else's secondhand trophy at a pawn shop. In both cases you end up with a trophy, and both trophies may be

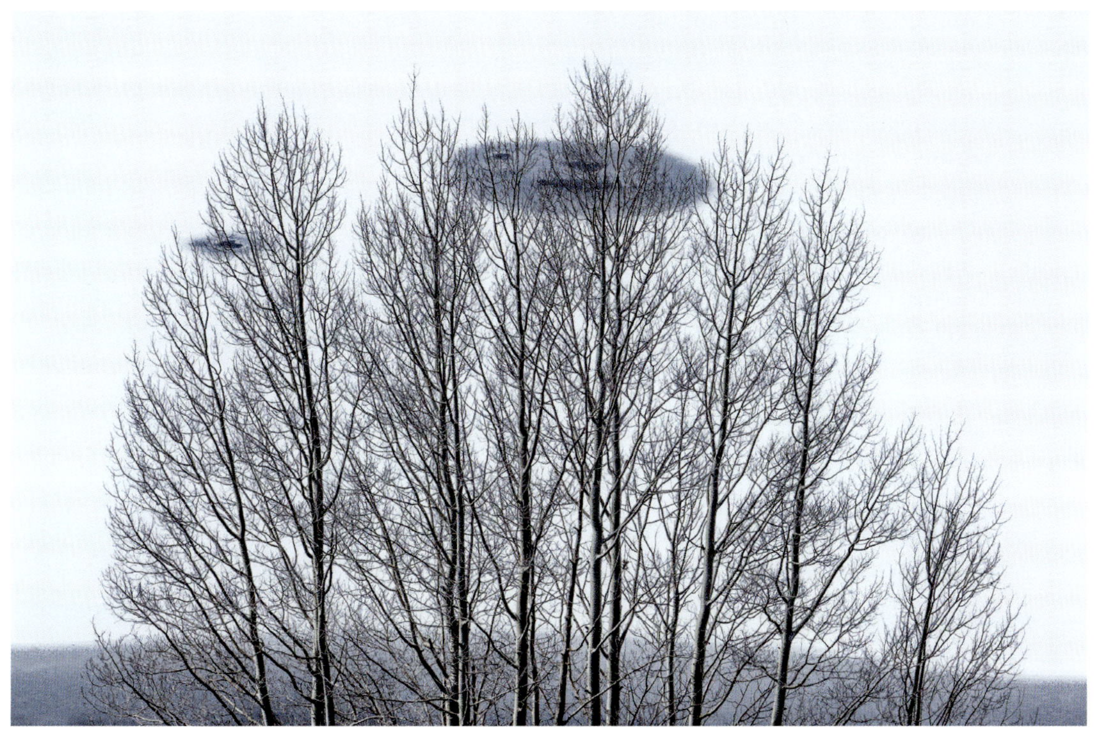

beautiful. An outsider seeing your trophy may never know the difference and may even assume you have accomplished something formidable to earn the trophy, but in terms of inner reward, the two scenarios are—by a long shot—not the same. Also worth considering is this: a beautiful, technically impressive trophy image, no matter how you earned it, is not necessarily a creative or an expressive image, and it is no guarantee that you got the most out of the experience of making this image.

To separate useful from unfounded advice about composition, it's worth keeping in mind that any reliable truth we know, or can know, about visual expression comes from only two sources: intuition and science. Being that, at this time, science can tell us very little about how human brains make meaning from visual information (and this knowledge so far is almost entirely within the realm of how we recognize and respond to obvious stimuli, not so much about how we experience art), intuition should be your primary focus. Keep in mind that, while we are all born with some intuition, we can also train and improve our intuition for expressive visual composition with practice and learning.

The turbulent history of visual art and the nascency of our scientific understanding of visual perception suggest that, when it comes to artistic expression, we are nowhere near the limits of human creativity and a very long way from a complete understanding (if that is even possible) of how art "works." Therefore, your intuition about what makes for a good composition may evolve over your lifetime. Indeed, based on how little we know today about how people experience art, it is likely that artistic visual expression will continue to evolve in new and unexpected ways long beyond our lifetimes. In this light, we can clearly see the futility of seeking easy answers about what makes for a "good" composition. Any attempt to distill even a tiny bit of what we know (let alone what we don't yet know) about visual expression into the scope of a book, a video, a list of tips, or "rules" for composition is on its face ridiculous.

No doubt, if you were to research composition, you'd likely come across such tropes as the "rule of thirds" or some reference to such things as the "golden ratio." Most people stop there and proceed to attempt to implement these concepts in their work rather than to research them further. Dig a little deeper and you will find that things are not quite as simple and straightforward as some authors want you to believe (or worse, that these authors themselves believe, leading them to perpetuate the mistakes of others).

In 1509, Luca Pacioli—a mathematician friend of Leonardo da Vinci—published a book titled *Divina Proportione* (divine proportion) discussing the relationship between mathematics and arts. In the book, Pacioli describes in mathematical terms the so-called "golden ratio." To his credit, Pacioli never suggested that the golden ratio had any special power to improve the aesthetics of architecture or art, although some assumed it to be the case anyway. While the golden ratio indeed makes for beautiful mathematics, there is no evidence that it has anything at all to do with visual aesthetics. In his analysis of the golden ratio, Mario Livio concluded:

> *The history of art has nevertheless shown that artists who have produced works of truly lasting value are precisely those who have departed from any formal canon for aesthetics. In spite of the Golden Ratio's truly amazing mathematical properties, and its propensity to pop up where least expected in natural phenomena, I believe that we should abandon its application as some sort of universal standard for "beauty," either in the human face or in the arts.*

Similarly, there is no evidence to suggest that such concepts as the rule of thirds or the rule of odds or any other so-called "rule of composition" are supported by scientific evidence, let alone point to any universal aesthetic ideal.

To the degree that such "rules" of composition are useful, it is only in prompting artists to think beyond the obvious function of representing subjects and to instead consider visual creations in terms of relationships—deliberate arrangements of elements (lines, shapes, colors, textures, patterns, tonal transitions) having a collective, synergetic meaning. In this sense, so-called "rules of composition" may be considered useful, not as templates to design photographs by but in demonstrating that images become more expressive when they break away from what John Szarkowski termed "habitual seeing." (In Szarkowski's words: "Photography, if practiced with high seriousness, is a contest between a photographer and the presumptions of approximate and habitual seeing.")

In their early attempts, most photographers aim to represent appearances, rather than to express meanings (in fairness, the idea that photographs *can* express meaning beyond representing appearances rarely even occurs to those who take up photography as a hobby in their early years). When our goal is to represent the appearance of some object, we naturally tend to portray this object in the center of the frame, to make it disproportionately more prominent than other elements in the frame—generally, to direct the viewer's attention toward that object and away from anything else in the frame. This is a good approach for purposes such as identification of birds or setting the expectations of travelers headed to some tourist attractions, when the goal is to provide viewers with a quick and obvious impression of what they may see themselves. When expression, rather than representation, is the goal, this approach has a severe handicap: it encourages oversimplification. When an image is too simple and obvious, why would viewers want to spend time with it beyond a single short-lived impression? Even if the impression is a wonderful, powerful one, it is unlikely that a viewer will consider contemplating the picture, meditating on it, seeking meanings and nuances in it. In the words of Edgar Degas, "When you always make your meaning perfectly plain, you end up boring people."

When our goal is to express meaning, rather than to depict appearances, it's not enough to portray things that may have a meaning; we must also signal to our viewers that we wish for them to attempt to decipher this meaning, to linger a bit longer, to contemplate our photographs beyond just a momentary impression. When our compositions transcend "habitual seeing" (i.e., how a random person will likely see an object or scene by default), we create the effect of visual tension: We throw the brains of our viewers a visual curveball. We show them something they are not

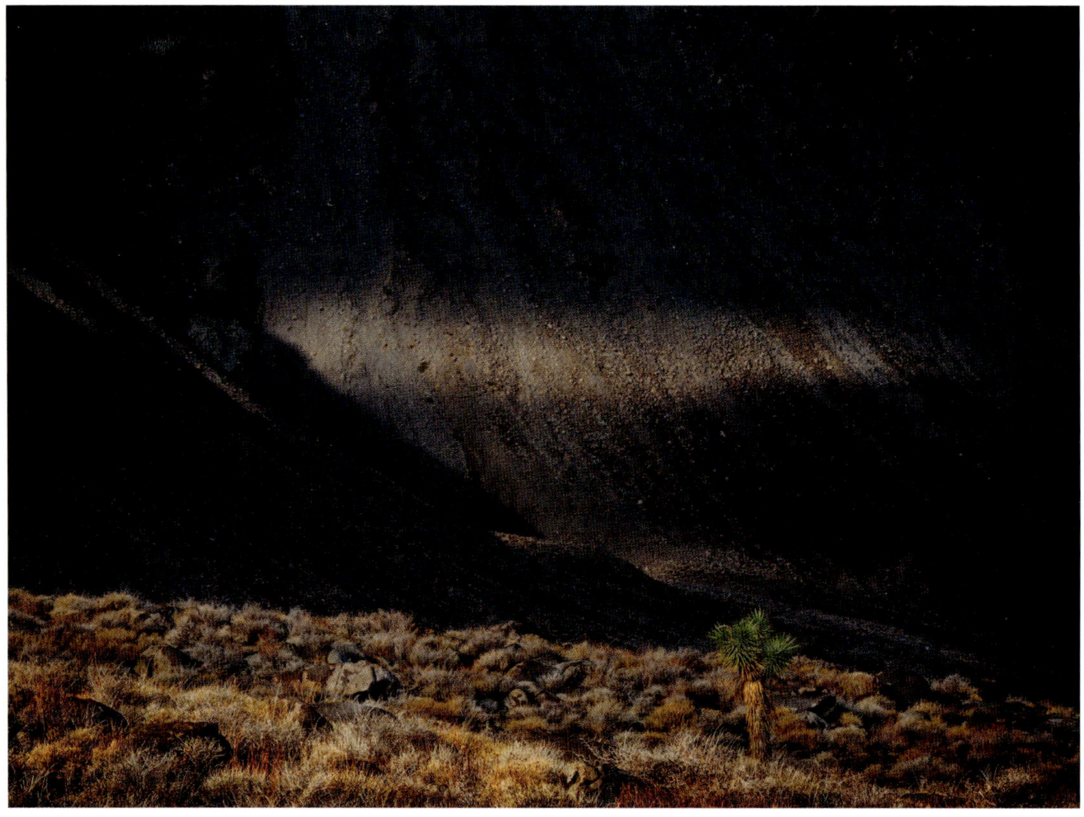

accustomed to seeing. We surprise them. We hope to arouse their curiosity so they'll want to explore further. This may seem like a good argument for applying compositional templates that are by design different from "habitual seeing," but, in fact, it is not.

Templates, even if they are visually attractive, are by their nature repetitive and formulaic. In time, they become habitual even if they were not so to begin with. For example, it used to be that fish-eye or ultra-wide lenses were rare and expensive, and their unexpected effects were an easy way to create tension in a composition. Today, when most people have seen a plethora of images made with such lenses, nobody finds their effect especially jarring. Photographs of the night sky also were once rare and difficult to make, but today making photographs of starry night skies and the Milky Way requires little more than traveling to a dark place at some precomputed (often by use of apps) "right time," and dialing in some camera settings by rote, and so night sky images have become commonplace too. This is the danger of templates, gimmicks, and other ephemeral novelties: They become progressively less impressive the easier and the more common they get. Also, they rely on viewers being surprised or impressed by some visual effect, rather than by a photographer's ability to express moods and feelings visually, by way of a deliberate, creative composition.

There are many more (perhaps infinite) ways to create expressive photographs than any list of templates can hope to encompass, or that any person can hope to memorize. So, why stick to just a small array of overused recipes, especially when their effectiveness is at best dubious? Rather than useful shortcuts to creative success, such recipes more often become lazy habits and creativity-limiting handicaps.

An important aspect of intuition is that it can be trained. All people are born with some innate aesthetic preferences. As we mature, we also acquire additional preferences from our environment, our experiences, our culture, the significant influences in our lives. Of course, not everyone likes or even understands the same things, especially when it comes to art. Cognitive abilities, including creativity and appreciation of art, can be trained deliberately just like physical abilities—by building up and exercising the relevant metaphorical "muscles"—the relevant brain circuitry.

Just as training programs for physical abilities rely on isolating specific muscles and picking exercises targeted to those muscles, we can isolate certain cognitive abilities and find exercises to target them. And just as with physical fitness, it helps to adopt lifestyles, habits, and attitudes that keep you in generally good shape in addition to the targeted exercises.

If we think of visual composition as a cognitive ability that we can train, then it doesn't matter that we don't know exactly how it works. (After all, how many gifted athletes can name every muscle, tendon, and nerve needed to perform their sport, let alone the underlying biochemistry and neural circuitry?) In practical terms, the analogy suggests that to be a good creative artist one must first adopt a lifestyle conducive to being in generally good "artistic shape." Such a lifestyle may involve nurturing mindfulness, evolving an interest in learning about art, setting aside time to practice your art, reading about art, attending exhibits, interacting with other artists, and doing so regularly rather than opportunistically.

Training for Visual Composition

I borrow some subject or other from life or from nature, and, using it as a pretext, I arrange lines and colors so as to obtain symphonies, harmonies that do not represent a thing that is real, in the vulgar sense of the word, and do not directly express any idea, but are supposed to make you think the way music is supposed to make you think, unaided by ideas or images, simply through the mysterious affinities that exist between our brains and such arrangements of colors and lines.
—Paul Gauguin

Although science, in principle, may offer more decisive guidance for expressive visual composition than intuition, at this point (and likely for the foreseeable future) the science of art is fairly limited, leaving us artists with intuition as the primary tool to rely on in conceiving expressive compositions. We should remember, though, that intuition is not a fixed quantity. We may evolve, grow, train, and improve our aesthetic intuition with deliberate practice. Also, not all intuition is necessarily useful. As we glean useful intuition by study, by experimentation, by inspiration, and by trial and error, we should also be willing to let go of, and to unlearn, those intuitions that in time may prove unhelpful or false.

To be clear, my goal is not to suggest that intuition should supplant science—on the contrary, I believe that knowing as much of the available science can be invaluable in guiding intuition. Intuition founded in science—in evidence—is far more useful than intuition founded in misconceptions, misinformation, habits, or historical errors. Put simply, I recommend that you take the time to study what science there is, and not rely blindly on just your gut feel[3]. Training intuition is not just about adding to the knowledge and skills you already possess; it is also about ridding yourself of intuition dispelled by science, regardless of popular beliefs or how self-evident it may seem.

---

[3]When it comes to the science of visual expression, two particularly useful disciplines are Gestalt Psychology and neuroaesthetics (both rely to a considerable degree on other disciplines, such as neuroscience and evolutionary biology). For Gestalt Psychology, a good place to start is Rudolf Arnheim's seminal book, *Art and Visual Perception*, which has been studied and vetted for several decades. In contrast, neuroaesthetics is a relatively young field and thus prone to a flux of new theories and discoveries, but a couple of good places to start are V. S. Ramachandran's eight laws of artistic experience and the overview provided in Anjan Chatterjee's book *The Aesthetic Brain*.

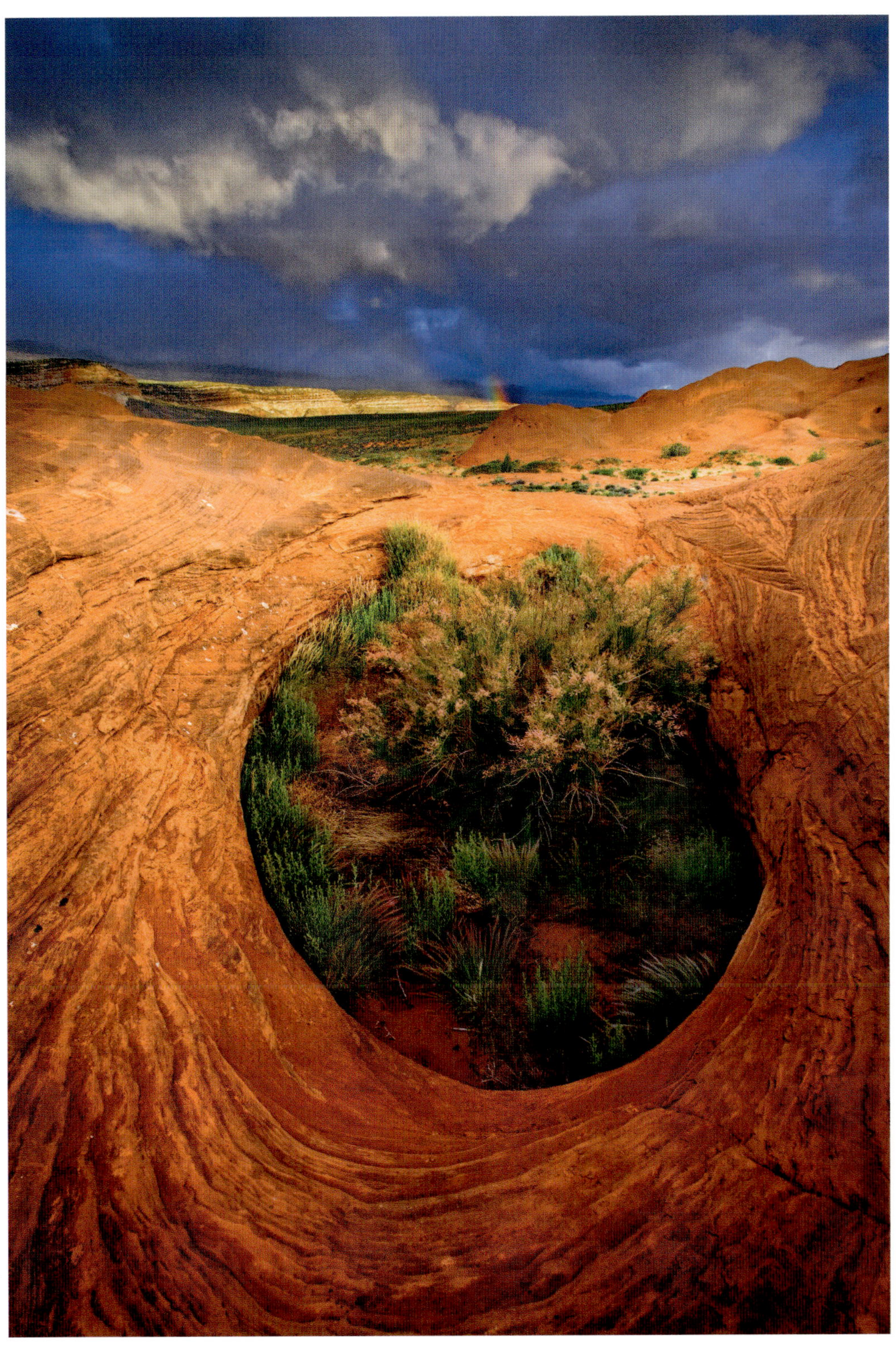

To get a sense of the current limitations of science when it comes to artistic expression, and for a good illustration of why, despite decades of scientific research, intuition remains an artist's most important resource, consider these words by neuroscientist V. S. Ramachandran. When asked in an interview how much science can tell us about how people experience art, he responded:

> *I think right now one percent or less is explained by neuroscience, but I think a time will come when we'll maybe understand 10, 20 percent of it.*

Training artistic intuition is a delicate dance among seemingly contradicting goals: using a structured approach to encourage unstructured thinking, using known patterns to improve our ability to depart from known patterns, and applying deliberate and conscious thinking to make our brains more flexible and fluent in their instinctive, subconscious responses.

A good way to think about training artistic intuition is in terms coined by psychologist and Nobel laureate Daniel Kahneman. Kahneman divided the workings of the brain into "System 1" and "System 2." System 1 is the intuitive system: It is the system that provides us with instant answers and perceptions. We have no conscious control of the workings of System 1. For example, when facing simple calculations such as "what is 2+2?" System 1 instantly presents us with the answer: 4. There is no effort or deliberate thinking involved. Just as important, there's nothing we can do to prevent System 1 from performing this simple calculation. System 1 is also responsible for such intuitive functions as recognizing facial expressions or diverting attention instantly to the source of a loud unexpected sound.

In contrast, System 2 is our conscious system. System 2 can perform difficult calculations, investigate complex problems, perform rational analysis, decide to consult other people or to research a problem. Faced with a complex task, such as "what is 23×17?" System 1 gives up instantly since the problem is outside its ability to respond quickly. System 2 takes over, and we get to decide if it's worth our while to invest the effort needed to find the answer.

Systems 1 and 2 are not fixed in their abilities. In fact, with enough repetition and practice, functions that may originally fall under the purview of the conscious and effortful System 2 may be taken over by System 1 and become intuitive and effortless. Think, for example, of driving a car. It takes time and effort to learn the controls and to get a sense for proper speed under different conditions, when and how hard to apply the brakes, and so on. In time, the brain creates and fine-tunes the neural circuitry needed to perform driving functions safely and efficiently until at some point these circuits become fast and reliable, and the brain allows System 1 to handle them, freeing System 2's resources for other tasks. An experienced driver rarely thinks consciously about how far to turn the wheel, when to slow down ahead of a turn, what position the shifter should be in, or how hard to step on the accelerator. We can say that when System 1 takes over functions that were previously handled by System 2, these functions became intuitive. Put another way, one's intuition had been augmented and extended by way of training and repetition.

Similarly, we can think of training our artistic intuition. This requires that we first consciously (using System 2) create the required neural circuitry: the thought patterns conducive to creative visual expression. Once these neuronal paths are created, we then must exercise and "debug" them by repetition until they become fast and reliable enough that they end up being taken over by intuition (System 1), which then applies them quickly and automatically when needed, even if we are not consciously engaged in artmaking. In simpler terms, our goal is to create "good" habits—habits conducive to creative thinking and artistic expression—by first deciding what these habits should be, then training them repeatedly until they become intuitive—fast, effortless, and subconscious.

In training ourselves to become better visual composers, it's important to consider that our goal is not just to evolve applicable skills but also to form and to practice general attitudes and personality traits conducive to creative expression. Of these, two that are supported by good science and are especially worth honing are: mindfulness (a practice) and openness (a personality trait).

Mindfulness is the practice of focusing conscious attention on qualities of your present experience—deliberately claiming whatever attention your brain may unwittingly spend (often waste) on distracting thoughts, worries, ruminations, and activities unrelated to your present experience (e.g., checking your work email while on vacation, or logging in to see what your friends are posting on social media). The goal of mindfulness is to train yourself to assign every bit of your attention toward recognizing and acknowledging what is happening around you and within you in real time, without judgment or overthinking. This is not easy. It means, among other things, training yourself to recognize distracting thoughts and feelings as they arise, and to have the power to detach from them emotionally and to set them aside for a period so they don't influence your mood, your contentment, and your gratitude for other, more elevated aspects of your present experience. Beyond just being useful to creative work, consider that gaining such abilities is also a powerful way of relieving anxiety, increasing happiness, and building up emotional resilience.

I should clarify that while mindfulness may increase your chances of coming up with creative ideas, you should not expect such ideas to come to your mind as you are being mindful. The point of mindfulness is to train your mind not to become distracted, to notice things relevant to the quality of your experience and that may be employed in creative, expressive ways (e.g., noticing subtle elements or arrangements that may yield a photograph, which you may otherwise miss), and to increase the odds of coming up with creative ideas as a matter of course.

You can't summon creative ideas on demand. Creative ideas require periods of subconscious processing known as incubation before they mature to a point where you become conscious of them. This is the reason such ideas sometimes seem to pop into your mind unexpectedly when you are distracted—when taking a walk or a shower, or on the verge of falling asleep. The point of mindfulness is not to force creative ideas but to prime your brain to consider creative ideas even when you are not conscious of doing so. Mindfulness gives your brain the raw materials for creative ideas, such as awareness of things you can use in a composition, as well as awareness of your inner states—your moods and emotions—that may be worth expressing in your artistic work (or letting go of consciously, if they are unproductive).

There are many ways to train yourself in mindfulness, ranging from meditation to a technique I teach in my workshops called *visual inventory*. A visual inventory is simply a list, whether written or mental, of things you notice in your environment. To produce a visual inventory, make yourself comfortable (I recommend sitting down and removing your backpack and eating or drinking if you wish) so you are not distracted by discomfort, then scanning your surroundings and enumerating as many things as you notice, regardless of whether you feel they have any photogenic potential. This technique is similar to meditation in the sense that it focuses attention consciously on your present experience (and away from distracting thoughts). It also prompts your brain to become aware of things without judgment or preconception—just noticing things around you. Unlike most meditation techniques, a visual inventory is directly conducive to considerations of visual composition. It gives you a rich list of ingredients that you may not otherwise notice, from which you may compose a photograph. (Simply put: you can't compose photographs from things you don't know exist.)

Openness (known in some psychological models of personality as *Openness to experience*) is a personality trait referring to the degree that you are receptive to a broad range of possibilities and experiences, trying new things, and venturing outside your comfort zone and default ways of thinking. People differ in their innate degrees of openness. Much like physical traits, personality traits are largely rooted in genetics. Openness, like other traits, may also be affected by external influences such as your socioeconomic status, your culture, your lifestyle, and your political ideology.

People who are liberal in their views generally possess greater degrees of openness than those prone to conservative thinking. If you are in the latter group and don't already have a high degree of openness, you may have to work hard, perhaps even need to overcome some discomfort, to transcend your default mode of thinking, if you wish to make yourself more open. It's worth reminding yourself that, while increasing your openness may be hard to do when it comes to such things as social, political, or religious views, art is different from these things in some

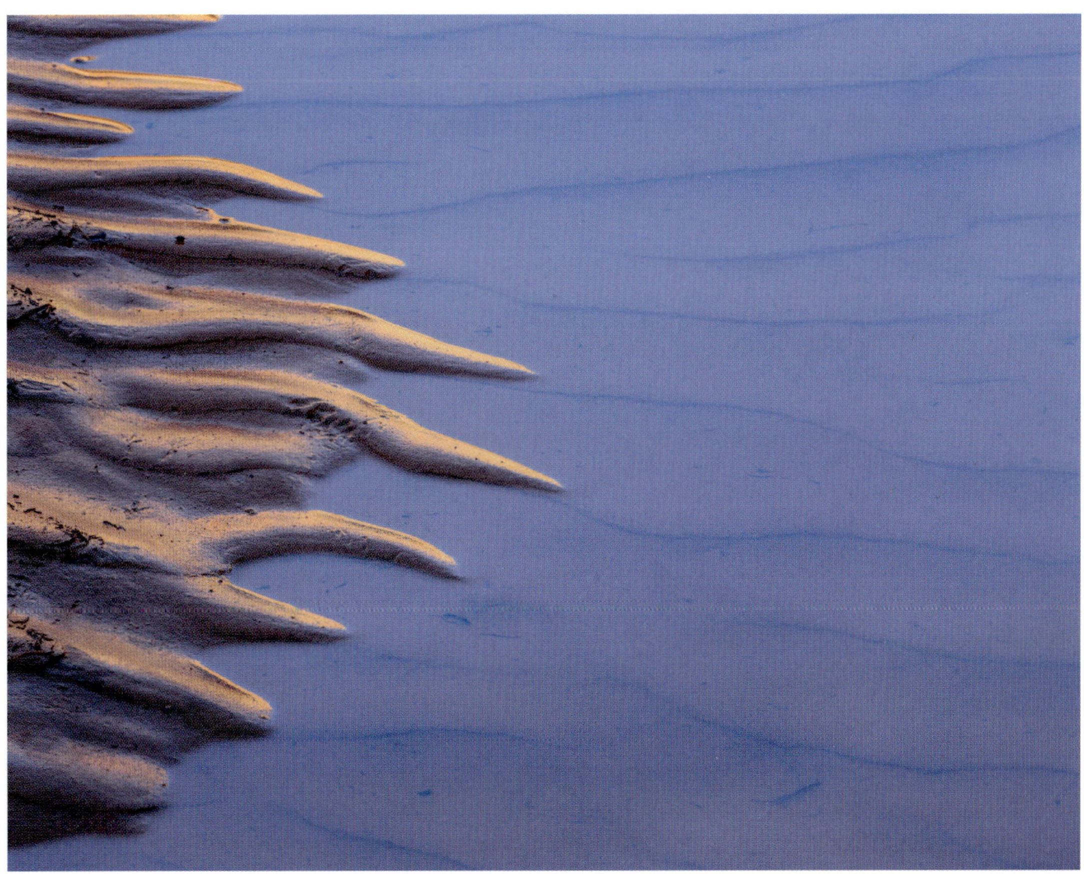

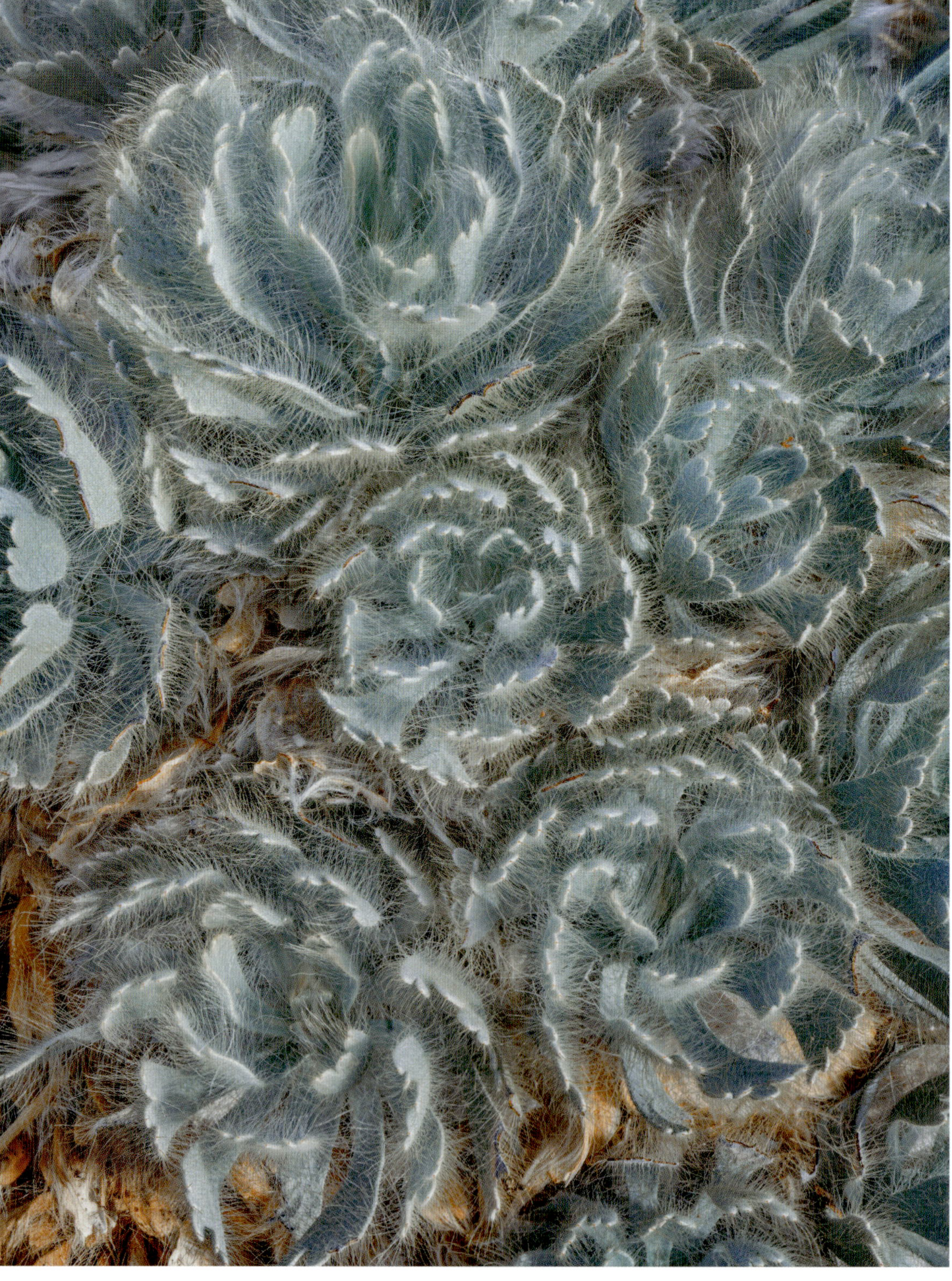

important ways. Art is largely a subjective and personal matter. There's no reason that a person can't hold traditional and conservative views in some aspects of life, and at the same time, also feel free to explore and experiment freely in art.

Making yourself more open is about, as the platitudes go, "pushing your envelope," prompting yourself to "think outside the box," examining your convictions and prejudices, and taking incremental risks even when it may feel uncomfortable. Ultimately, it may be that your predisposition to a certain degree of openness, rather than how hard you try, may limit how far you can push yourself. In this sense, openness is no different from such traits as athletic predisposition or extraversion—different people are wired differently. This means your goal should be to strive to become as open as you can be within your physical and cognitive capacities, and not judge your artistic accomplishments relative to those of others who may be more naturally predisposed to creative ideas. (Don't necessarily envy such people, as the cognitive traits that make them more artistically creative may also make them lacking, or even miserable, in other important ways.)

To summarize, you may train your intuition by such exercises as meditation or making visual inventories, and by pushing yourself consciously to become more open. You can also train yourself to become a better divergent thinker (i.e., force yourself to tackle creative tasks with no preconceptions and to come up with as many possible solutions as you can before deciding on the "right" one).

Now we come to the point where the proverbial rubber meets the metaphorical road: how to put all this to use when faced with a photographic opportunity. For this, I offer a reductionist approach. Think of composition as an optimization problem—a problem of finding optimal solutions to three components of composition: *framing*, *perspective*, and *balance*. (Being interrelated, all three components should be considered simultaneously, and not in any order.)

Framing is deciding where to draw the frame boundaries: where to cut off the composition on the top, bottom, left, and right. Framing is obviously important in deciding what to include in and what to exclude from your composition, but that's just the beginning. Many gestalt principles governing what viewers will pay attention to and what impressions viewers may experience depend on where things are within the frame and the relationships between visual elements. To become a better visual composer, I recommend training yourself to frame your compositions in your mind, without looking through a finder or a composition card. This will free you to consider a variety of aspect ratios, inclusion and exclusion of certain elements, and so on, without the discomfort of having to manipulate physical objects or being limited arbitrarily to your camera's aspect ratio.

Perspective is, as Ansel Adams put it, "knowing where to stand." More precisely, perspective is the spatial relationship (referring to relative positions in space) between your camera and your subject. Beyond just knowing where to stand, perspective also depends on the magnification of the lens you use (higher magnification, as in long lenses or macro photography, will have a "compression" effect, whereas lower magnification, as in wider lenses, will have a "stretching" effect). Think of how many things you can control just by moving yourself around: you can include or exclude certain things, bring things closer together or pull things apart from each other, juxtapose some things against other things, make some things larger or smaller relative to other things, hide things behind other things, and so on. Note that perspective is the one parameter you cannot easily modify in post-exposure processing. Be sure to consider your possibilities carefully before departing from the scene.

Balance may be the most nuanced of the three considerations of visual composition. Balance is about distribution of weight. For our purposes, the goal is to balance what's known as "visual weight." Think of visual weight as a gravitational force for attention; the more visual weight an element within the frame has, the more it will draw a viewer's attention. A balanced composition is one in which the distribution of visual weight guides viewers' attention toward those elements you wish for them to notice. Visual weight is affected by placement, color, visual relationships, and other factors.

A good composition, by this approach, is one in which framing, perspective, and balance are chosen optimally. Unlike so many rule-based or recipe-based approaches, optimizing framing, perspective, and balance does not imply doing so within the constraints of any template or in any order. Also, the very act of considering these parameters explicitly will have the long-term effect of training your brain to think about these concepts intuitively. The more you practice it, the better you will get and the less effortful it will seem.

Concept and Visualization

A photograph is not an accident—it is a concept. It exists at, or before, the moment of exposure of the negative. From that moment on to the final print, the process is chiefly one of craft; the previsualized photograph is rendered in terms of the final print by a series of processes peculiar to the medium.
—Ansel Adams

Visual perception—how our brains make meaning from visual information—relies on both objective and subjective factors. This means that, even if there are some "rules" of visual expression known to inspire predictable effects in viewers of art, at best only a portion of those rules is universal. Even if following such rules may prove effective in a given photograph, this evidence should be considered anecdotal. To suggest that so-called "rules of composition" be accepted as universal truths just because they work in a handful of anecdotal cases is what philosophers refer to as *argumentum ad consequentiam* (Latin for "appeal to consequences")—a type of logical fallacy wherein something is considered as true only because its presumed consequences are desirable (or as false if these consequences are undesirable).

Viewers intuitively derive meaning from a picture by how individual elements are arranged within the boundaries of the frame, and relative to each other. This collective unified meaning is referred to as *gestalt*. Gestalt research is fairly mature, and we now have a good understanding of some universal rules for how the human brain decides what to pay attention to in the frame, how the brain may attempt to connect elements that seem to have common qualities (consistency, continuity, and so on), and other useful information. While *gestalt* is a good term to use in scientific study of visual perception, for artists I think that a better way to refer to this collective meaning is as a *concept*. In plain terms, the concept for a work of art is the thing that the picture is *about* (as opposed to the things the picture is *of*)—the thing an artist wishes to express to viewers, or the emotional effect an artist intends for the work to impart (in cases where the work is not intended to express any singular, decisive meaning).

A concept can be as simple and obvious as inherent aesthetic appeal (pretty flower, bucolic scene), or as complex as mood, emotion, humor, fatalism, symbolic meaning, metaphor, surprise, a visual riddle intended to prompt viewers to fill in their own meaning, or even meaning that has no word equivalent. A photograph aiming to express a concept (that is, a photograph intending to achieve something other than just portray an obvious, recognizable subject) is, as the term suggests, an *expressive* photograph (as distinct from a *representational* photograph). A good way to think of expressive photographs is as photographs intended primarily to convey and elicit subjective meanings, rather than to portray objective appearances. (Certainly, these are not hard-and-fast distinctions, and some overlap is to be expected, especially in photography, which relies on material objects as input.)

Studies of consciousness offer some useful analogies to characterize the effects of expressive art. Both artistic perception and consciousness are complex cognitive processes arising from simpler functional components. Consciousness has been a lively topic of research and philosophical thinking in recent years, with many scientists attempting to unravel the "neural correlates of consciousness" (NCCs)—the physical components and activities in the brain that give rise to having a conscious experience: the ability to recognize, feel, and respond to things in our environment.

Philosopher David Chalmers suggested that studies of the NCCs, even if successful, will only solve what he termed "the easy problem of consciousness"—the mapping of certain perceptions to certain brain regions or processes. In contrast, Chalmers coined the term "the hard problem of consciousness," referring to how these disparate brain activities come together to form qualia—the (perhaps illusory) sense of having subjective experience: of being a singular, unified, conscious, free-willing entity. Similarly, we can define "the hard problem of composition" as the challenge of unraveling how our known responses to individual visual stimuli (lines, shapes, patterns, colors, recognizable objects, and so on) may combine to give rise to a greater unified perception (i.e., gestalt) of an image composed of these stimuli. As with the hard problem of consciousness, at this time science can tell us little about the hard problem of composition, especially when it comes to art.

In his book *The Aesthetic Brain*, Anjan Chatterjee sums up the current state of our knowledge of how the human brain perceives and responds to art:

> *We encounter limits of what neuroscience can contribute to aesthetics when we consider meaning in art. Neuroscience has something to say about the way we recognize representational paintings. We know something about how we recognize objects or places or faces. . . . But this knowledge is about our general understanding of these categories of objects and not about the particular response to a Cézanne still life, or a Rembrandt portrait, or a Turner landscape.*

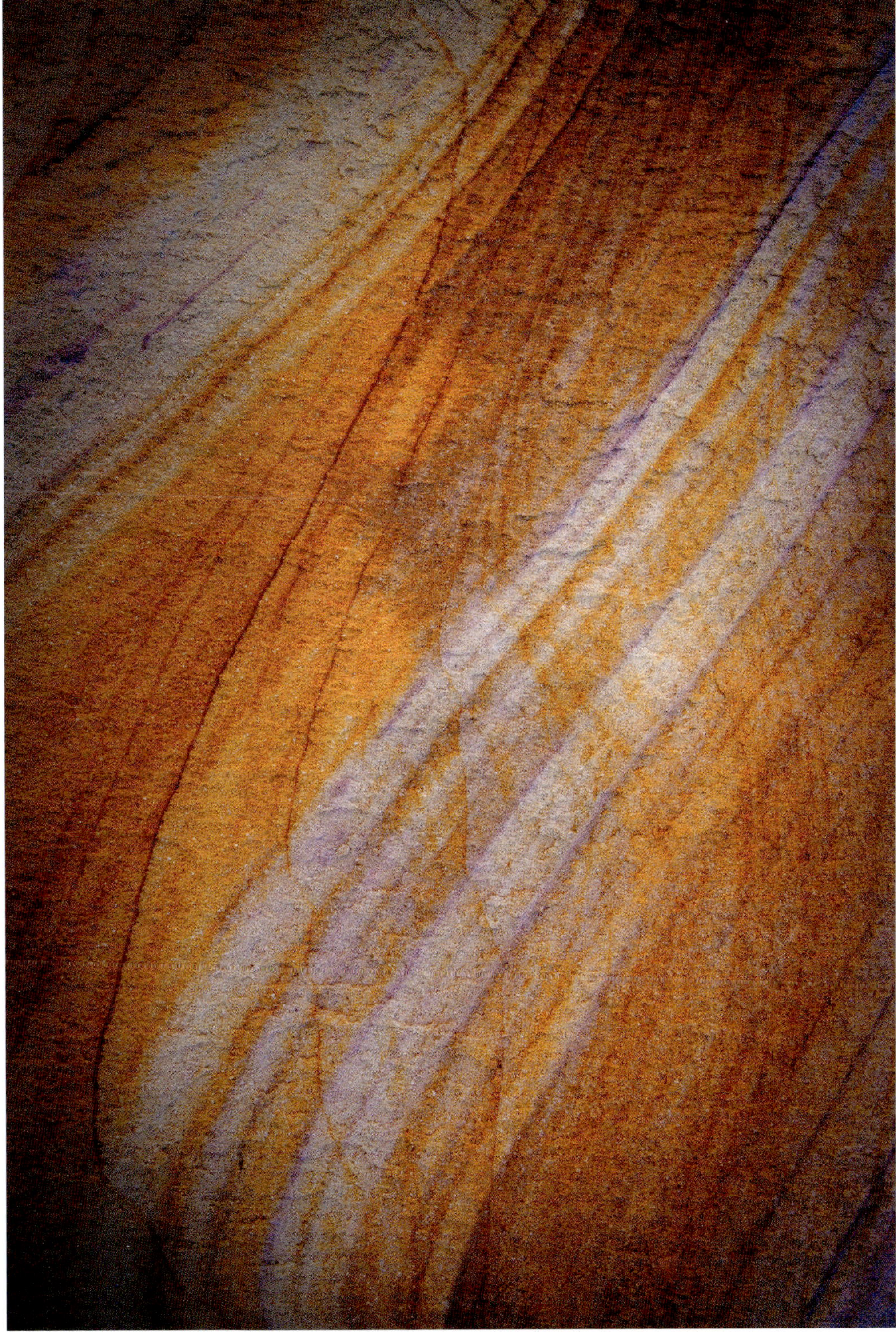

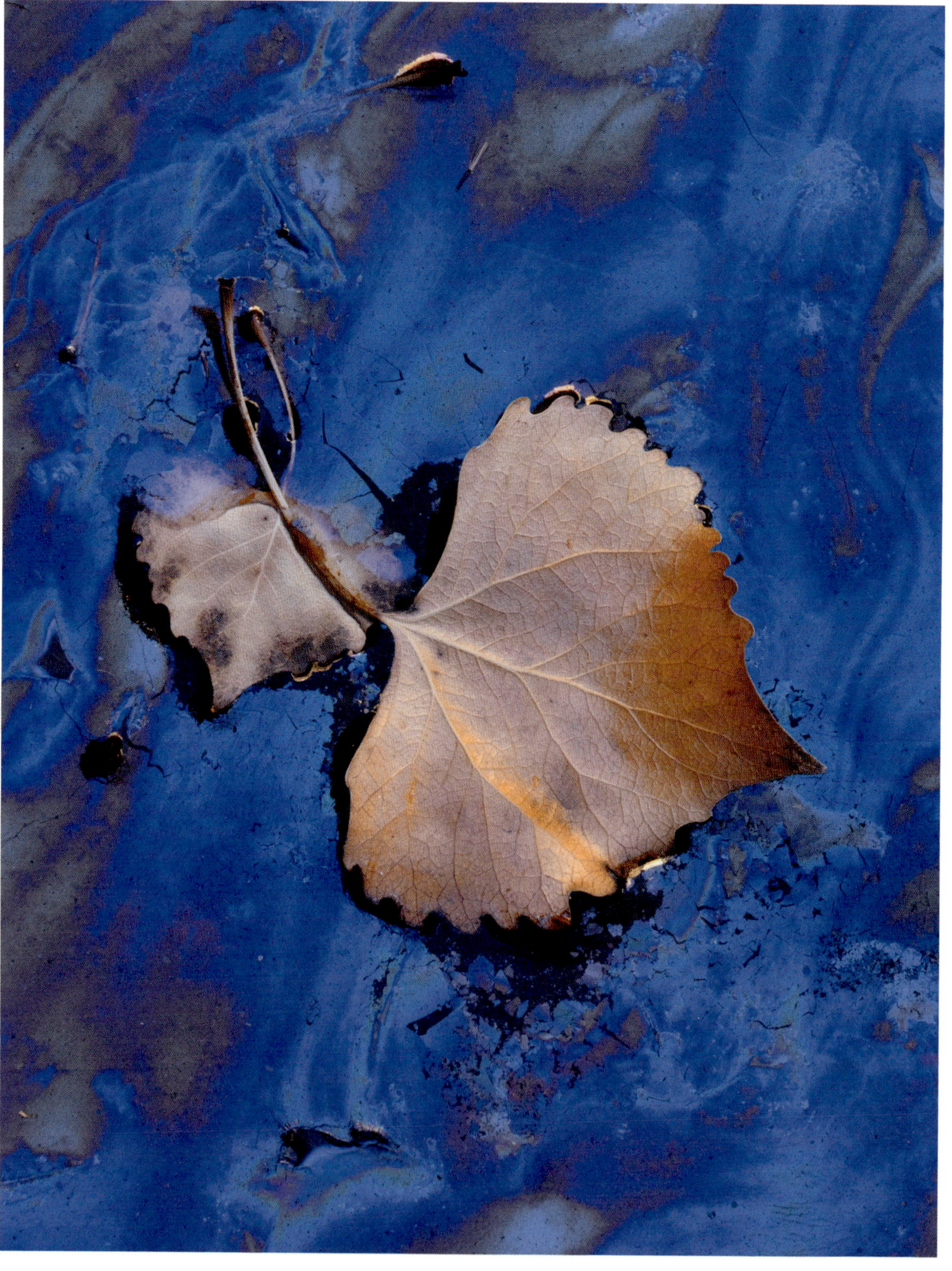

It's no surprise that art keeps evolving and changing in disruptive and unpredictable ways. Since no rules for making or perceiving art are known to exist beyond some simplistic knowledge of how we may respond to certain elements (colors, shapes, faces), artists continually discover new ways of expressing various concepts visually. Classical art doesn't look like impressionist art; impressionist art doesn't look like abstract art, and so on. It's all but certain that art movements yet to come will look little like today's art. It is also certain that these movements will not arise from the ranks of those who stick only to commonly established patterns. More pertinent to photography, these movements are also not likely to come from those who hold overly conservative notions of what's "appropriate" or "ethical" to portray in a photograph. Alas, photography as a medium for art suffers from such conservatism to a considerably greater extent than other, more established, media.

The consistent rising of new movements, new ways of thinking, and ultimately new artistic expressions relies on the human capacity for creativity. Adhering too closely to rules, to traditions, and to established templates suppresses creativity. Applying known templates and following prescribed recipes relies on what's known as *convergent thinking*—thinking that aims to use known methods to arrive at known (preconceived) outcomes. On the other hand, creative ideas require a different kind of thinking: *divergent thinking*—coming up with solutions on the fly without having a preconceived outcome, considering many possible solutions at each point of decision before settling on a course of action.

Creativity also suffers when things are made too easy, such as reducing an activity to stepwise processes or to a list of tips. The easier something is to accomplish, the less creative it is likely to be, and the more likely it is that others have already done it before. Ease also hinders the experience of flow, which requires, according to pioneering psychologist Mihaly Csikszentmihalyi, "a voluntary effort to accomplish something difficult and worthwhile."

Suppose one acknowledges the benefits of striving for creative expression in photography and is willing to invest the effort needed to gain the rewards of flow and discovery, and perhaps even make some significant contribution to the evolution of visual art. Now what? If the art of visual composition is indeed so mysterious that it cannot be reduced to lessons and rules, and science can tell us relatively little about it, then how does one get good at it?

Although we don't know enough to articulate the rules of expressive visual composition, we do have a way of testing our compositions—to tell successful compositions from unsuccessful ones. Each of us has a brain capable of consuming and interpreting visual art. We may not be able to articulate whatever rules of compositions may exist, but we know they are encoded in the vastly complex neuronal networks in our brains. The challenge, therefore, is not so much reducing visual composition to simple rules but conceiving original compositions and using our intuition—both innate and learned—to contrast them against each other. This is the essence of visualization.

We may not know how our brains decide what a good composition is, or what a given work of art expresses, yet we do these things all the time. We feed images into the neuronal "black box," and we make intuitive judgments about them: like or dislike, works or doesn't work, expresses X or expresses Y, interesting or dull, obvious or complex, appealing or boring, tasteful or kitsch. This black box—our intuition—has the answers (granted, at least in part, subjective rather than universal answers). We can use this intuition to separate good, expressive compositions from poor, inexpressive compositions to pare down possibilities we conceive in the process of divergent thinking. This, in summary, is visualization: the ability to conceive in the "mind's eye"[4] images that don't exist in any objective sense and decide whether they are worth bringing into existence—the very definition of creation.

[4]As I wrote this piece, *The New York Times* published a story revealing that different people may differ profoundly in their ability to visualize. The story highlights an uncomfortable truth: not everyone is equally capable of producing expressive art. Just like different people may score differently in IQ tests or in various personality traits, artistic ability is also not distributed evenly. This is a fact, not a judgment. There are two important conclusions to be drawn from this fact.

The first important conclusion is this: just like it is pointless for most of us to compete in some athletic pursuits against people whose body types are more suitable to these activities, it is pointless to judge one's art based on how it compares with others' art. The point of artistic work is not to win contests but to enrich and elevate one's life. I believe that just like most people can enjoy running or playing basketball even if unfit for the Olympic team, anyone can also reap the inner rewards of pursuing creative work, regardless of outcome.

The second important conclusion is this: art is among the most subjective pursuits that a person may choose to engage in. So long as we do not impose on others, we are each free to pursue our art in whatever manner, using whatever tools, and with whatever intention satisfies us most. Different people may find satisfaction and creative success in different aspects of photography (or any other creative pursuit), in different parts of the process, in different activities. The greatest rewards don't come from doing any one thing better than (or even as well as) others. The greatest rewards come from deep and prolonged immersion in a creative activity, however one chooses to pursue it.

Incubation and Creative Blocks 4

Creativity involves not only years of conscious preparation and training but unconscious preparation as well. This incubation period is essential to allow the subconscious assimilation and incorporation of one's influences and sources, to reorganize and synthesize them into something of one's own.
—Oliver Sacks

Anyone involved in creative endeavors likely is familiar with creative blocks—times when creative ideas fail persistently to materialize for prolonged periods. When the creative well runs dry, we often become anxious and seek reassurances, we remind ourselves of the inevitability of blocks, their transitory nature, perhaps even of times when creativity returned with renewed vigor after such episodes. We look for tips and strategies to break the block, we try to force ourselves to work despite the malaise, we wish for things to go back to the way they were. Still, as the days turn to weeks or months, anxiety and doubt keep building. Will this time be an exception?

There's another way to think about creative blocks: not as hindrances to creativity but as harbingers of creative renewals, as necessary breaks for the mind to replenish its creative resources, to clean house, to organize and assimilate new ideas and information.

Psychologist Eric Maisel speculated that to a creative person, creating is a way of making meaning. When we are not productive, according to Maisel, we lose our sense of meaning and spiral into depression. In his book *The Van Gogh Blues*, Maisel wrote, "This is why creating is such a crucial activity in the life of a creator: It is one of the ways, and often the most important way, that she manages to make life feel meaningful. Not creating is depressing because she is not making meaning when

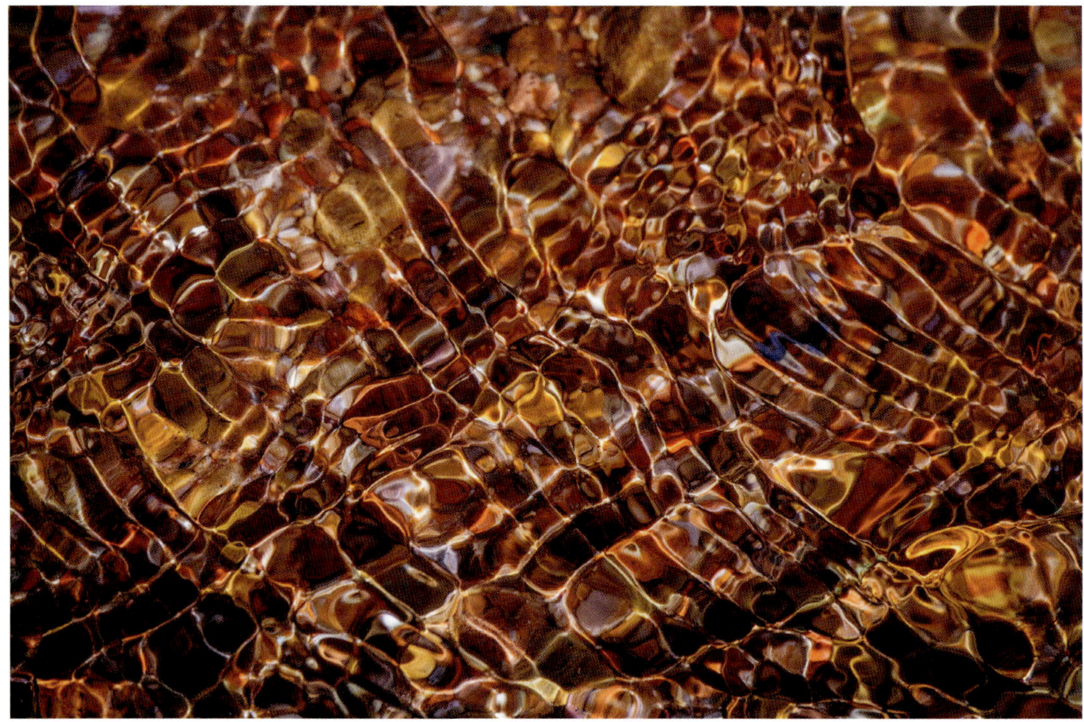

she is not creating." I think Maisel's point is true regarding creativity, but I also think it's worthwhile to point out a common misconception, which is this: to be creative is not the same thing as to be productive.

A creative product may (or may not) be the outcome of "creating," but a person may be creating, in the sense of being engaged in a creative activity, for prolonged periods before arriving at an idea that may lead to any tangible outcome. As it turns out, some of the brain processes involved in giving rise to creative ideas are not conscious. The phase of subconscious processing, before an idea or a solution comes to mind, is known as *incubation*. When incubating, creators may be "creating" without even knowing they are engaged in creative thinking. Even when doing other things. Even when asleep. These periods of incubation, therefore, are easy to confuse for creative blocks.

I am no stranger to creative highs: the experience of flow when immersed in creative work, the "aha!" moment of revelation or discovery when an exciting idea comes to mind, the sense of accomplishment and pride when creating a satisfying photograph, an article, or a book. The more original and personally significant the work, the greater the satisfaction, and the more energized I feel afterward to tackle my next challenge. Still, the reverse is not true: I don't feel that my life has lost meaning when I am not productive.

Some of my most meaningful experiences involve the assimilation of various dimensions of my experience—sensations, contemplations, awe, beauty—leading to intense emotions, sometimes to ideas whose usefulness may not be immediately apparent, and that are not ostensibly associated with any product. Such experiences may still count as creative if feeding into the subconscious parts of creative thinking, which for me are constant by virtue of the fact that I strive constantly to live a creative life: to shape my attitude toward and engagement with the world by constantly seeking and aspiring to discoveries, new ideas, and new knowledge. There is no doubt in my mind that these are essential to the conception of future creative expressions, even if I may not know what they are or apply any conscious effort toward them at a given time.

Certainly, those indoctrinated into associating such things as duty and self-worth with work may instinctively associate lack of productivity with such feelings as shame and distress. This is unfortunate. Susan Sontag observed this effect among photographers, writing, "Using a camera appeases the anxiety which the work-driven feel about not working when they are on vacation and supposed to be having fun. They have something to do that is like a friendly imitation of work: they can take pictures." Bertrand Russell, in an essay titled "In Praise of Idleness," wrote, "A great deal of harm is being done in the modern world by belief in the virtuousness of work."

When it comes to creative work, creativity—incubation and all—must precede work. As Timothy Egan put it in a *New York Times* opinion piece, "Creativity comes from time off, and time out." It is good for artists feeling blocked to remind ourselves that what we may perceive as a creative block is perhaps better described as a productivity block. Our creative faculties most likely are intact, perhaps even working subconsciously on new ideas, even if at any given time we may fail to come up with actionable ideas. It is also true, however, that work involving states of flow—even if not outright creative—often begets creative ideas by suppressing distractions and anxiety. This may suggest that one way to get through creative blocks is to work through them—clean the studio, do yard work, study, tend to accounting or other uncreative demands. In doing so, we may free up cognitive resources for those parts of our subconscious mind engaged in whatever it is they do while incubating new ideas. As psychologist Adam Grant put it, "It's only when you're told that you're going to be working on this problem, and then you start procrastinating, but the task is still active in the back of your mind, that you start to incubate. Procrastination gives you time to consider divergent ideas, to think in nonlinear ways, to make unexpected leaps."

Creative blocks, when they are short-lived, can be unpleasant, and often lead to a sense of relief when productivity and the flow of ideas return to their normal levels. Still, I think that there is something unique about notoriously persistent blocks—those that refuse to yield, for weeks or months. I believe that such blocks generally accompany significant change in one's life, especially for artists committed to self-expression in their work. When the self—the person—changes, former styles and methods that may have been expressive of the person one was may no longer express the person one has become. It may be that these prolonged and difficult blocks, in fact, are indicative of the subconscious mind exploring new ways to assimilate changes in personality, outlook, lifestyle, or philosophy. It's no longer about finding creative ways to express what one already knows how to express but about adapting to new knowledge, which by necessity takes longer and may be contingent on rare moments of insight before resolving itself.

My advice to anyone in the throes of a prolonged creative block is this: Before attempting to stem the block, first cut yourself some slack. Meditate on changes in your life, open your mind to novel ideas, make yourself comfortable with letting go of older formulas that may no longer satisfy, and with accepting that your subconscious mind may be telling you it's time to try something new that you may not yet know how to do. Most important, don't make an already vexing situation worse by interpreting what may ultimately be a necessary phase of incubation and creative growth as any indication of diminished self-worth, or as reason for self-flagellation. As psychologists like to say, give yourself permission to use this time to rest and renew, to explore possibilities, to indulge.

If the time has come, not just for new work but for new ideas, epiphanies, directions, or style, don't stand in your own way. Give it time. Let the creative circuitry in your brain do what it needs to do to adapt and to conceive new ways of thinking and producing work.

Anecdotally, one means of grappling with a creative block that has often worked for me is to write about creative blocks—to dredge from my mind what I know and what I have experienced regarding creative blocks. If nothing else, it helps keep things in perspective and to regain the confidence that, as the adage goes, "this too shall pass."

Limitations of Language 5

Pablo Picasso, speaking with his friend Brassaï (aka Gyula Halász)—the photographer nicknamed "the eye of Paris"—commented, "When you see what you express through photography, you realize all the things that can no longer be the objective of painting. . . . Photography has arrived at a point where it is capable of liberating painting from all literature, from the anecdote, and even from the subject. In any case, a certain aspect of the subject now belongs to the domain of photography. So shouldn't painters profit from their newly acquired liberty, and make use of it to do other things?"

Although no medium has yet been invented to "liberate" photography in the same way Picasso thought photography has liberated painting, photographic technology has advanced so rapidly since the medium's inception that to a large degree photography has liberated itself from many of its own former constraints—primarily its strict dependency on realistic representation and qualities of found color and light. Shouldn't photographers also, in the words of Picasso, profit from our newly acquired liberties and make use of them to do "other things"?

This may seem a rhetorical question today when so many photographers already do more with the medium than to work within the former constraints of, to use Picasso's terms, literature (documentation), anecdotes (right place, right time), and mimetic representation of various subjects. Like any other advancement in art, the liberation of photography from constraints of former traditions, styles, expectations, attitudes, and technical limitations has drawn the ire of some purists. For better or worse, however, there's no putting the genie back in the bottle.

Nearly a century and a half after Monet's *Impression, soleil levant* rattled the sensibilities of the art world of its day, no one today thinks of impressionism—the art movement inspired by the painting's title—as anything but a perfectly valid style of painting, and hardly a revolutionary one at that. Soon the same will likely be true of any number of now-novel styles of photography emerging from the greater freedoms afforded us today by technological advancements, by the constant efforts of creative photographers to explore and expand the boundaries of the medium, and by the ongoing evolution of thought in art. This evolution has trended so far toward greater abstraction, more personal expression, and challenging the roles that art may play beyond illustration and beyond realistic representation.

Just like impressionism expanded the expressive vocabulary of painters beyond realistic representation, and later movements (cubism, fauvism, and so on) continued to expand the expressive range of paintings even further, so will many of today's trends in photography ultimately—hopefully—expand photographers' expressive powers in time, beyond representation, and likely even beyond anything possible in painting. Those perturbed by such prospects will do well to consider that many who previously decried various artistic revolutions have often found themselves, as the expression goes, "on the wrong side of history."

Perhaps a more interesting question arising from Picasso's comment is not whether photographers today should do "other things" (the nature of progress makes that a practical inevitability) but, given that different media have different means and ranges of expression, should artists in general strive for those realms of expression exclusive to or best suited for their chosen medium, rather than those that may overlap with other media?

Picasso believed that painters should venture beyond realistic representation, not because realism is impossible in painting, but because photography is better suited for the task. Photographers, too, have expressed similar sentiments. Ernst Haas wrote, "To compete with the painter is not really our destiny; we are on the way to speaking our very own language. With it we will have to create our own literature." Edward Weston wrote cynically, "The camera then, used as a means of expression, must have inherent qualities either different or greater than those of any other medium; otherwise, it has no value at all, except for commerce, science, or as a weekend hobby for weary businessmen—which would be fine if they did not expose their results to the public as art!"

Considering that every medium has a range of expression that is unique to it, or for which it is better suited than other media, attempting to quantify and to compare the products of one medium in terms of another only works in those areas where the two media overlap in their expressive capacities. When it comes to art, "a picture is worth a thousand words" is as silly as "a book is worth a thousand bananas." (To be sure, I've had bananas that were more satisfying than some books, and I know some short quips that are more expressive than most pictures.)

Some things are expressible equally well in multiple media, some things can be expressed better in one medium over another, and some things can be expressed *only* in one medium and *not* in any other. The photographs I think of most highly (my own and others') tend to fall within that last category: they express things visually, not only better than words can but in ways that no number of words can. Indeed, I now strive to make only these kinds of photographs: photographs that may be augmented by words but whose effect can't be described entirely or at all in words—not a thousand, not a hundred thousand, not a million, not any other number.

Berenice Abbott wrote, "Photography can never grow up if it imitates some other medium. It has to walk alone." I agree with the first part but disagree with the second. Photography *can* walk alone, but it doesn't have to. There are many examples where photography can overlap with, augment, and collaborate with other media to expand an artist's expressive range beyond what photography alone can accomplish. In art, the mechanics and aesthetics of any medium are just means to expressive ends. For some expressions, pure "straight" photography may work best. For other expressions, perhaps other styles of photography may work better, or a combination of photography with words or music or other media. For some expressions, no form of photography can equal or surpass other media.

It is because different media have different ways and means of expression that I believe there is great value for any lover of art in studying a broad range of artistic works—not only by other artists but also in media other than one's own. Admittedly, I'm perplexed by such attitudes as "photographic celibacy," if only for the fact that I love photography, art, and expressions of creativity. It seems odd to me to deny myself these things just because they were made by other people or because I can't

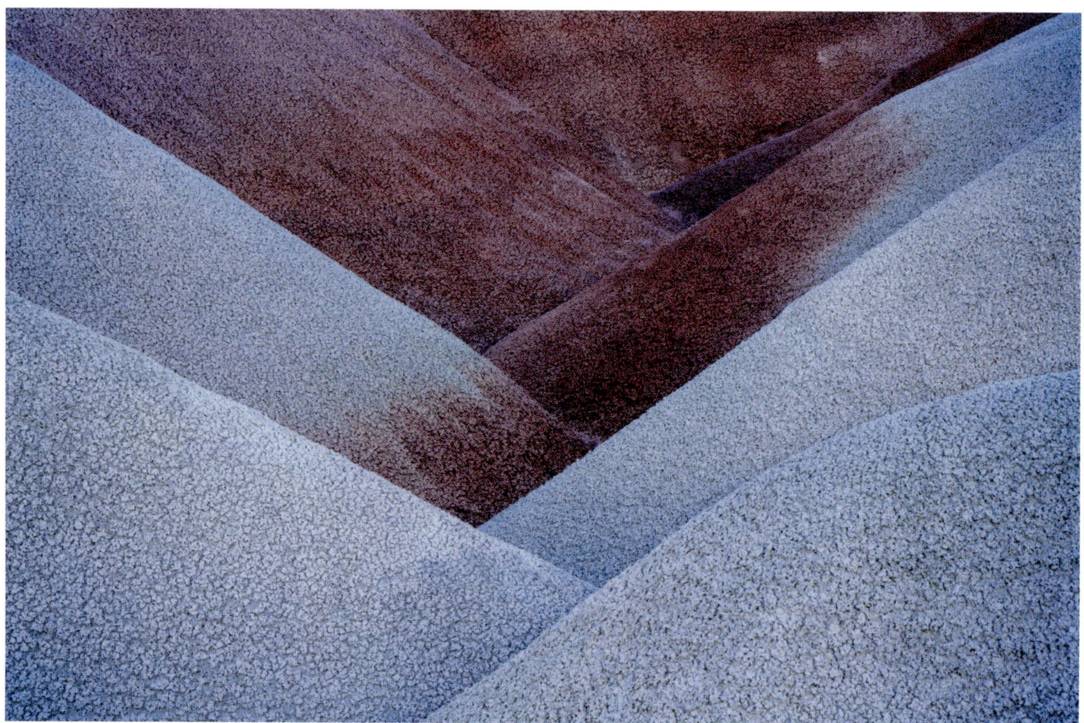

trust my own ethical conscience and creative skills to keep myself from copying others outright without making some creative contribution of my own. Seeing and assimilating as much art and knowledge as I can is not only a wonderful way for me to find inspiration and to learn from the genius of others; it is also a useful way of informing myself of things others had already done so I can better isolate my own expressive voice and distinguish it from others, and so I can chart a course for myself that is more likely to lead me to discovery and to progress rather than repetition, plagiarism, and creative stagnation.

I found it interesting when a photographer recently described to me a method he hoped would help him find his expressive voice. He selected a large number of photographs he liked, then spent considerable time writing down what he (thought he) liked about them, looking for commonalities he may then apply in his own work. While I believe there is value in spending time examining and being inspired by good photographs for one's own edification, I don't think that attempting to describe in words what one likes about these photographs is ultimately very useful.

Beyond perhaps identifying favorable subject matter or simple concepts such as color combinations or the use of certain specialized lenses, attempting to express

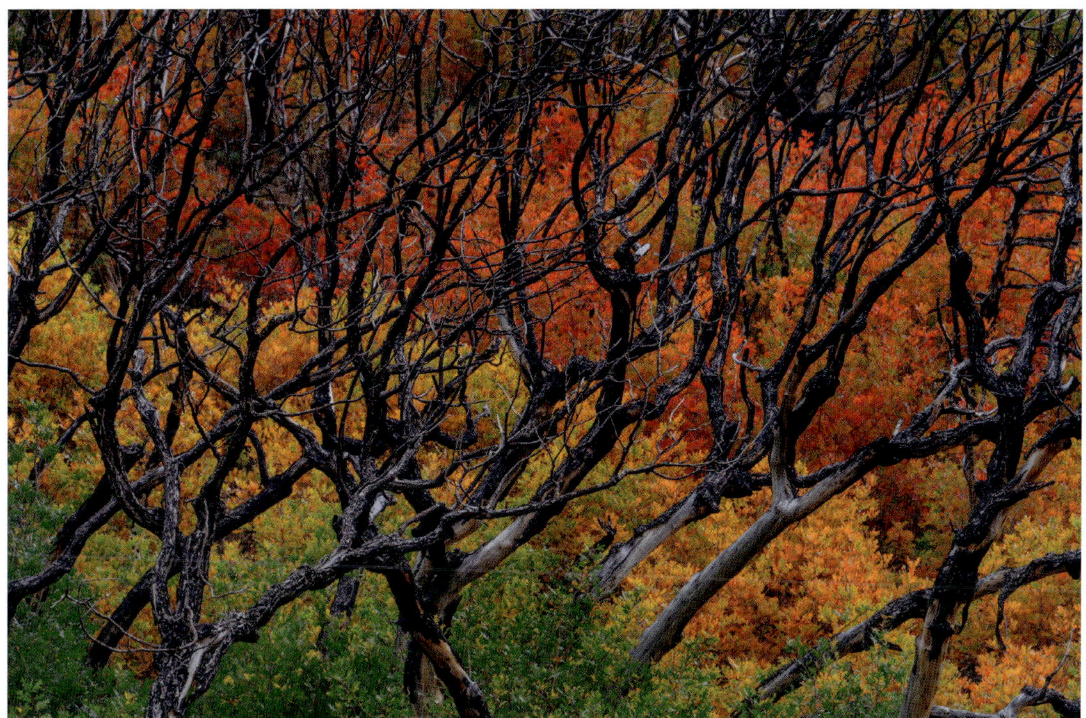

in the language of words things originally expressed in the language of photography comes with the risk of mischaracterizing the true reasons one may like or dislike a photograph. For one, some visual impressions may transcend the precision and expressive range of words. More important, some impressions may arise from subconscious intuition, rather than from formal qualities of a work. One of the great differences between verbal language and nonverbal, artistic expression is that words generally have precise and specific meaning, while artistic expression (distinct from documentary representation) are by nature and by necessity ambiguous.

The more ambiguous, complex, or abstract a work of art is, the less likely it is to be adequately describable in words. Perhaps it is fair to say that the most important and profound art is that which cannot be expressed in words. As Gustav Mahler put it, "For myself I know that, as long as I can summarize my experience in words, I would certainly not make any music about it." Or, as Ansel Adams put it, "A true photograph need not be explained, nor can be contained in words." (Presumably, by "true" Adams meant "artistic.")

When it comes to "finding" a personal artistic style, your best bet is ultimately to rely on your own intuition, on striving to broaden your knowledge and experience, and on constant learning by trial and error. Beyond what you may be able express in words, intuition reflects not only the foundations of your formal knowledge and understanding of art but also your sensibilities and the complexity of your personality at a point in time. The process of evolving as a person and as an artist to a point where your work takes on a consistent and recognizable style—an artistic voice—may be inefficient, effortful, and time-consuming. These may seem like detriments but, in fact, they are not. There are no shortcuts to finding one's own artistic voice. Even if there were, there would be a penalty to pay in taking them: the penalty of denying yourself the creative experience—the sense of flow, discovery, and pride in original creation. Time and effort are essential in forming and maturing a deeper understanding of yourself, your art, and the expressive powers of your medium.

The language of words evolved for specific purposes, and it imposes expressive limitations sometimes rooted in obsolete ideas (ask any writer about the challenge of writing gender-neutral narratives in most current languages). As Ludwig Wittgenstein put it, "Language sets everyone the same traps; it is an immense network of easily accessible wrong turnings." Don't let the limitations of the words become the limitations of your ability to express yourself in other media: in the language of music, in the language of painting, in the language of mathematics, in the language of photography. Each has its own breadth and means of expression, and each possesses at least some range of expressive powers that transcends those of other media.

The immersive multisensory panorama of your perceptual scene, right here and right now, is a reaching out from the brain to the world, a writing as much as a reading. The entirety of perceptual experience is a neuronal fantasy that remains yoked to the world through a continuous making and remaking of perceptual best guesses, of controlled hallucinations.

You could even say that we're all hallucinating all the time. It's just that when we agree about our hallucinations, that's what we call reality.

—Anil Seth

In daily life, we rarely doubt the reality we exist within. Our brains construct our perception of reality based on information detected by our senses, by our intuitions, or by inductive reasoning: our ability to derive reliable predictions based on prior experiences, knowledge, and common assumptions about causes and their effects.

We rarely consider that information coming from our senses is incomplete (and most of it is discarded before we ever become conscious of it), that our intuitions are often incorrect and prone to bias, or that inductive reasoning by its nature is never guaranteed to yield truthful conclusions. Our perception of reality therefore rests on incomplete evidence and potentially flawed assumptions, and on our limited capacities to infer meaning from these foundations quickly enough to respond in a timely way to events requiring attention and to avoid bumping into things. We are also bombarded constantly with potential distractions attempting to hijack our attention, emerging both from our own minds and from unexpected things in our environment.

A discussion of realism—in art, in photography, or in any other context—must begin with this concession: realism is never, and cannot be, an absolute and measurable quantity. Realism is always a matter of degree, approximation, and subjective judgment.

It's easy to become mired in the tangled philosophical implications of so many studies in physics, psychology, biology, and neuroscience (let alone such thought experiments as were proposed by philosopher Nick Bostrom suggesting a high probability that we may be living in a simulation)—that put to question common understandings of so many things we intuitively accept as real: ontology, materiality, temporality, cause-and-effect relationships, consciousness, even the belief that we are free-willing agents.

By unraveling the extent of the rift between empirical reality and subjective experience, science and philosophical thinking have given us, perhaps as an unintended bonus, some useful means of articulating the relationship between art and reality. Acknowledging that what is empirically real and what we perceive to be real are different things, we can say that while science concerns itself primarily with the former—with measurable and verifiable information—art concerns itself primarily with the latter—with subjective interpretations and manufactured realities. Nonetheless, we should concede that what a person feels, senses, believes, or imagines, even if at odds with objective reality or with the beliefs of others, is at least in some sense real to that person.

The raison d'être of all art, at least at this point in the evolution of art, is to affect its viewers' subjective experiences, not to report on objective facts. This may seem obvious to artists working in most media but raises some obvious challenges for those working in the medium of photography—a medium intended by design to render objective appearances of things as a random person will likely see them. This means that for photography to serve as a medium for artistic—subjective—expression, artists must knowingly and deliberately, at least to some significant degree, overcome, transcend, and depart from photography's default mode of objective representation. As photographer Minor White put it, "Camera objectivity has a way of getting into every photograph. I am calling this residue of objectivity, this glimpse of it, carelessness."

So as not to become mired in irrelevant technicalities and philosophical hyperbole, in this discussion I will use terms like "reality" and "realism" to refer to aspects of experience that most people will likely accept intuitively as objective realism. For example, people standing at a scenic viewpoint will likely agree about the existence, arrangement, color, and other visual qualities of the physical objects within their

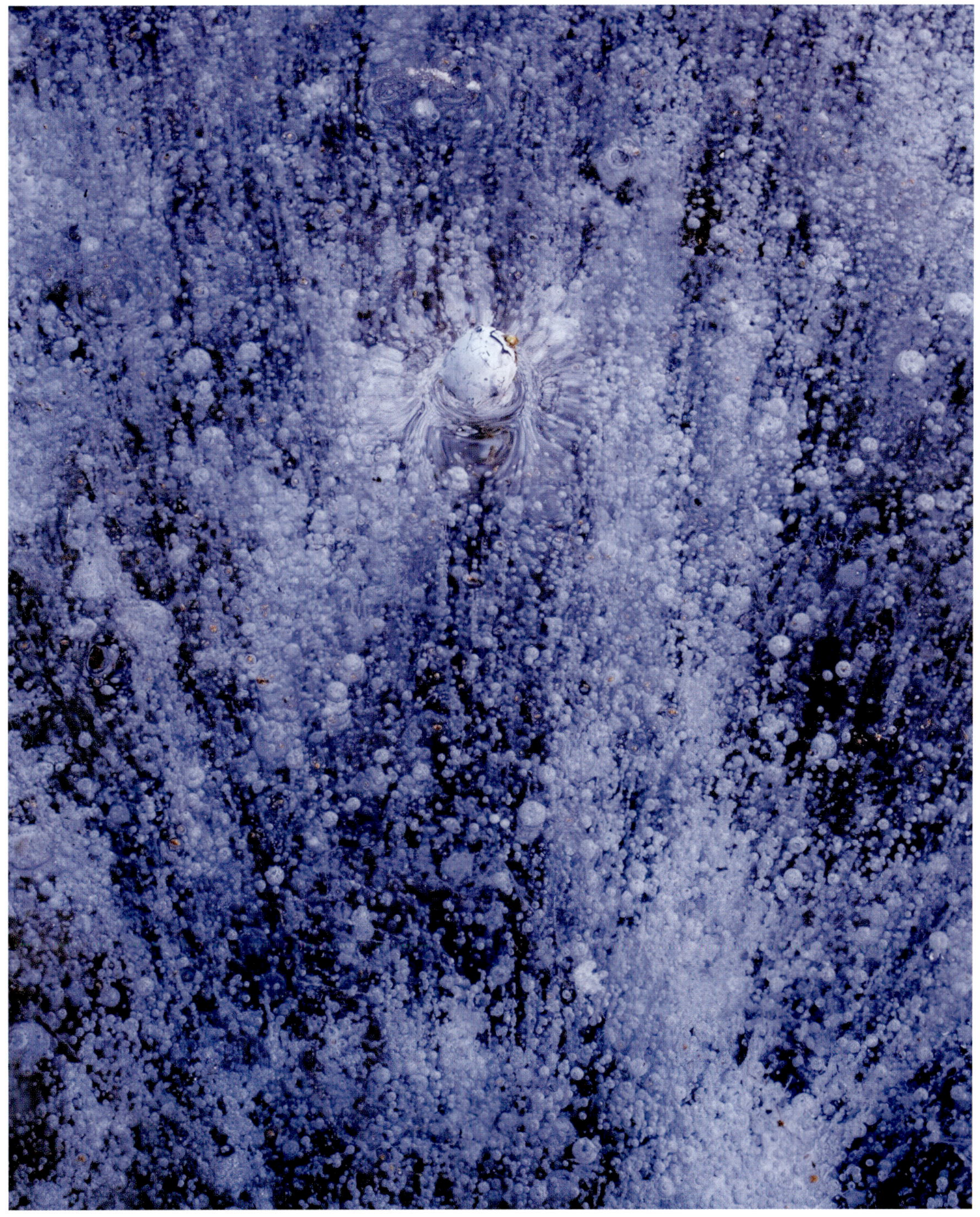

field of view. These people will likely also agree that certain objects and qualities are universally worthy of being considered beautiful, impressive, austere, or some other adjective.

*　*　*

Realistic views eliciting predictable and desirable impressions—pleasure, inspiration, calmness, excitement, yearning, awe—when captured as-is, even without creative contribution from the mind of a photographer, are the primary interest of most who pursue landscape photography as an art form. Alas, such "interest in things as they are" (in the words of Susan Sontag) is ostensibly at odds with current conceptions of art that place greater emphasis on creativity and expression, rather than on representation and depiction. The transition to this mode of thinking dates back at least to the late 19th century, when realism in painting gave way to impressionism and later movements. It's fair to say that photography, invented shortly before the advent of impressionism, has largely remained stuck in the realms of Realism and/or Romanticism that have long been supplanted by newer ideas in other artistic media. Indeed, the invention of photography, which relies on technology—rather than on honed manual skill—to do much of the "heavy lifting" of realistic rendition, has played no small role in nudging other artistic media away from realistic depictions.

Being that art, at least of the past 150 years or so, is generally concerned with subjective expression rather than objective realism, photographic artists who are committed to maintaining strict fidelity to realistic appearances risk limiting their expressive repertoires to just views and subjects that predictably elicit known emotional impressions. Although this may not seem like a severe limitation, in fact, it is. It explains, at least in part, why so much photographic work, especially in what is commonly considered "landscape photography," is repetitive if not outright plagiarized—same places, same subjects, same composition and processing styles.

This, however, doesn't mean that photographic media and processes are incapable of subjective expression. As Alfred Stieglitz put it (in 1899!):

> *The statement that the photographic apparatus, lens, camera, plate, etc., are pliant tools and not mechanical tyrants, will even to-day come as a shock to many who have tacitly accepted the popular verdict to the contrary. It must be admitted that this verdict was based upon a great mass of the evidence—mechanical professional work. This evidence, however, was not of the best kind to support such a verdict. It unquestionably established*

Photography as a medium for art is disadvantaged compared with other media, but not because of photography's mechanics. The greatest disadvantage facing artists working in the medium of photography is the pervasive prejudice that photography's only valid and acceptable use is objective representation—scientific, journalistic work. Viewers of photographs have been led to believe that what they see in a photograph is what they would have seen themselves if present at the same place and time the photograph was captured. Photographs are commonly expected to serve primarily some utilitarian purpose: to be a picture *of* something before they are considered also to (perhaps) serve some expressive purpose: being *about* something. In the minds of many, a photograph first has to fall into some descriptive category—a "street photograph," a "landscape photograph," a "portrait photograph"—before it may be considered secondarily for any artistic merit it may have. The notion that some photographs' primary, sometimes *only*, purpose is artistic expression and not representation of some quality inherent in the objects portrayed is an odd one to many people. Still, this limited view of photography's range of expression is a matter of belief, not any handicap inherent in the capabilities of the medium itself.

Alas, largely to blame for the limited acceptance of subjective expression in photographs are attitudes promoted by some of the historical "greats" of the medium. Consider that it's been well over a century since such movements as Realism and impressionism were considered contemporary in painting—about the same timescale as when pictorialism was the dominant style in photography, later to be supplanted by "straight" photography. If a painter today wanted to make impressionistic paintings, few would even think of deriding such work despite the fact that impressionism is no longer the dominant style in painting. But try presenting a pictorial (or other nonrepresentational) photograph in most mainstream media today, and you may find yourself assaulted and accused of such grave ethical violations as "manipulation" or "Photoshopping." For many consumers of photography, there is only one "true way." In my mind, fundamentalism has no place in art, and to arbitrarily limit an artist's range and means of expression is as a matter of principle a bad idea.

*   *   *

I am a photographer and an artist. I'm also an avid consumer of photographic art. In my own work, realism and natural aesthetics are important, but not because I feel myself under any obligation to remain true to them. My work is faithful to realistic appearances to a significant degree (not always perfectly) because I choose for it to be so, given that my aim is to express moods I experience in remote and lonesome natural places, owed largely to the effects that such environments have on my psyche. Considering myself a creative artist, I strive to show my viewers images that venture beyond anything they may have seen themselves or that have been done by others; and I strive to be self-expressive in my work, meaning that the moods and feelings I wish to inspire in viewers are ones I have felt, not contrivances or visual clichés manufactured for aesthetic appeal or popularity, but not rooted in a genuine emotional experience.

As a consumer of artistic photographs, my sensibilities and tastes extend greatly beyond just the kind of photographs I like making myself. The photographs that

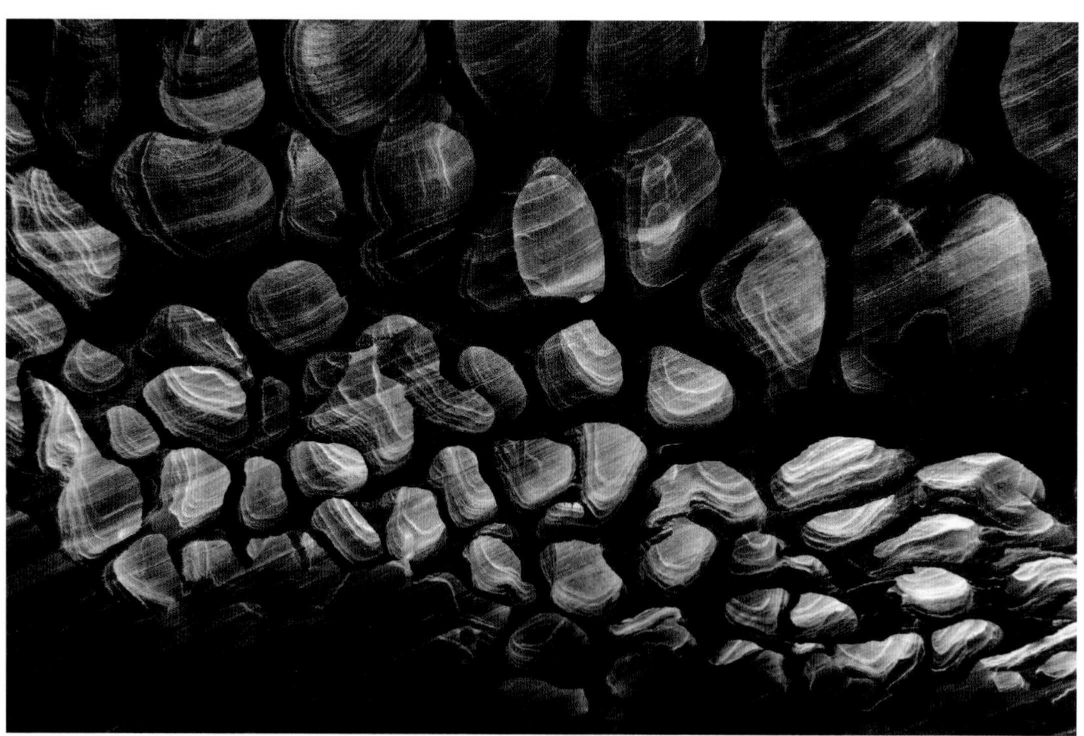

interest me most today are those designed primarily to express subjective moods, regardless of subject matter, rather than those that venture no further than to portray fortuitous objective appearances. When viewing a photograph presented as art, it doesn't bother me in the least if, to better accomplish a subjective expression, a photographer chose to depart to whatever degree from objective representation. In fact, I think that any creation worthy of the designation of art must involve such departure. Certainly, I have no expectation that the same composition or visualization would have been obvious to me in the same circumstances. That would mean the photographer's imagination played little or no role in composing the photograph, making it uncreative and unartistic, even if pleasing in some other way.

For any medium to be useful to an artist, it must allow a generous degree of plasticity: it must lend itself readily to subjective expression of concepts and feelings originating in the artist's mind and not just those inherent in or commonly associated with the subject. In the words of Henry Peach Robinson, "to the artist there is no merit in a process that cannot be made to say the thing that is not." There is little doubt in my mind that photography is not such a medium. Photography absolutely provides ample room for subjective expression, up to and including repudiating entirely the objective reality of the things photographed. This is evident by, if nothing else, the prevalence of so many discussions about whether photography should be *allowed* to depart from realism—a moot point if photography wasn't *capable* of such departure.

Indeed, there is no medium I know of—including photography—that is entirely limited by its nature to objective representation, having no ability to depart from realistic depiction and to be used as a means for subjective expression. Presented with this truism, some traditionalists may respond, "People believe photographs." This may be true for many viewers of photography, but it also concedes that the expectation of realism is a matter of belief, not an imposition of the medium. Beliefs by their nature are matters of choice. If this weren't the case, the very idea of belief would be unnecessary. Progress demands that beliefs must on occasion be challenged, expanded on, and, when appropriate, repudiated and abandoned in favor of more truthful or useful ones.

It is appropriate to believe that photographs are realistic when these photographs are presented as realistic and can be verified as such. When presented as art, the more appropriate belief is that a photograph is intended to express a subjective truth, not an objective appearance. To believe otherwise would be at odds with the purpose of artistic expression and likely lead to (justified or unjustified) feelings of deception and disappointment. Put another way: people shouldn't believe photographs; they should believe photographers. At least those photographers who are honest about the kind of reality they strive to express—photojournalism, expressive art, postmodern abstractions, fictional worlds, or anything else. All are real in some sense. They are just not all real in the same sense.

A person aspiring to become a photographic artist would do well to consider these questions: Do I want to describe things or to express things? Do I want to show my viewers what they would have seen if standing next to me, or do I want to impart to my viewers something about what I experienced that they couldn't know otherwise, even if looking at the same things I was? Even if the answer is some combination of expression and representation, leading to some overlap, the two can never be equal in importance without confusing viewers. One must be primary and the other secondary. This is because to do either one well, a photographic artist must also answer this follow-up question: If I want to describe something, what is it I want to describe? Or, if I want to express something, what is it I want to express? Most people have no problem answering the former but find it much harder to answer the latter.

There are several reasons we may struggle to articulate verbally what we wish to express in a photograph beyond objective appearances and common perceptions. One reason is that some things we may wish to express in a photograph are not, or not entirely, describable in words. Another is that often we are not consciously aware of our own feelings, their origins, their appropriateness, or whether they are worth sharing with others. It follows that to be a good photographic artist, it's not enough just to be a good photographer (just like in order to be a good artistic painter, it's not enough to know how to draw; and in order to be a good writer, it's not enough to know proper spelling and grammar). Just like a good painter must evolve a unique style, and a good novelist must have good stories to tell, photographic artists must also live, think, and shape their attitudes such that they have concepts and feelings worthy of expression, and also find the courage to express them publicly, in full knowledge that—like all art—not everyone may understand, like, or even accept their creations as intended.

Objective aesthetics are relatively easy to find and reproduce photographically. There's no shortage of resources to guide a willing photographer to any number of scenic locations that are impressive by their nature, regardless of any creative or expressive contribution from the photographer. There are also special-purpose lenses, filters, gadgets, software packages, and processing techniques that reliably produce interesting and popular visual effects requiring little effort, forethought, or emotional engagement. There are well-established compositional templates known to impress viewers, requiring only mechanical skills but no expressive intent. Art raises the bar. Art requires from the artist a degree of emotional investment and an elevated subjective experience, as well as the skill to express visually concepts beyond just "here's something pretty," "look where I've been," or "see how lucky I was."

There is undoubtedly value, even joy, in producing an attractive, impressive, or technically challenging photograph independent of artistic merit. It is the same kind of joy one may get from playing a game well or from successfully preparing a scrumptious dish by following a recipe. But this joy is different from creative joy, from expressive joy, from artistic joy, where accomplishment is not only measured in virtuosity of technical skill, volume of work, or popular appeal but also in the degree that one's work is uniquely their own, perhaps even breaking new ground, and giving tangible form to subjective experiences not otherwise available to anyone other than the artist.

Some people pursue photography as a shared passion that brings them together with others, fostering common interest and camaraderie founded in rewarding shared experiences. Others pursue photography with the goal of personal creative expression, which in some ways may be the opposite of sociability. To be creative is to be original, to distinguish oneself from others as an individual and not as a member of a group, to venture beyond other people's expectations and boundaries (possibly even involving degrees of risk, discomfort, or conflict). Whereas artisanship may be a group activity, art is an individual pursuit. Art requires the courage to distinguish one's subjective experience from others' objective perceptions. One's art should be faithful first and foremost to one's own states of mind and not be arbitrarily bound to—or by—imposed objectivity or social conformism.

Realism in painting has been superseded by numerous successive movements, but realistic painting still remains a valid and useful style favored by many. Likewise, photography should come to terms with its own potential to be a suitable medium for both subjective expression and objective representation, also without denigrating those who wish to remain realistic in their work nor those aspiring to chart new creative waters. Not only is such an attitude demonstrably more conducive to artistic evolution and progress (as evident in the histories of other artistic media), but it is also better aligned with our growing understanding and acceptance of the extent and variability of subjective realities. Genuinely expressed feelings, even if the mode of their expression ostensibly departs from realistic appearances, may be just as (sometimes more) real in their effect as anything a viewer may derive from representational depictions of superficial appearances.

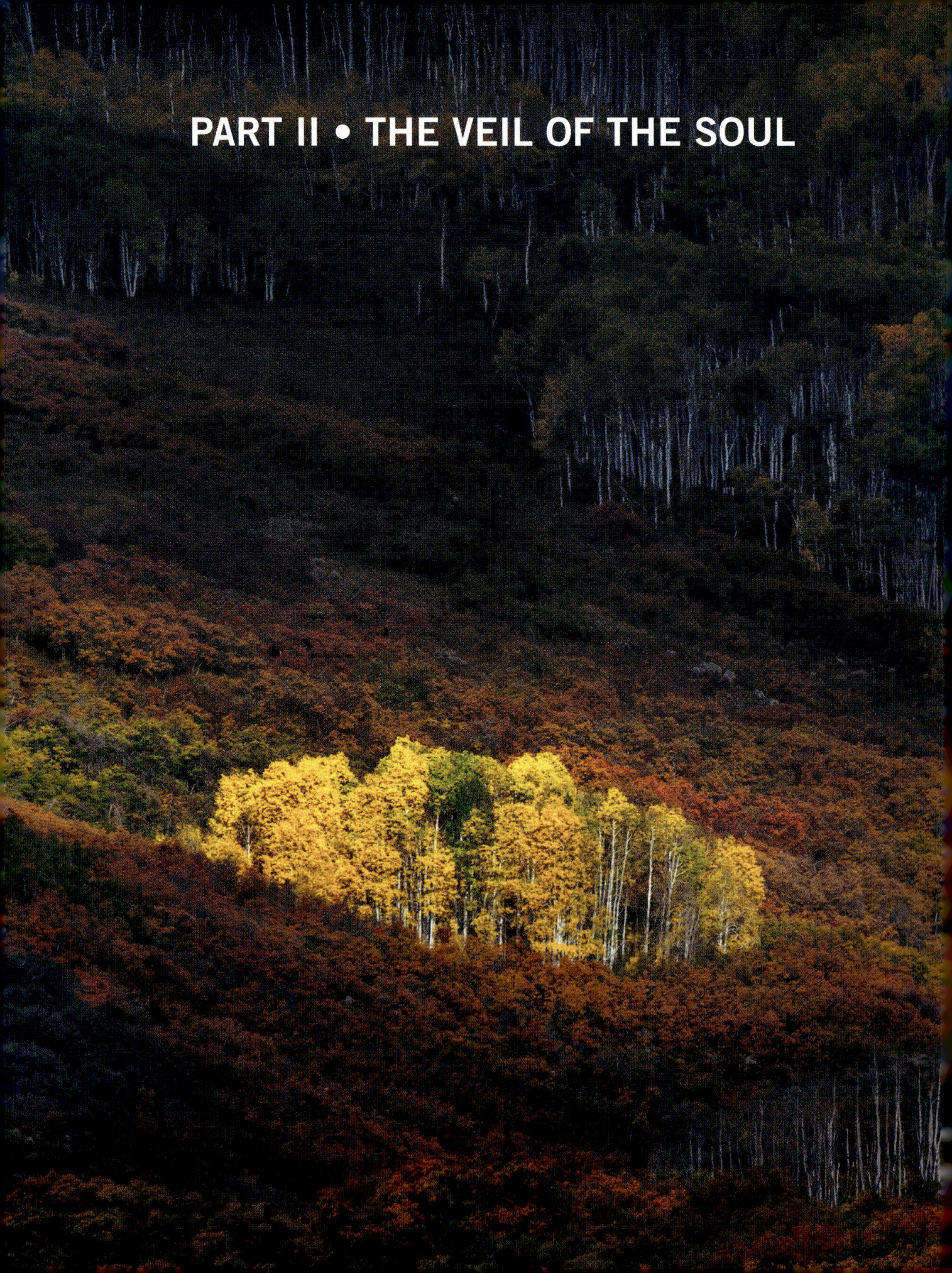

PART II • THE VEIL OF THE SOUL

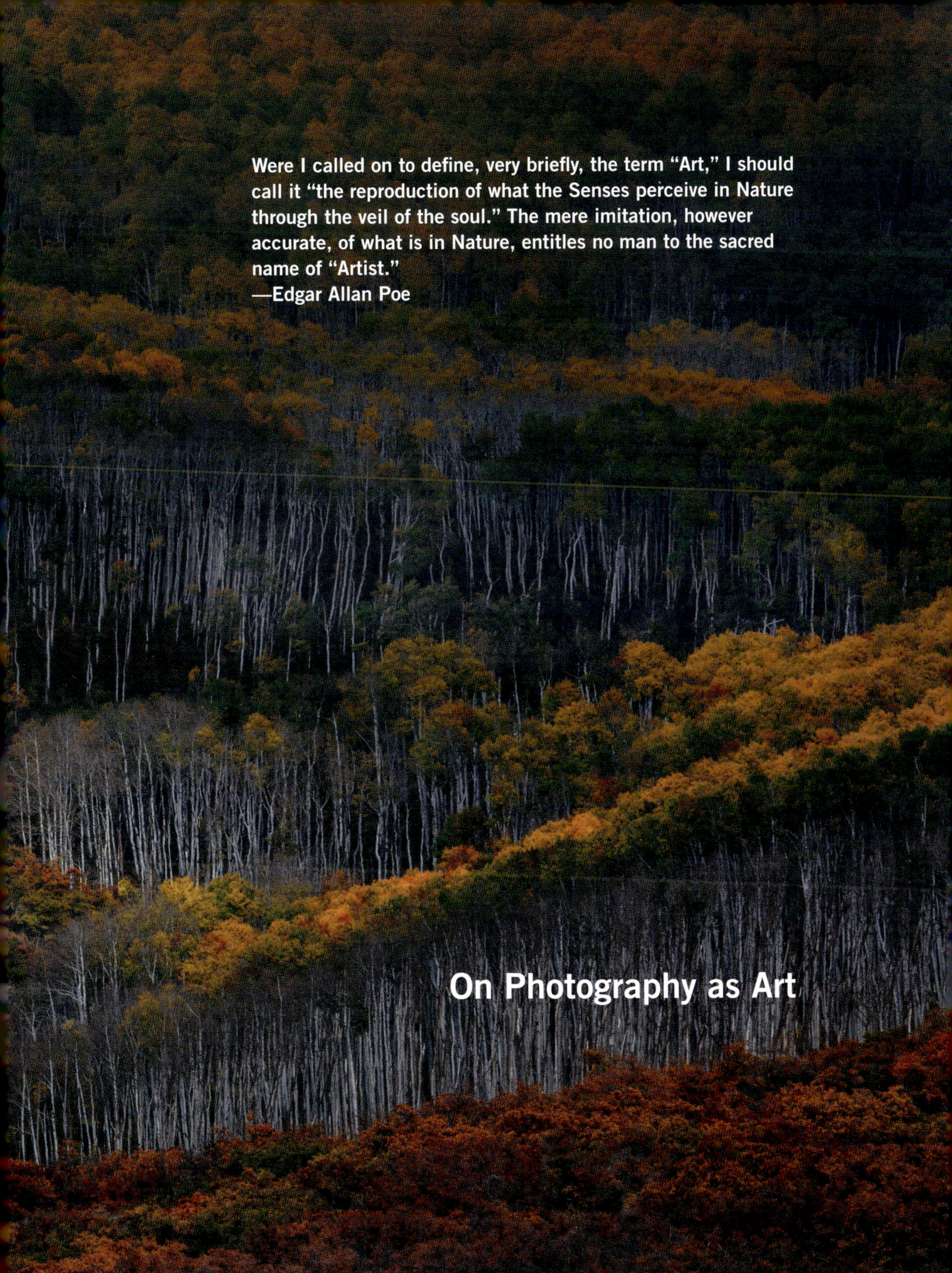

On Photography as Art

7 Artistic Merit in Photography

In our time it seems entirely appropriate that the widest choice be open to artists. Those using the camera or other photographic means to produce works of artistic merit should seek to exploit their medium in the most adventurous ways. . . . The derogatory use of the term *artifice* is more often than not a bugaboo. Art is artifice. Its reality is of another nature than that of the purely physical world.
—Aaron Scharf

In 1859, not long after the invention of photography, French poet and critic Charles Baudelaire penned a scathing critique of the medium and its (lack of) artistic merit. According to Baudelaire, "This industry [photography], by invading the territories of art, has become art's most mortal enemy."

History has deemed Baudelaire wrong (at least about photography). Both art and photography have come a long way since his diatribe, and the question of whether photography is (or is not) art has been settled numerous times. In brief: the question of whether photography is art is nonsensical in its very premise. Photography, without further qualification, is no more an art than writing, baking, or whittling. Photography is an activity—a means of producing images, some of which are artistic and many of which are not. That something is a photograph does not make it art, but that some photographs are art is not in dispute except, it seems, among those ignorant of the history of art and photography.

It seems a common misconception among many photographers to consider the designation of "art" as a badge of honor, as if art is—always and unequivocally—better than "non-art." This is patently nonsensical. There is no shortage of impressive and important photographs that are not art, just as there are many photographs that may qualify as art by some definition yet can be considered (at least subjectively) trite, banal, or kitsch. Just because something happens to be a work of art does not mean that this thing is necessarily venerable or important.

The term *art* has been largely settled, at least among scholars, to refer to objects created by human skill and imagination (i.e., creativity). Anything that meets these qualifications is art. There are, of course, other definitions for the term that may encompass almost anything—artifacts produced by skill but without creative imagination, random naturally occurring phenomena, even strategies for war. It is fair, therefore, when a person presents something as art, if that thing does not fit obviously within the "product of human skill and imagination" criteria, to ask that person this question: by what definition is it art? The point being that not all definitions are equally venerable. Knowing the definition by which a claim to art is made is an important factor in evaluating a work's artistic merit.

For example, a person may present a beautiful and expertly produced photograph as art even if that photograph is a plagiarized copy of another person's photograph. Such a photograph may fit some definition of art, but it obviously fails to meet the "imagination" criterion (i.e., it is not creative). This is an important bit of information for one attempting to assess the photograph's artistic merit. Despite being similar to the original work, a plagiarized copy, it's fair to say, is considerably less venerable than an original, despite perhaps making an excellent piece of decoration.

Another useful criterion for judging artistic merit is expressiveness—whether, and how well, a work of art expresses an artist's thoughts and feelings. To the degree that a plagiarized photograph may be considered expressive, one should consider that the photograph, in fact, expresses the feelings of the artist who made the original work, not those of the photographer who copied the work, even if the copy was produced with great skill.

If we accept the definition of art as a product of human skill and imagination, then Baudelaire's premise for dismissing photography as a medium for art becomes moot. The medium used to produce a given work may indeed factor into one's subjective judgment of artistic merit, but it has nothing to do with whether a given work meets the definition of art. For a medium to be deemed *un*suitable for art, this medium should require no trained skill and allow no room for creative expression. Photography is decidedly not such a medium.

What remains ambiguous and open to subjective judgment is not whether a thing is or is not art but whether, and by what criteria, that thing may be considered

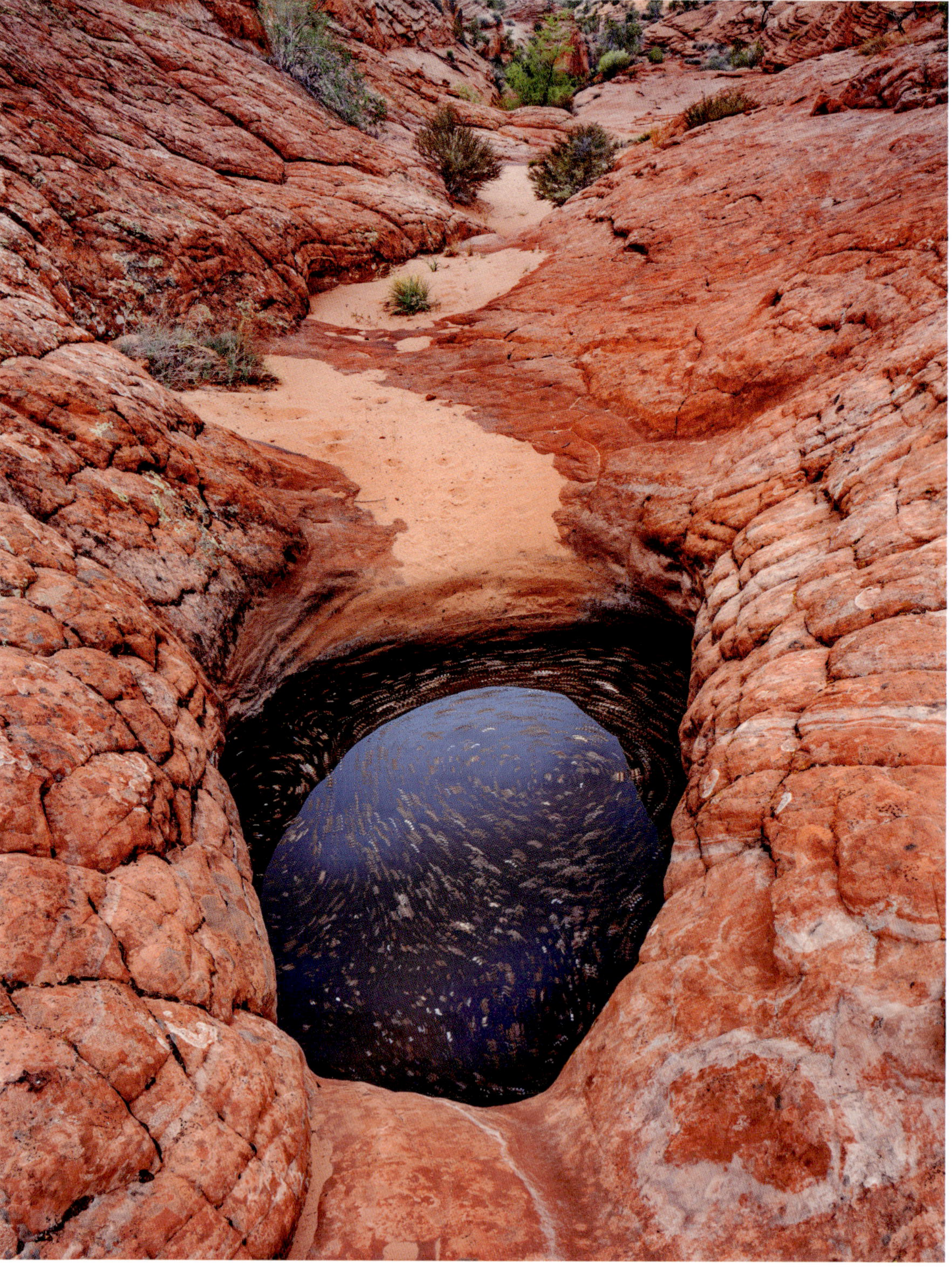

"good" art. This is, and should always remain, a matter of opinion. If we all agreed on objective criteria for good art, art would become meaningless. This is because the definition of art relies on creativity, and creativity means the invention and creation of new things, some of which may challenge or even contradict the zeitgeist of their day, things that may offend some people's sensibilities and challenge long-standing traditions. This is how art evolves and progresses—by novelty, not by compliance. This is a lesson we should have learned by now from the history of art: practically all major progress in art was considered revolutionary in its day, and was often greeted with skepticism, ridicule, and attempts by some to characterize novel media and novel creations as bad art, or as no art.

What amounts to one's subjective judgment of artistic merit ultimately comes down to the importance a given person may assign to specific qualities of a work of art. For example, to some, beauty may be the primary measure of art. To such a person, any work that possesses great aesthetic appeal is, by necessity, a great work of art, regardless of other qualities it may or may not possess (e.g., originality or skill). Others may place greater importance on creativity, expression, difficulty of production, or avant-gardeness. We must be cautious never to demand that all judges of art must be in agreement about the validity, value, or importance of any art or any artist. To do so is akin to declaring that no further progress in art is possible. For this reason, however, it is also eminently important for judges of art to be explicit about the criteria used in their judgment, why they believe these criteria are important, and what qualifies them to judge these criteria fairly. This is important as a means of checks and balances, and as insurance that art may continue to evolve: judges get to judge art, and the public gets to judge the judges.

It is to the great detriment of photography as a medium for art that most of those nominated to judge artistic merit in photographic contests are not held to scrutiny about their qualifications (beyond perhaps being famous or commercially successful), nor asked to articulate in unambiguous terms the criteria they use in their judgment. Those whose work prevails by such judgment sometimes themselves evolve to become judges and perpetuate the practice of biased and lacking judgment. It is part of the reason I advise those aspiring to produce important photographic art to avoid most competitions and to focus instead on seeking knowledge and inspiration, and to strive to produce original work, even if it may not appease some judges.

Those immersed in the photographic zeitgeist may relate to these words by Bertrand Russell:

> *It is impossible for art, or any of the higher creative activities, to flourish under any system which requires that the artist shall prove his competence to some body of authorities before he is allowed to follow his impulse. Any really great artist is almost sure to be thought incompetent by those among his seniors who would be generally regarded as best qualified to form an opinion. And the mere fact of having to produce work which will please older men is hostile to a free spirit and to bold innovation. Apart from this difficulty, selection by older men would lead to jealousy and intrigue and back-biting, producing a poisonous atmosphere of underground competition.*

Defining art as a product of human skill and imagination suggests that these qualities—skill and imagination—may be used as measures of artistic merit. Judgment of skill is predominantly judgment of difficulty—an evaluation of abilities that some possess and excel in, but not others (at least not to the same degree). Possession and excellence of expert manual and cognitive skills may be an outcome of random chance or honed training. Few would argue that photography requires much less skill to produce excellent results than, say, woodcutting, sculpture, poetry, painting, or playing the violin. This may prejudice some to judge all photographic works as inherently inferior in an artistic sense to art rendered in other media. In truth, it only means that skill is a poor measure of the artistic merit of photographs, not that photographs are inherently less artistic than, say, paintings.

Skill and aesthetic appeal being relatively easy to accomplish in a photograph doesn't mean that photography is an inferior art medium; it just means that skill and beauty are not good measures of artistic merit in photography. Qualities such as creativity and expressiveness, on the other hand, are much better criteria for judging artistic merit since they reflect the excellence of an artist as a person, rather than the abilities of the medium or the aesthetics of the subjects photographed. This is not to say that skill and aesthetic appeal are unimportant. In fact, I believe the opposite is true. Being that skill and finding aesthetically interesting subject matter are relatively easy to accomplish in photography, I expect them to be qualities of excellent photographs, in the same sense that I expect properly mixed pigments in an excellent painting, proper key in excellent music, and graceful movement in an excellent ballet performance. Having these qualities is no guarantee of good art, but not having them is very often the mark of bad art.

Creativity is judged differently in art than in other fields (e.g., science or business). Creative works in areas other than art are expected to possess demonstrable and objectively verifiable value. In art, value always is (or should be) a subjective judgment. However, one measure for creativity that is ubiquitous in all fields is originality.

Conceding my own subjective bias, nothing will make me pass on the work of a photographer faster than to find that the photographer's work is comprised primarily or entirely of copies and imitations—compositions or styles directly copied from others, with no creative "added value" contributed by the photographer. No matter how skillfully executed, how beautiful, or how enjoyable these works were for the photographer to make, as art I consider such photographs deficient in or altogether devoid of merit. When I see photographs I know to be copies of other people's photographs, I don't see art—I see copies of art, imitations of art, pretensions of art, sometimes delusions of art.

Some measure the artistic merit of photographs by qualities inherent in the subjects photographed, such as impressive scale, interesting features, dazzling colors, rarity, or serendipitous qualities of found light. I consider such things favorably (after all, I choose to photograph natural things, not so much because of my love for photography, but more so for my love of nature). Still, in evaluating artistic merit I always consider what proportion of the appeal of a photograph comes from qualities of the subject or fortuitous circumstances, relative to the proportion of appeal that comes from the creative mind of the photographer. Photographs that are more biased toward qualities of subjects and good fortune may still be good—even great—photographs, but without a significant and discernible creative contribution from the photographer, I don't consider them good art.

Expression, in addition to creativity, is the other quality I believe deserves the distinction of having great importance when it comes to artistic merit. Photographs may show me only what I would have seen myself in the same circumstances, in which case these photographs lack expression. Expressive photographs are those that venture beyond merely being an objective record of what the photographer had seen; they also suggest to me how the photographer felt, allowing me to estimate how well the photographer's feelings are expressed *using* the things the photographer had seen. As such, artistic photographs that are also expressive, especially when these feelings are expressed in unique and unobvious ways, are to me considerably more venerable than photographs that relay to me only how lucky or technically skilled a photographer is.

Unlike other qualities of photographs that can be assessed as singular dimensions (e.g., how pretty or interesting a photograph is, how skillfully it was captured or processed, how novel and original it is), assessing the expressiveness of a photograph relies not only on how well a photographer has expressed a feeling but also on the nature of the feeling expressed. The more complex, nuanced, and personally relatable the feeling is to me, the more artistic I consider the photograph to be. This illustrates that, regardless of understanding what the criteria for artistic merit are, their judgment is always subjective. In practical terms, it means that we must not rely exclusively on anyone's judgment, and strive to become good judges ourselves. Other people's judgment should be considered only as guidance—as advice to be considered and then consciously accepted or rejected.

That the medium of photography may be used to create art is not in question—it is born from formal, clear, and unambiguous definitions of art. How we value and relate to discrete works of photographic art, however, is for each of us to decide. As artists invested in the art of photography, we also stand to gain from helping our audiences become more educated and discerning about ways we may value photographic art: to explain, as I have attempted to do here, what qualities we each find important, and why we consider them important. By doing so, we may hopefully someday be able to move beyond rehashing old arguments and allow photographic art to mature in the same ways as other artistic media that, having established themselves as artistic, have moved on to considerations of styles, movements, and philosophies.

Measures of artistic merit aside, I would be remiss if I did not caution here against making "good art" one's sole motivation to practice photography. Such an approach seems to me to defeat what I consider the most important reason for any person to engage in art, which is to elevate a person's own living experience. I believe that good art should not be an end but an expression—a byproduct—of meaningful, mindful, passionate, and satisfying living. It is one thing to endure some suffering for the sake of one's art, and quite another thing to suffer *because* of one's art.

Photography and the Technological Sublime 8

Technology is the knack of so arranging the world that we do not experience it.
—Max Frisch

You take risks. You search. Sometimes luck is with you, and sometimes not, but the important thing is to take the dare. A new fact has recently become clear to me: It is not variety that is the spice of life. Variety is the meat and potatoes. Risk is the spice of life. Those who climb mountains or raft rivers understand this.
—David Brower

In his book *The Desert*, John C. Van Dyke describes lying awake in the desert at night, looking into the sky, wondering, "What is it that draws us to the boundless and the fathomless? Why should the lovely things of earth—the grasses, the trees, the lakes, the little hills—appear trivial and insignificant when we come face to face with the sea or the desert or the vastness of the midnight sky?"

The feeling Van Dyke described—the feeling that transcends mere aesthetic appeal to such degree that beauty alone seems trivial and insignificant in comparison—is what some philosophers referred to as the sublime—the quality of greatness. For centuries, thinkers contemplated how to define the sublime, and what distinguishes it from mere goodness or beauty. Some proclaimed the sublime to be beyond the reach of human attainment, and some even considered it beyond the reach of human perception—an experience so powerful, so pure, so complex, or so vast as to transcend the capacities of the human mind; or some ideal one never expects to reach but whose acknowledgment or pursuit may still elevate one's living experience.

Although contemplations of the sublime date back at least as far as the first century CE (in writings attributed to an unknown Roman soldier referred to as Longinus), current thinking about the sublime is rooted to a large degree in a 1757 treatise by philosopher and statesman Edmund Burke, titled *A Philosophical Enquiry Into the Origin of Our Ideas of the Sublime and Beautiful*. According to Burke, beauty and sublimity differ primarily in their origin: beauty originates in pleasure, whereas the sublime originates in pain. Not just any pain, but outright terror—the sort of pain one may feel when encountering things that are vast, powerful, and mortally dangerous.

According to Burke, existential fear is the strongest and most primal of all emotions; and therefore, terror can elicit more powerful emotional responses than any feeling rooted in pleasure. In Burke's mind, the "delight" (as opposed to pleasure) we find in the sublime is our response to feeling astonished. In his words, "Astonishment . . . is the emotional effect of the sublime in its highest degree; the inferior effects are admiration, reverence, and respect."

Philosopher Immanuel Kant, at odds with Burke on numerous philosophical and ideological subjects, was nonetheless influenced deeply by Burke's thoughts about the sublime. Kant himself contemplated the idea of the sublime in his own work *Critique of Judgment* and characterized the sublime (relative to the beautiful) a bit differently from Burke. According to Kant, the sublime differs from beauty in that the sublime is boundless, transcending the imagination. The effect of the sublime arises, according to Kant, from the human mind attempting to grasp what is beyond its capacity to comprehend, and inevitably coming up short. He wrote: "Whereas the beautiful is limited, the sublime is limitless, so that the mind in the presence of the sublime, attempting to imagine what it cannot, has pain in the failure but pleasure in contemplating the immensity of the attempt."

For most of the history of Western art, the effect of the sublime was associated with powerful, majestic, and vast feats of nature—the very things that today make up a great proportion of subjects favored by landscape photographers. No doubt, many photographers intend their photographs of sublime phenomena to inspire in viewers at least a degree of the responses described by Burke and Kant: astonishment, admiration, reverence, awe, and respect, ostensibly expressing feelings the photographers themselves have had in the presence of the things photographed. Yet, in our jaded and cynical world, it seems that such photographs, having become common and abundant, often elicit responses more in line with a sense of benign

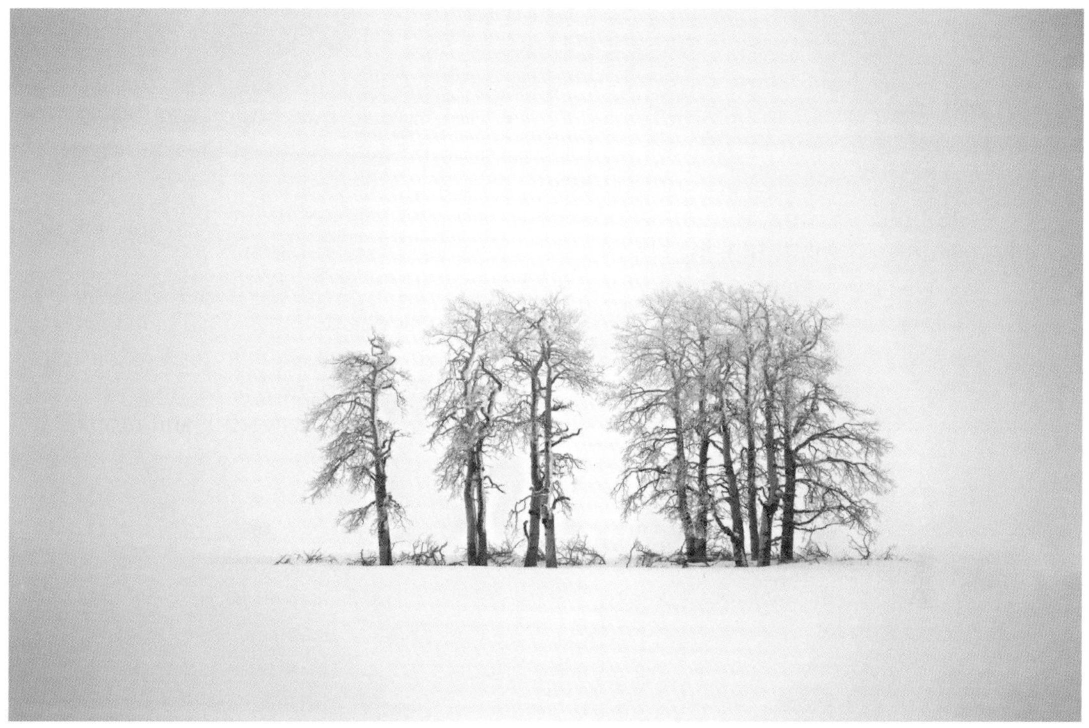

pleasantness rather than with the more powerful effects of encountering the sublime. In the words of Susan Sontag (originally referring to war photographs): "Photographs shock insofar as they show something novel. Unfortunately, the ante keeps getting raised."

It is fair to ask whether photographs, beyond just having the capacity to appear beautiful, are also capable of inspiring a sense of the sublime. Photographer Henry Peach Robinson (in his book *Pictorial Effect in Photography*, published in 1869) believed, to the dismay of many landscape photographers, that the answer was no. He wrote:

> It is an old canon of art, that every scene worth painting must have something of the sublime, the beautiful, or the picturesque. By its nature, photography can make no pretensions to represent the first, but beauty can be represented by its means and picturesqueness has never had so perfect an interpreter.

It is not clear to me whether Robinson's words "by its nature" refer to the nature of photography or to the nature of the sublime. Still, his assertion is difficult to argue with if we accept the characterization of the sublime as Burke and Kant defined it—a feeling inspired by terror, or a feeling of something limitless. Clearly, no photograph can impose such impressions by means of vastness comparable to that of mountains, oceans, or the night sky, nor by displays of astounding force comparable to storms or volcanic eruptions, even if portraying these subjects.

The degree of separation between a photograph and the things portrayed in a photograph may vary, but I think it's fair to say that the circumstances of viewing a photograph—usually in a safe and comfortable setting, physically removed from the things portrayed, even if those things are ostensibly impressive or terrible—is sufficient to prevent viewers from feeling the instinctive sense of terror and existential threat that Burke proposed as the feelings that elicit a sense of the sublime, nor that these effects are limitless. It is much easier to divert attention away from a photograph of a majestic scene than it is to disregard such a scene or dismiss its effects when one is physically in it.

Enter the *technological sublime*, a term perhaps most closely associated with the works of David Nye and Mario Costa, who considered technology the latest incarnation of the sublime. (Some previous incarnations were characterized as "the rhetoric sublime" of ancient philosophies, "the natural sublime" of the 18th century, and "the industrial/metropolitan sublime" of the modern era.)

Things like rampant industrialization, computing, mass communication, space exploration, cyber-warfare, and scientific advances in such fields as quantum mechanics and neuroscience not only transformed the way we live but also the things we consider sublime. Alain de Botton offers this summary of the transition in recent decades: "Over the course of the nineteenth century, the dominant catalyst for that feeling of the sublime had ceased to be nature. We were now deep in the era of the technological sublime, when awe could most powerfully be invoked not by forests or icebergs but by supercomputers, rockets, and particle accelerators. We were now almost exclusively amazed by ourselves."

Having some familiarity with the sublime as Burke and Kant described it, I consider humanity's transition from a nature-inspired sublime to a technological sublime an extremely unfortunate one, amounting to an ongoing impoverishment of human living experience, or at least to impoverishment of the range of opportunities available to people to elevate their living experiences. Proud as we are of our technological accomplishments, we tend to forget that at the end of the day we are still animals: biological entities possessing certain naturally evolved emotional "programming" that governs the qualities of our subjective experiences—programming we can't simply switch off. This programming makes us respond strongly and innately to certain stimuli, and to certain experiences that we cannot simply substitute other experiences for, even if we believe them to be equivalent.

One reason many today may believe that impressive technology can be as sublime as an awe-inspiring manifestation of nature is that most of us do not, and may never, experience true terror—a precondition for the sense of the sublime as Burke described it. Most of us may never encounter existential threats outside the protective envelope of "managed" and predictable experiences, within reach of a supportive community, safe harbors, and specialized emergency services. In the absence of terror, our technological accomplishments may still reward us with profound beauty, inspiration, and gratification, but if we never venture outside our "safe zone," if we never encounter life-threatening forces beyond our ability to control or to resist, whatever we may call "sublime" is not the same sublime that Burke and Kant described. In this sense, a technological sublime is not, and cannot be, equivalent to the sublime of Burke and Kant. It is something altogether different and, in some important ways, inferior.

My sparse social circle is mostly comprised of people who tend to live more adventurously than most—hikers, climbers, river runners, explorers, artists. Often, I have heard safety-conscious people express puzzlement, or even anger, at those who partake in such "extreme" activities as mountain climbing, venturing alone into remote and wild places, or tackling powerful river rapids. Such responses illustrate to me that many people, lacking personal experience with such activities, fail to acknowledge that these pursuits—because they involve mortal risk—may yield states of minds and consciousness that, as those familiar with them will likely testify, may eclipse in their power, vitality, and emotional rewards any rewards possible by other, safer means.

What does this have to do with photography? Being more dependent on technology than most other artistic pursuits, photography—especially photography founded in natural aesthetics—has been gravely affected by the transition in perception from experiential sublime to technological sublime. The reason can be summed up in this simple truism: although there may be ways of comparing various kinds of sublimity in historical, quantitative, or conceptual terms, when considered in terms of subjective experience, one kind of sublime is not like another.

I recall in my younger years reading accounts of photographers in the medium's early days: hauling heavy and sensitive equipment into places and situations never before photographed, or even witnessed, into the unknown, into the mysterious and the terrifying. We owe much of what we know about the world today to these adventurers, explorers, and artists. Technology has evolved to allow us to produce technically better photographs (sometimes astoundingly so) than those produced by our predecessors, usually requiring little or no risk or discomfort. We don't often acknowledge that this technological progress, despite making photographic tools and processes attractive and fascinating, has also dulled our experience in making photographs. Photographers who wish to experience the sublime can no longer hope to find it in the course of making predictable photographs in predictable places. The technological sublime, if it can even be compared with the sublime as originally defined, is a tame sublime, a quasi-sublime.

While it is easy to understand why many photographers are unwilling to take existential risks voluntarily, it is much less obvious why so many are also reluctant to take creative risks. In the age of the technological so-called-sublime, many have come to believe a plethora of false equivalencies: awe has been supplanted by popularity, novelty by conformity, and authentic experience by manufactured evidence implying experiences the photographer did not actually have—experiences of

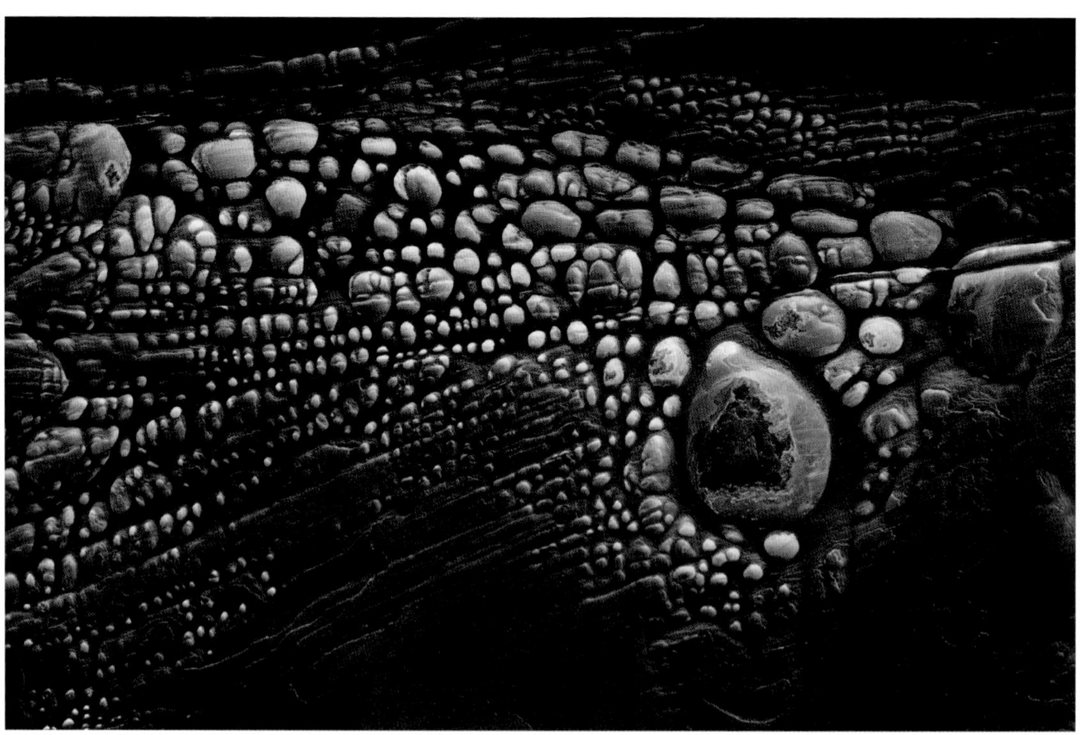

wildness, remoteness, disconnectedness, solitude, adventure. So many photographs suggesting such experiences are in actuality produced by following directions, from the safety of easily accessible viewpoints, and often mimicking photographs already made by others. These photographs—fitting Hermann Hesse's characterization of some poems as "planned productions, fabrications, pralines for the public"—often are presented as equivalent to creative accomplishments, or to experiential accomplishments. They are not, at least when it comes to the photographer's experience in making them, even if viewers can't tell.

Objectively, technologically impressive photographs may indeed impress their viewers as much as, or even more than, photographs resulting from true awe or amazement, from deep emotional engagement, from physical immersion, and from creative epiphanies, but in terms of subjective experience, there is no comparing the inner rewards of making safe and predictable photographs to what one may gain from making photographs in the throes of amazement, fear, uncertainty, mystery— circumstances that test a photographer's mettle and grit, and not just their camera skills. Whether such mischaracterization has any practical or ethical implications is a question for another discussion. The question for this discussion is this: why would photographers—or any persons aspiring to experience the sublime, or anything close to it—choose knowingly to cheat *themselves* out of such experiences?

I propose that it may be of value to, at least on occasion, scare ourselves: to let go of certainties, to challenge ourselves to create, if not in the face of mortal danger, at least in the face of doubt and the possibility of failure, to allow for unpredictable things, to venture into what wildness remains without planning and preconception. By this I don't mean putting ourselves recklessly in harm's way without forethought, but to be at peace with a degree of risk that inevitably will increase as we gain in skill and fortitude, not for the sake of any praise, not to prove anything to anyone, not for celebrity or bragging rights, but so we may remain open, should circumstances allow, to awe, to amazement, to humility, to the sublime as described by Burke and Kant, for the sake of enlarging and enriching our own lives.

Take it from one who has had successful careers in both technology and photography: in terms of photographs, the technological sublime may have the quantitative upper hand, but in terms of qualitative depth of subjective experience, the commonality between the experiential sublime and the technological sublime begins and ends with the misguided choice of characterizing both experiences using the word "sublime."

9 Commitment and Doubt

The relationship between commitment and doubt is by no means an antagonistic one. Commitment is healthiest when it is not without doubt but in spite of doubt.
—Rollo May

Paul Cézanne famously said he wanted to die painting, and he did. My commitment to photography is not quite so decisive. I can't say that I want to die photographing, or even to die a photographer. Frankly, so long as my death is swift and painless, I don't really care about its circumstances. My commitment to photography is not absolute; it is founded in a simple condition: so long as I find value and meaning in photography, I'll keep doing it.

To the degree that I am, and have been, committed to photography, my commitment has not always been the same. Long ago, photography was just a fun and gratifying thing to do, an enjoyable hobby to augment and to enrich my solitary explorations. It soon became a passion, then an obsession, and then, as is the fate of any long-term relationship, it got considerably more complicated. Some days I feel I can't do without photography, and other days I can't stand the thought of it. Some days photography is a source of happiness, and other days a source of despair. Some days photography is a gift, and other days a burden.

In my early years as a "serious" photographer, if you asked me why I photograph with such great dedication, I may have responded with some naïve trope about photography being my "creative outlet," or about showing people the beauty of nature, perhaps even contributing to public awareness of the need to conserve wild places. In truth, none of these was ever really, or at least not entirely, the case. At different times, these explanations felt as real as any other I've had. In hindsight, I confess,

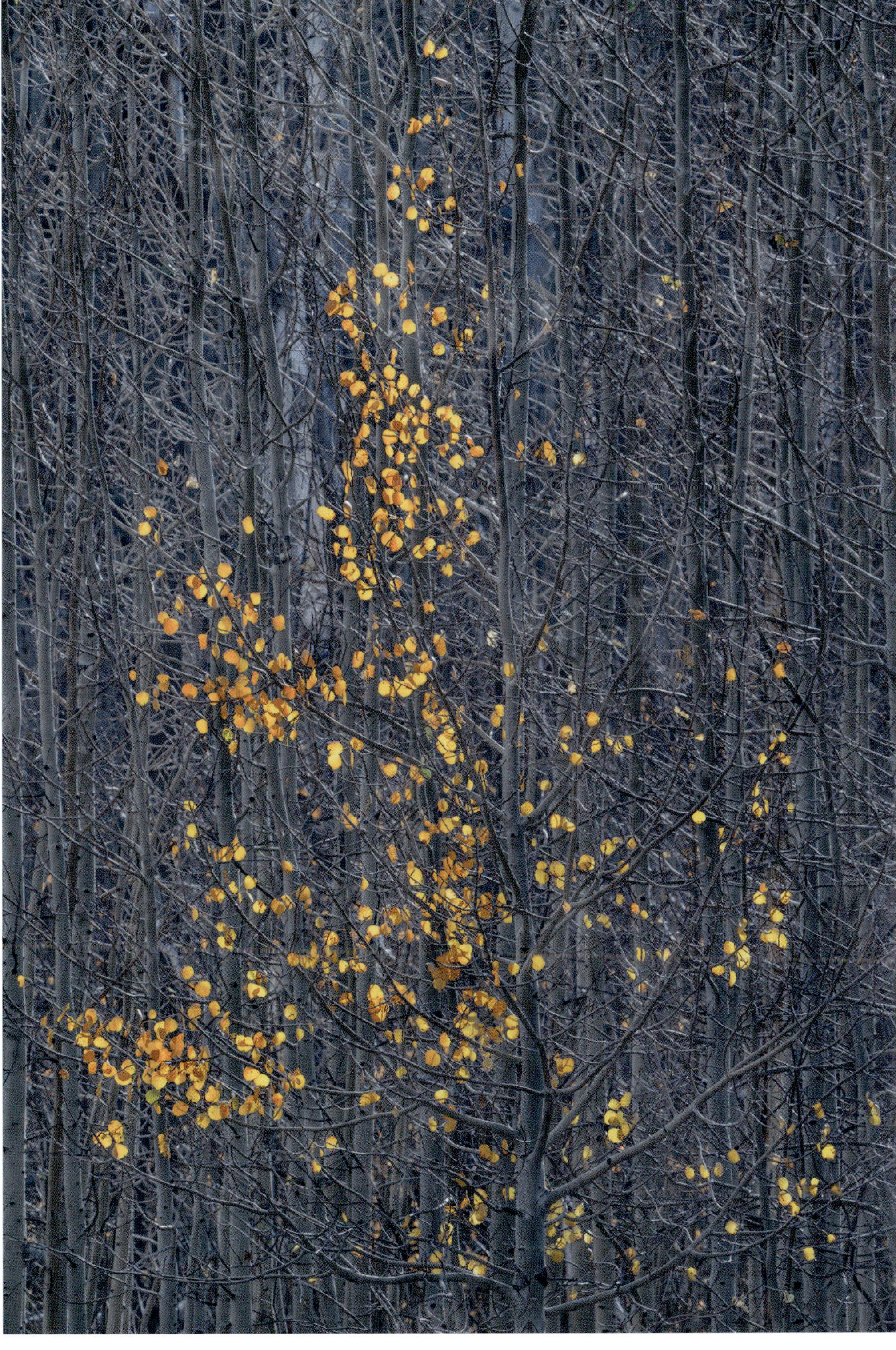

photography was never something I've done for any particular purpose. I practiced photography because it added yet more enjoyable dimensions to experiences that already were, still are, and likely will always be, indispensable to my well-being.

My commitment to photography today (and likely tomorrow, and probably also next week, but that's as far as I'm willing to commit) is as my tool of choice for making expressive art. What I mean by this is that photography seems to me so far to be the medium best suited for expressing the kinds of things I most want to express: epiphanies, aesthetics, moods, and feelings inspired by my experiences in the natural world. Just as important, photography for me is about the process of making, not about any predetermined use I may (or may not) have for the resulting photographs. To me, a photograph becomes much less interesting once I consider it finished.

Part of my commitment to photography comes from the fact that the mechanics of the medium allow me to create in places and circumstances that are not as well-suited for other media but that happen to be the places and circumstances where I feel most inspired. Another part of my commitment comes from the long-term rewards I gain by continually training my mind to seek interesting and photogenic subjects. The result of such training is that I have become more mindful and aware of dimensions of my experience—things and relationships, both real and metaphorical, both grand and subtle—that I may otherwise not take notice of. These aspects of photography—its immediacy when I feel inspired and its long-term benefits in enriching my living experience—are the primary reasons I am committed to photography. (The resulting photographs, when they are successful, are of course satisfying as well, but not to the same extent.)

In a 1967 article titled "Post-Visualization," photographer Jerry Uelsmann wrote, "It is interesting to note that much of the experimental photography that we revere today has been done by individuals whose commitment to photography is but one aspect of their commitment to art." In my case, I would throw another commitment into the mix: my commitment to natural places and the experiences they inspire.

It used to be that nature, photography, and artmaking were so closely related in my mind that I could regard them as perhaps just separate dimensions of one thing: my commitment to life as I wish to live it. But after so many years of living this life, nature, photography, and art have slowly drifted apart for me. Each has become complex and significant enough to warrant its own mode of appreciation and its own manner of commitment. My degree of commitment to each is rooted in a hierarchy of importance: I often doubt my commitment to photography as my artistic medium; I sometimes (but rarely) doubt my commitment to art in the greater sense; but I never doubt my commitment to nature. I will always be a naturalist—I will die a naturalist. I almost certainly will always be an artist of some kind, but I'm at least open to the idea that some other form of expression may someday seem more appealing to me than photography.

Beyond sometimes doubting my commitment to photography, I also sometimes doubt my commitment to presenting myself to the world as a photographer. This is not only because I have other passions and interests but also because of expectations and prejudices that often go with the designation "photographer." Most people, I've learned, have a simplistic, and often lesser, opinion of photography as an art form compared with such things as painting or music. Beyond just having a penchant for "taking pictures," few consider photography an emotional and intellectual pursuit, in the same sense that poetry or creative writing are. What to me is a "work," to many is a "shot"; what to me is a creative act, to many is just being in the right place at the right time (if not outright dumb luck); what to me is the culmination of a prolonged experience, to many is just a random moment frozen in time; what to me is subjective expression, to many is objective representation.

Although I likely would enjoy photography even if I could not earn a living by it, not a week goes by that I don't question my desire to photograph professionally. Often, in considering viewers' responses, I question my desire to explain my motivations and intents, and why I qualify my work as art. I constantly find myself in need of a reminder that the greatest rewards I find in my photographic work come from doing the work—from my joy in finding creative ways to express aspects of my most cherished experiences and my most profound states of mind. That is not just enough; it is considerably more than enough. My commitment to photography remains, and likely always will be, as Rollo May put it, not without doubt but in spite of doubt.

10 Taking (Back) My Time

If we take eternity to mean not infinite temporal duration but timelessness, then eternal life belongs to those who live in the present. Our life has no end in just the way in which our visual field has no limits.
—Ludwig Wittgenstein

My relationship with photography began, as affairs of the heart often do, with mindless lust. I wanted to play with beautiful machines, to see spectacular things, and to make the kind of tantalizing photographs I saw in glossy magazines and coffee-table books. In time, lust blossomed into love—a committed kinship, founded in intimate familiarity, implicit acceptance, and mutual respect. Short-lived infatuations don't produce the same depth of mutual appreciation as love, which must evolve at its own pace, with ongoing investment of care and attention, through bliss and despair. No matter how passionate initial encounters may be, before anything may be considered love, time must pass.

Works of significance and beauty often and aptly are described as timeless, although the implications of such characterization often are not fully acknowledged—such works are, literally, without the dimension of time. Their meanings are not bound to any anecdotal event; their relevance is not limited to just some period; their importance is not dependent on any fleeting fashion.

Like all amorous affairs outside of storybooks and sappy movies, so is my otherwise blissful union with photography sometimes plagued with complications, pet peeves, and impure thoughts (admittedly originating most often from my own failings and eccentricities), one of which is the fact that I am one who takes great pleasure in prolonged, meandering contemplations. I lose myself in streams of consciousness, often allowing them to flow unimpeded to see where they may lead. I am interested not only in ideas but also in the evolution of ideas. I relish time spent imagining possibilities and scenarios, even when they have no practical implications to me. I mind every aspect and detail of any creative endeavor I engage in, not only for the sake of feeling in control (one of my eccentric obsessions) but also as a way of extending my joy in being immersed in such experiences, delaying on purpose their inevitable culmination, even when I could complete them in shorter times with the same quality of output.

When working outdoors, I may stay in one place for hours, sometimes days, watching the light move and transform, revealing and obscuring elements. I hate feeling rushed when working. If a spectacle of ephemeral perfection unfolds before me when I am not ready to photograph it, I just pause to appreciate it, feel grateful for my good fortune to witness it, and do not bother with the camera. Frantic camera work would only diminish my experience beyond what even a "great" photograph will compensate me for.

In my work, I deliberately avoid anything requiring swift action. To the extent that I can help it, I aim to unburden my work of any time constraints. When photographing, I like to consider and visualize every perspective available to me, every way I may select, arrange, juxtapose, and fine-tune elements in my environment. I like to take my time to assess whether I may be better off returning at another time, in different light, in a different season, or in a different state of mind. I take time to make sure my tripod is at exactly the position I need it to be. I take pleasure in studying the finder image, deliberately and carefully. I savor the tactile feel of buttons, rings, and dials as I manipulate them (their smoothness, precision, and resistance as important criteria to me in choosing them as any optical quality or technical function they may possess). Without such prolonged immersion in my work, I stand no hope of finding flow in it.

I'm never tempted to pounce at short-lived photographic opportunities, knowing from experience that whatever work may ensue from a lesser, shorter, anxious, and hurried experience, no matter how beautiful or impressive, will not be very satisfying to me and likely will be poorer in comparison with using my time and cognitive abilities to appreciate nature quietly, with reverence, awe, and wonder. If the prospect of a good photograph requires being distracted from or entirely sacrificing such elevated feelings, then to hell with that photograph.

When processing my work, I also take my time. I mull over every decision, consider every possibility, and stop on occasion to examine the image-in-the-making and to visualize possibilities I may otherwise miss. I check and double-check for technical imperfections. I work every pixel to perfection, or as close to it as I can get—not for perfection's sake but because I enjoy the process of striving for it, pushing my imagination and skills as far as I can in pursuit of it.

Photography is not always tolerant of and does not always yield to "unproductive" mindfulness, however enjoyable. As a medium, photography sometimes tempts one to be abrupt and decisive, demands rapid responses, limits one's windows of opportunity, insists that one finds some significance in ephemeral moments. It's not rare for me, when recognizing such impulses, to assert consciously: "Shut up, brain." Although the wording may not be what mindfulness trainers will teach you, the ability to recognize such temptations when they arise, to acknowledge their detrimental effect, to overrule them consciously, and not to regret the decision are exactly the skills cultivated by prolonged practice of mindfulness.

I enjoy seeing my labors coming to fruition, and I take pride in a finished work as much (although perhaps not for as long) as anyone. But the reason that, after three decades of photography, I still have no intention of giving it up is that my joy of being immersed in elevated states—awe, sublimity, flow, mindfulness—far exceeds my desire to just add trophies to my archive.

After many years of practice, I recognize that my greatest rewards from photography require certain preconditions. I must be consumed in compositional meditations and deep contemplation. I must push myself relentlessly to keep refining until I get everything "just right." Such conditions require that my subject remains mostly static. Any abrupt change may "reset" my creative counter back to zero. I joke sometimes that in my favorite conditions to photograph, a photographer like Henri Cartier-Bresson would likely have died of boredom waiting for some "decisive moment" to occur.

After each such experience, I recognize in hindsight that I have lost track of time, that I have been so elated and enraptured by my experience that the click of the shutter sometimes jars me back to "normal" reality, as if I have woken up from a beautiful dream, the memory of which will stay with me for hours and days afterward, and likely be rekindled later in my studio as I process the image.

If the practice of photography fails to elicit such states of mind for some, it may be because so many photographers, often without giving it much thought, take the attitude of hunter-gatherers: always on the lookout, ready to pounce, waiting for some "decisive moment" to emerge randomly from the steady stream of otherwise mundane and insignificant events. Other photographers take the approach of careful planning and preconception, deciding on their photographs before, and independent of, having a meaningful experience. It rarely occurs to photographers that,

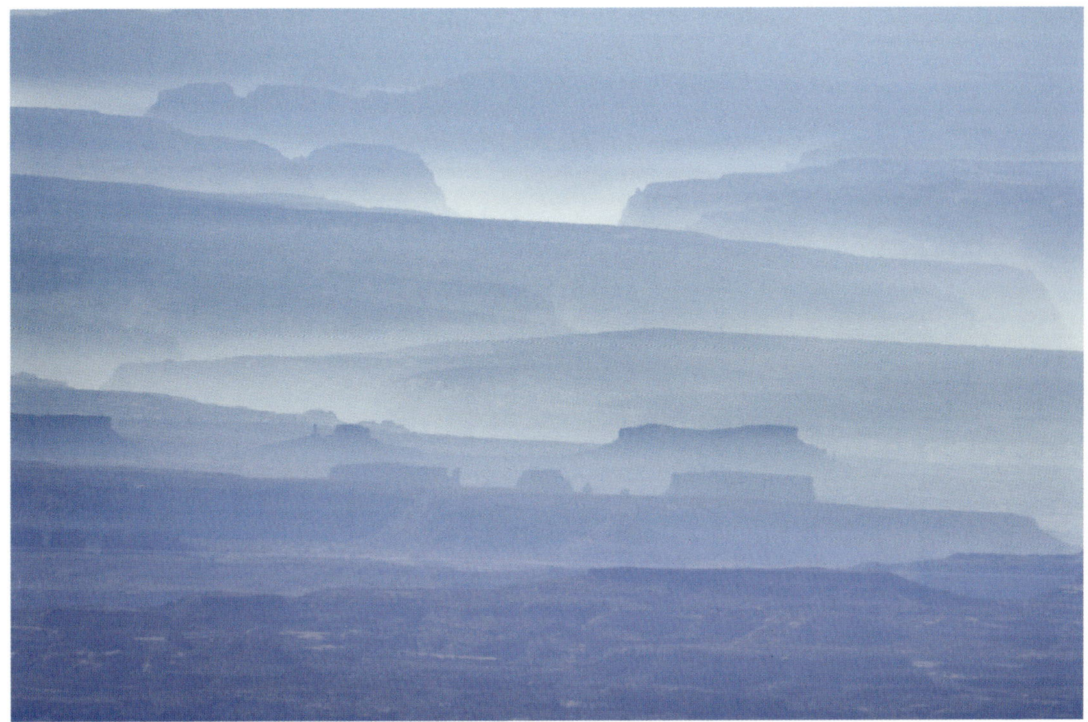

by adopting a contemplative approach, they can spare themselves the need to wait for any ephemeral occurrences or to decide anything in advance. Certainly, it rarely occurs to photographers that, by doing these things, they risk diminishing their own experiences and likely rob themselves of the great joys of flow and emotional engagement with their subjects.

The planning approach is by its nature uncreative and unexpressive. Adopting this approach means giving up in advance on any reward that creativity and expression may yield. This approach may be useful for photographers working on assignment or for some commercial purposes. When it comes to artmaking, where one may benefit tremendously from creative work and from experiencing powerful emotions worthy of artistic expression, this is by far the worst (i.e., least rewarding) attitude that a photographer may adopt.

The "decisive moment" approach relies on photogenic anecdotes to emerge randomly from an ongoing stream of banal and insignificant events. In contrast, the contemplative approach puts the choice to photograph into the photographer's hands, rather than making the photographer a slave to circumstances. Photographers who constantly and deliberately seek elevated and intensified

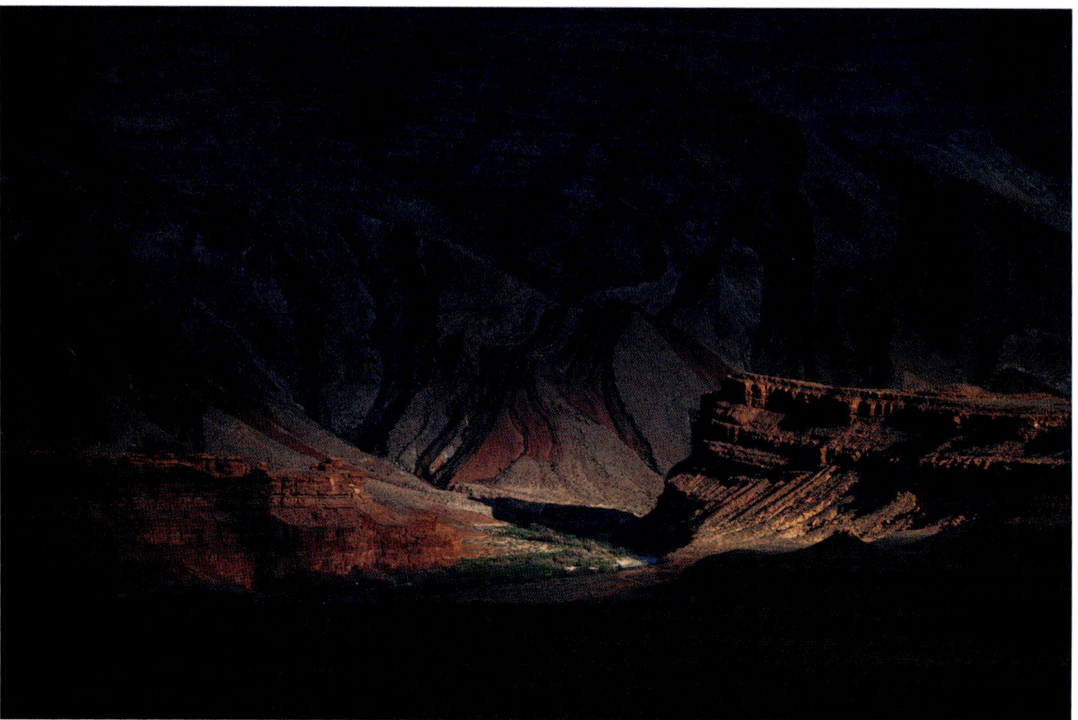

experiences in the course of daily living, regardless of photography, will likely find many more such experiences than either the planners or the hunter-gatherers. Such photographers may find things to photograph—to express creatively—almost any time they feel inspired to create.

Timelessness is not just a desirable quality of our finished photographs; it can also be something to aspire to in the way we live and photograph. We don't have to decide in advance what the "right" time may be to photograph. We don't have to submit passively to random circumstances. We don't have to record only occasional highlights that random luck may throw our way at certain times. Are we not better off if we evolve the capacity to create at any time, in spite of time, without regard to time?

Photography as an Art Language 11

Photography has been called an irresponsive medium. This
is much the same as calling it a mechanical process. A great
paradox which has been combated is the assumption that
because photography is not "hand-work," as the public say—
though we find there is very much "hand work" and head-work
in it—therefore it is not an art language. This is a fallacy born of
thoughtlessness.
—Peter Henry Emerson

The words above, by photographer Peter Henry Emerson, are from his book
Naturalistic Photography for Students of the Art, published in 1890. The book influenced
many photographers of the time, including Alfred Stieglitz, who quoted from it in his
writings. The book also was, in the words of Emerson, "an attempt to start a departure from the scientific side of photography." In the book's latter pages, Emerson
posed this question, which gave me pause: "The promising young goddess, photography, is but fifty years old. What prophet will venture to cast her horoscope for the
year 2000?"

Emerson offered many brilliant observations on photography as art (distinguishing art from scientific and industrial uses for the medium). In time, he had also witnessed the great influence that his book had on some of the leading photographers
of his day. Then, just a couple of years after publishing his book, Emerson published
a follow-up titled *The Death of Naturalistic Photography*, recanting many of his original
positions and conceding he was wrong in thinking that direct reproduction of nature
could be a form of art on par with artistic expression in other media. In his despair,
Emerson wrote, "I have, I regret it deeply, compared photographs to great works of

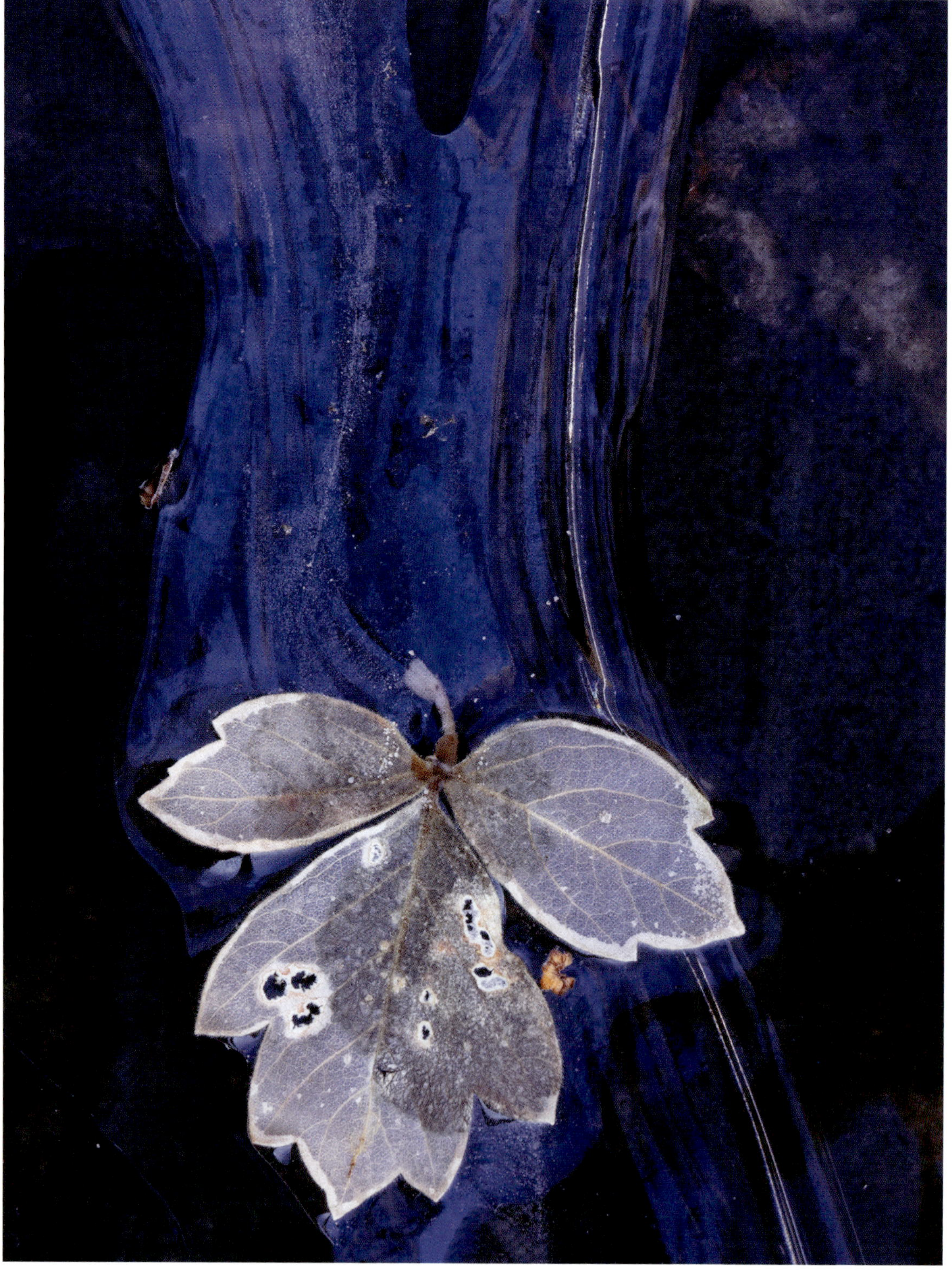

art and photographers to great artists. I was rash and thoughtless and my punishment is having to acknowledge it now."

I have often contemplated thoughts similar to Emerson's, both about photography as a worthy medium for art (i.e., photography as "an art language") and about the reasons that so much photography (rightly, in many cases) fails to earn the distinction of *art*.

To this day, photography struggles for acceptance in many art venues and is still maligned by some as an inferior medium for art—not only by some artists of other disciplines but also by some photographers who still consider photography only a mechanical process, to be regarded strictly as a technology for mimetic representation—for capturing and recording objective appearances, rather than creating and expressing subjective notions.

It seems to me that part of the reason photography has struggled to gain acceptance as an art form is that the discussion about photography's artistic merits has been largely academic, often requiring a depth of knowledge of art and its history that is not of universal interest. But there is another, more pervasive, reason, which is this: many such discussions are doomed from the outset to lead to ambiguous conclusions because they begin with the question, "Is photography art?"

To ask whether photography is art is akin to asking whether a pen or a word processor is art, or whether the English alphabet is art. It is a nonsensical question, yielding by necessity subjective, vague, and often nonsensical answers ("yes" not being the least of them). I believe that a more useful question is, as Emerson characterized it, whether photography can be an *art language*. To this question, I propose that "yes" can be asserted and defended as a useful and objectively defensible answer.

Among the definitions of the word "language" in the *Merriam-Webster Dictionary* is this: "a systematic means of communicating ideas or feelings by the use of conventionalized signs, sounds, gestures, or marks having understood meanings." Few would argue that pictures cannot communicate ideas and feelings. As evidenced by experiments in Gestalt psychology and other fields, people associate certain perceptions and feelings with visual cues such as lines, shapes, and colors, and from the ways these cues can be arranged (composed) together to complement or contrast with each other. Photography is as capable of leveraging these associations to express meaning as any visual medium. In other words, photography meets the definition of a form of language. Now, we may ask: What distinguishes "language" from "art language"?

Human beings acquire language skills gradually. In early childhood, toddlers lack the ability to express themselves in specific ways (i.e., using words). When in need of calling attention to themselves, they just scream. Likewise, many photographers in their early attempts may hope to command viewer attention by equivalents of visual screaming—intense colors, visual gimmickry, extreme perspectives, or abstraction for abstraction's sake.

As children begin to gain command of words and grammar, their modes of communication become less loud and more specific. Still limited in their vocabulary and in their capacity to form complex expressions, children tend to be descriptive and literal, rather than metaphorical or lyrical, in their verbal expressions. The same is true of most photographs made by budding but inexperienced photographers and laypersons lacking depth of skill in visual composition; their images tend to be descriptive, literal transcriptions, and the concepts they express are limited to appealing qualities of the subjects photographed (color, elegance, rarity), rather than attempting to convey (using qualities of the subjects) ulterior meanings originating from the photographer's mind.

In time, as people mature, they acquire richer vocabularies and the ability to alter the meanings of words and expressions by intonation of voice; by use of metaphors, parables, or idioms; as well as linguistic tools such as humor and sarcasm. In photography, such degree of expression—clear, unambiguous, effective, purposeful, and well-crafted—may be considered the hallmark of seasoned commercial workers.

Having mastered a degree of language extending beyond just practical need, most people proceed to find ways of using language to broaden their knowledge according to personal interests, to express complex concepts, to socialize, to consume various forms of entertainment, and so on. Such progress in language beyond mere utility can be seen in photography too—in online forums, in camera clubs, in photography-focused workshops, contests, events, educational books, and video tutorials.

It is here that a minority of people choose deliberately to depart from just practical and common uses for language and evolve further interest in not just the meaning of words and expressions, or in communicating known concepts, but also in the aesthetics of language. Members of this minority become poets and wordsmiths, novelists and short-story tellers, essayists and science-fiction writers, rhymers and spoken-word artists; authors of haikus, slogans, koans, aphorisms, and maxims; coiners of new metaphors, terms, and expressions. These few use language not just as a means of communication but also as a means of creative expression, not just to relay information and wisdom but also to challenge their audiences with riddles and abstractions, imparting rich and complex experiences beyond utilitarian descriptions and explanations, to be consumed and appreciated for their own sakes. These are the people who turn common language into art language.

Likewise, artists in photography—those who use photography not just as language but as art language—can, have, and do express more in their photographs than literal transcriptions, more than just surface appearances, deeper and more complex concepts than just what something looked like. Such artists also sometimes photograph for reasons having nothing at all to do with communication or with realism, intending for their photographs to be experiences in themselves, their purpose being to arouse feelings and thoughts, which are not necessarily or entirely related to any object portrayed in the photograph.

As artists, we must acknowledge that, just as some may lack the skills, interest, or depth of feeling to find meaning in poems, so do some lack the knowledge or depth of understanding to find meaning in visual art. But in those cases where a lack of understanding and appreciation of photographic art is owed to honest ignorance rather than to prejudice, I believe that there is great value in going out of our way to educate our audiences rather than to become indignant about our work being misunderstood. Being that we are invested in photography as a medium for art, we stand to gain from expanding our potential audience by helping people see the value of poetic, artistic expression in photography—to help people distinguish explicitly photography as language from photography as art language.

Let us go beyond decrying our medium as the victim of prejudice or misunderstanding. Instead, let us be teachers and educators. Let us work positively to eradicate artistic illiteracy among photographers and in the general population. Rather than blame the prejudiced, let us move the world beyond the prejudice, until the prejudiced become a minority. This must begin with those of us who proclaim ourselves—openly and proudly—as artists, and our work as art, distinct in purpose, methods, and modes of appreciation from other forms of photography.

To say that photography is (or is not) art is a bit like saying that English is (or is not) beige. It's a meaningless characterization. Art may be rendered by any medium, and no medium is artistic in itself. Photography, like English or any other language having sufficient richness of expression, can—in artistic hands—become more than just a language. It can become an art language. Let us speak it, use it, teach it, and build upon it.

12 Disinterested Interest

> **The criterion for art is no longer just the visual world. One of the major changes evidenced in modern art is the transition from what was basically an outer directed art form in the nineteenth century to the inner directed art of today. The contemporary artist draws upon new levels of consciousness, creating a span of aesthetic that is without precedent. To date, photography has played a minor role in this liberation. We have kept blinders on our eyes, restricting the potential imaginative freedom that photography is capable of.**
> **—Jerry Uelsmann**

Nearly 40 years before the invention of photography, philosopher Immanuel Kant presciently confronted what would later become one of the most contentious questions haunting photography as a medium for art: the question of whether realism should matter in the judgment of aesthetic value (and by extension in the judgment of works of art whose primary purpose is to impart aesthetic beauty, those works we today refer to as "fine art").

In his *Critique of Judgment*, Kant wrote, "Where the question is whether something is beautiful, we do not want to know, whether we, or anyone else, are, or even could be, concerned in the real existence of the thing, but rather what estimate we form of it on mere contemplation (intuition or reflection)."

Kant proposed that emotions resulting from aesthetic beauty are different from emotions inspired by other kinds of experience. Because of this difference, aesthetic judgment should also be different from other kinds of judgment (such as moral judgment, factual judgment, or logical judgment). The quality that distinguishes aesthetic judgment from other forms of judgment is what Kant referred to by a term that, to the misfortune of present-day English speakers, had been confusingly translated as "disinterestedness."

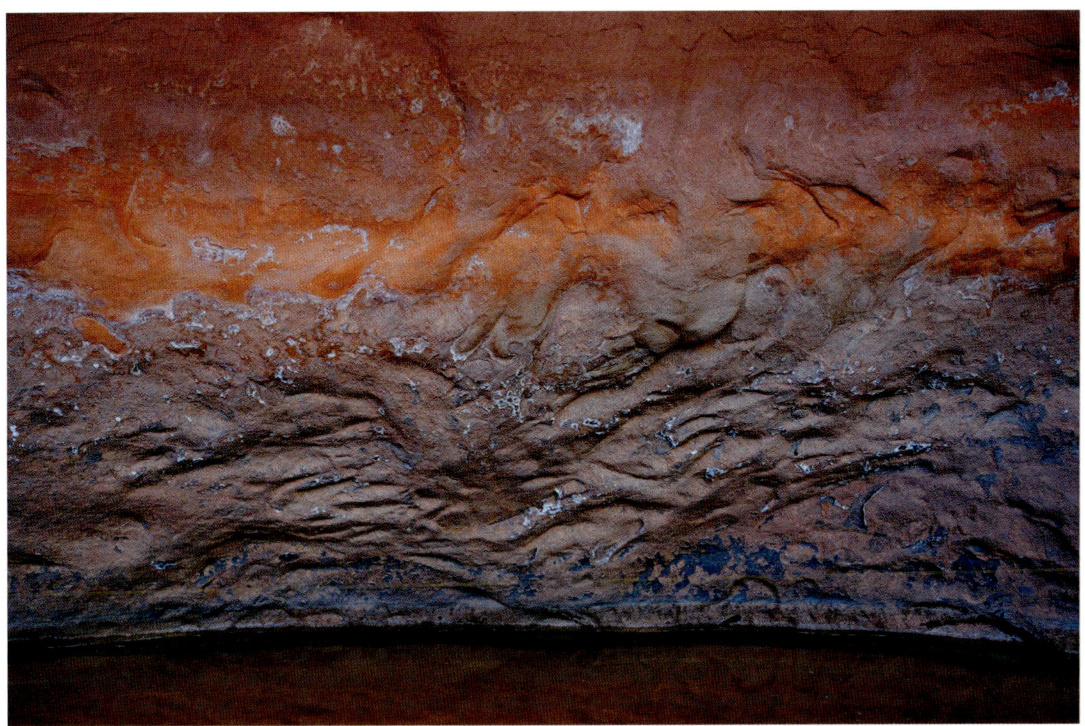

To understand disinterestedness as Kant intended it, it's important to first consider what Kant meant by "interest," which is a bit different from how we use the term today. The interest Kant is referring to is, in his words, "the delight which we connect with the representation of the real existence of an object." Kant did not dispute that there is such delight (and value) in realistic representation, but he claimed that this delight is of a different kind from the delight we take (or should take) in artistic beauty. Disinterestedness, therefore, does not mean a general lack of interest, nor that interests other than beauty are without value. What it means is that to fully appreciate beauty, we must omit from our judgment such personal interests as whether the thing represented is "real" (however one wishes to define the term) since such considerations may distract us from experiencing in full, and most powerfully, those emotions ensuing directly from beauty.

Although Kant may not have been the first to contemplate such thoughts, his formulation of them has become widely discussed, and largely accepted as eminently important in philosophical writings about appreciation of art. To wit, Jerome Stolnitz, author of *Aesthetics and Philosophy of Art Criticism*, went as far as to declare

that, "We cannot understand modern aesthetic theory unless we understand the concept of 'disinterestedness.'"

Lest Kant's ideas be considered irrelevant to photography (which did not exist in his time), or because these ideas preceded more recent thinking about the value of photography as a documentary, representational medium, consider that Dorothea Lange—a consummate and celebrated documentarian—expressed the very same idea as Kant did in her writings too. Lange wrote, "The good photograph is not the object, the consequences of the photograph are the objects. So that no one would say, how did you do it, where did you find it, but they would say that such things could be."

No lesser a documentarian and photojournalist than Ernst Haas—former president of Magnum Photos—also alluded to the effect of disinterestedness in realistic representation in the context of art. Haas wrote, "Disinterested in scientific objectivity, I want to transform reality with a poetic conception by relating the unrelated into vision—forcing the viewer to feel what I felt as well as to think what I thought" (read: not necessarily to see what I saw).

To be sure, the idea of disinterestedness as the quality distinguishing judgment of artistic beauty from other forms of judgments—moral, factual, logical—does not imply that these other forms of judgment are without value, only that their value is different from aesthetic judgment, and thus must be determined by different criteria and attitudes.

In regards to photography, the idea of disinterestedness highlights the fact that photography is not just one thing to be judged by one set of criteria regardless of the purpose of a given work. Photography may be a medium for journalism and documentary representation just as it may be a medium for creative artistic expression. Photographer W. Eugene Smith articulated this dichotomy well when he wrote: "I am constantly torn between the attitude of the conscientious journalist who is a recorder and interpreter of the facts and of the creative artist who often is necessarily at poetic odds with the literal facts."

Had Smith read Kant, perhaps he would have realized there was no reason for him to feel torn. Both attitudes are equally valid; they are just valid in different contexts. Feeling torn between photography as journalism and photography as art doesn't suggest that one is better or more "right" than the other, only that each deserves to be judged by the criteria appropriate for its purpose and that the two should not be conflated. Because photography may be used in different ways and toward different purposes, it is both fair and useful that each of these purposes be valued and judged by the criteria relevant to what it is, and not penalized for failing to be what it is not meant to be. Disinterestedness specifically separates the criteria for judging artistic work from the criteria for judging representational work.

Confusing artistic judgment with such unrelated judgments as ethics or fidelity to objective appearances ultimately only muddies the waters of all judgments regarding photography. Rather than judge documentary and artistic photographs by their intended purpose, some critics have come to consider the two antagonistic rivals when they may just as well be considered mutually supportive allies. The prevalence of the antagonistic attitude among photographers likely is responsible for photographic art remaining mired in century-old debates about realism, and why photographic art has largely failed to progress much beyond aesthetic canons that in other media have been accepted and transcended since the days of impressionism.

Rather than grapple with what disinterestedness *is*, it may be easier to understand it by considering what it *is not*. This is the approach taken by philosopher Iris Murdoch and others. Rather than investigate *disinterest* in the context of art, Murdoch chose instead to investigate what Kant meant by "interest" as the thing to avoid when judging aesthetic value.

The interest that Kant (and Murdoch and others) refers to is not a general interest in the existence of artistic subjects, but specifically, various forms of self-interest—what these objects are, where they are, how they were rendered, or whether they really looked "like that." We should also consider that interests such as ethical judgments and possessive or acquisitive desires (the wish to see, to acquire, to own, or to experience in person things portrayed in artistic works) may vary among individuals and therefore, should not be considered universal factors in the judgment of aesthetics. In contrast, appreciation of beauty (according to Kant) is universal and innate to all people—we all recognize instinctively (to use his term, *a-priori*) some things as beautiful and others as not.

Recent studies seem to support this universality of some aspects of beauty. One such study by neurobiologist Semir Zeki and colleagues showed that people who possess no understanding of advanced mathematics could still classify some mathematical equations as more beautiful than others in the same way as professional mathematicians do. When evaluating these mathematical formulas, people showed activation in the same brain regions (the medial orbitofrontal cortex) used in judgment of aesthetic beauty in art. Neuroscientist V. S. Ramachandran even postulated that some universal judgments of beauty may extend beyond just the human species. In his book *The Tell-Tale Brain*, Ramachandran wrote, "I suggest that

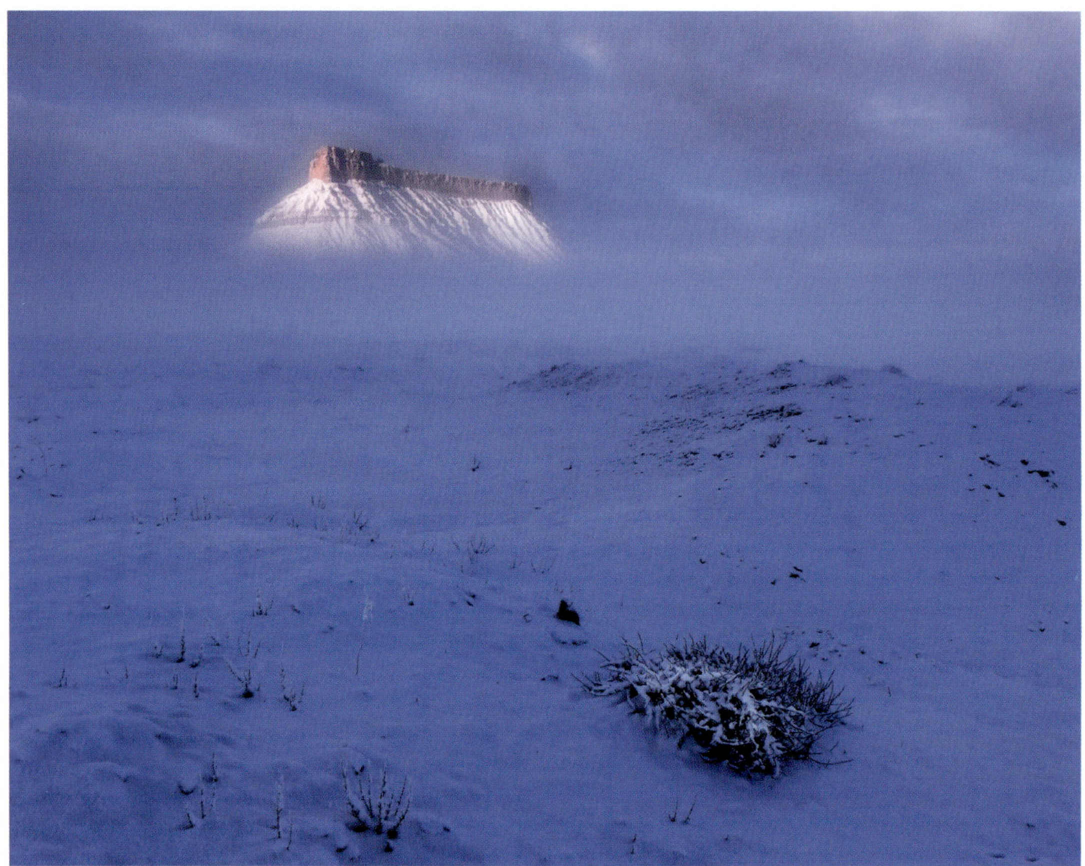

there are laws of aesthetics that are universal, cutting across cultural and even species boundaries."

In Murdoch's analysis, disinterestedness means transcending one's self-interests, focusing instead on the greater and more universal emotions inspired by aesthetic beauty. Murdoch therefore referred to the effect of disinterested judgment as "unselfing," which she defined as "unpossessive contemplation"—finding value in the experience of beauty for its own sake, independent of any acquisitive impulse or ethical judgment, and consciously transcending personal (selfish) interests in order to experience beauty in its purest form.

Philosopher Bertrand Russell, reflecting on the idea of disinterestedness, lamented the struggle of artists facing audiences who may bring their personal "baggage"—their self-interests—into their judgment of art. Russell suggested that such audiences may ultimately hinder their own experience and deny themselves the full extent of the potential rewards of the aesthetic experience. In his book *Proposed Roads to Freedom*, he wrote, "It is difficult for an artist to live in an environment in which everything is judged by its utility, rather than by its intrinsic quality. The whole side of life of which art is the flower requires something which may be called disinterestedness, a capacity for direct enjoyment."

Perhaps a good way to understand disinterestedness in the context of photography is with an example. Consider a photograph of a mountain that is (for the sake of this example) universally agreed to be beautiful. An "interested" judgment of such a photograph (which may be appropriate if the photograph were presented as a documentary record meant to possess some utilitarian value) may be this: "Hey, this is Mount Something-or-other, but it doesn't look like that in reality! I have been deceived!" In contrast, a disinterested judgment (appropriate for photographs presented as art) may be this: "Oh, this is such a beautiful rendition of a mountain, I feel uplifted and inspired by it."

Both judgments may be considered equally truthful and logically valid. They are only in contradiction if one fails to account for the photographer's intent. To illustrate the self-defeating effect of applying "interested" judgment where a disinterested judgment is more appropriate, consider this: if the photograph were offered as a work of art, rather than as a documentary record, those making the "interested" judgment (relying on self-interest in such things as the name of the specific mountain or the ethics of the photographer) would have needlessly sabotaged their own aesthetic experience. By failing to align their judgment with the stated purpose of the work, rather than feel inspired, they ended up feeling deceived, to their own detriment and to the detriment of the photographer whose ethics were unfairly called into question.

By a simple calculus, we can say that those who know to consciously align their form of judgment with the nature of a given work will be better off. By distinguishing works that should be approached with disinterestedness from works intended to serve some utilitarian function by their realism (i.e., by judging art as art and representation as representation), viewers may reap the full rewards of both. In so doing, viewers may also spare themselves such self-inflicted penalties as a misplaced sense of having been deceived or manipulated to some nefarious end.

It seems to me in the best interest of both artists and documentarians to become familiar with and to promote the idea of disinterestedness in the context of photographic art: not only to accept but also to celebrate that our beloved medium, photography, is so versatile as to be able to serve more than just one purpose.

13 Art and Flow in Photography

The true artists are almost as rare a phenomenon among painters, sculptors, composers as among photographers.
—Paul Strand

Almost since its inception, photography has drawn criticism from painters and art critics. Examples are not difficult to find. In 1859, Baudelaire declared photography "the refuge of every would-be painter, every painter too ill-endowed or too lazy to complete his studies." Almost 120 years later, writer Gore Vidal, criticizing the work of photographer Cecil Beaton, expressed a similar sentiment, claiming photography to be "the 'art form' of the untalented."

To this day, at least in some quarters, tribal rivalry between photographers and painters often leads to friction, whether in the form of barbed, cynical comments, in excluding photography from art venues, or in more subtle ways, such as websites and headlines referring to "art and photography" as if the two are inherently separate entities. Alas, competition and tribalism are innately human qualities, often transcending reason in their premises, pettiness, and extent, sometimes culminating in outright rancor and intolerant attitudes. Such manufactured rivalries may seem like just good-natured jabs in some cases. But the fact that prejudice against photography as an art form still persists and excludes some photographic artists from various venues strictly because of their choice of medium suggests that these attitudes have real-world consequences for photographic artists.

I concede that there are good reasons to question the artistic merits of some (perhaps even a lot of) photographs when applied on a case-by-case basis, but to malign the medium of photography as inherently inferior to other artistic media is more aptly characterized as prejudice rather than as valid criticism.

To be sure, considering photography as artistically inferior to painting is not unique to painters. For example, Edvard Munch, despite being known primarily as a painter, was also an avid photographer, yet he did not think that photography could live up to the expressive powers of painting. Cartier-Bresson started off as a painter, then became one of the most accomplished photographers in history, only to return to painting in his elder years, saying in one interview, "Photography has never been more than a way into painting, a sort of instant drawing."

In reading such accounts about the superiority of painting to photography as a medium for art, I had to ask myself honestly and objectively whether they are true. Despite my confidence in the creative and expressive qualities of my own work, I still wondered if I was missing something important. Perhaps I was biased subconsciously to rationalize in hindsight my choice of photography as my artistic medium, which, admittedly, was not the result of careful, objective consideration. There was never a point when, realizing that I wanted to become an artist, I stopped to compare different media and to determine by some rational analysis that photography was the worthiest or the most rewarding one.

I evolved into a photographic artist not by deciding to become one, but rather, by way of practicing photography in various ways, driven by various motivations, reaching on occasion various points of saturation that prompted me to seek some "next thing" to challenge myself with. It took nearly three decades for me to realize that my trajectory was leading me toward making art and away from other uses for photography, which became gradually less interesting and comparably less rewarding. Without planning to become one, I was already a committed photographic artist when I finally stopped to wonder whether I would be (or would have been) better off if I had used those years to pursue painting instead.

Considering the many ways that art and media may be compared, I realized I needed metrics by which to make a meaningful comparison. I also had to define my questions in terms conducive to such a comparison. Beyond considerations of popular acceptance or income, the question I sought to answer was this: Will I gain anything in terms of the quality of my artistic experiences if I switched to a medium other than photography?

With quality of inner experience as my main interest, I settled on the psychological condition of flow as my metric. In his book *Flow: The Psychology of Optimal Experience*, Mihaly Csikszentmihalyi describes what he means by flow being an "optimal experience." He wrote, "We feel a sense of exhilaration, a deep sense of enjoyment that is long cherished and that becomes a landmark in memory for what life should be like." My question then, is this: Can engagement in photography elicit flow as effectively as painting (or other activity)? I believe the answer is yes. Also, I believe that the choice of medium by which one may accomplish flow matters much less (perhaps not at all) than one's attitude when creating art, in any medium. Flow does not depend on *what* one does but on *how* one engages with what one does. In the words of Csikszentmihalyi, "The goal in itself is usually not important; what matters is that it focuses a person's attention and involves it in an achievable, enjoyable activity."

Discussing his experimental findings, Csikszentmihalyi wrote:

> *We found that every flow activity, whether it involved competition, chance, or any other dimension of experience, had this in common: It provided a sense of discovery, a creative feeling of transporting the person into a new reality. It pushed the person to higher levels of performance and led to previously undreamed-of states of consciousness. In short, it transformed the self by making it more complex. In this growth of the self lies the key to flow activities.*

These words imply what I believe is the crux of the issue. Activities such as painting or sculpting, which rely on practiced manual skills, may impose on an artist a mode of work that is more conducive to flow (i.e., more challenging and requiring more attention) than photography, which relies to a great degree on automated technology and allows almost anyone to make technically competent photographs by following simple directions, without great investment of effort or attention.

The conclusion: photography may be as rewarding a medium for artists as any other, but it also allows for tempting shortcuts to high-quality results—and these shortcuts may come at the cost of hindering or preventing a photographer from experiencing flow. Therefore, photographers may need to deliberately set for themselves challenges requiring prolonged investment of effort and focused attention. Whereas other media may impose such challenges by their nature, in photography an artist must choose these challenges consciously and have the discipline to abide by them.

It is important here to distinguish between different kinds of challenges in art. There are technical challenges, and there are creative/expressive challenges. Technical challenges may involve mastering difficult manual skills or knowledge of manipulating certain materials. Such challenges may give rise to flow by virtue of consuming an artist's attention for prolonged periods. The technical challenges of photography are comparatively easier than those of other media. Some

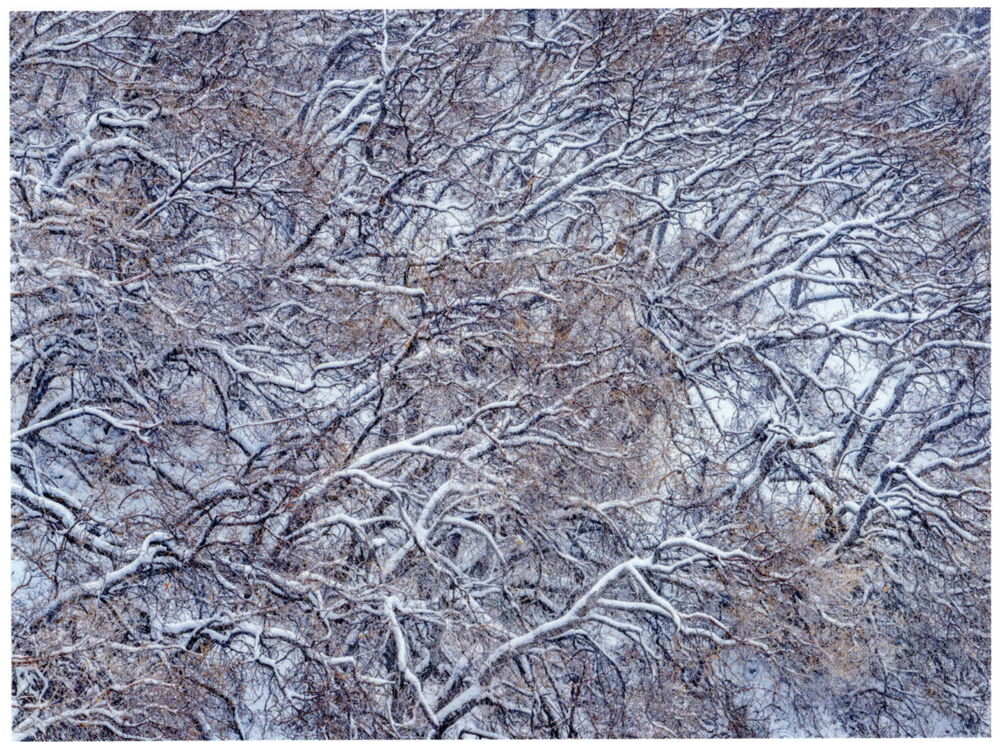

photographers, perhaps seeking flow, may choose to deliberately introduce greater technical challenges into their work by such strategies as working with analog processes or by employing difficult digital processing techniques.

I think that a better way to challenge yourself in photography is to accept the gifts of technical ease and powerful automated tools, and instead focus on creative/expressive challenges—cognitive (intellectual, emotional) challenges, rather than technical ones. This is because it's the nature of technical skills to become easier in time. It is also the nature of technology to evolve toward greater ease for its users. Creative and expressive challenges, by contrast, are infinite in nature. As Ted Orland and David Bayles put it in their book, *Art and Fear*, "Compared to other challenges, the ultimate shortcoming of technical problems is not that they're hard, but that they're easy."

According to literature, the flow experience ensues from certain conditions. Flow requires having sufficient skill to accomplish a desired goal (without such skill, one may be driven to frustration rather than flow). Flow also requires that one should have a sense of control over one's work. Lastly, flow requires a high degree

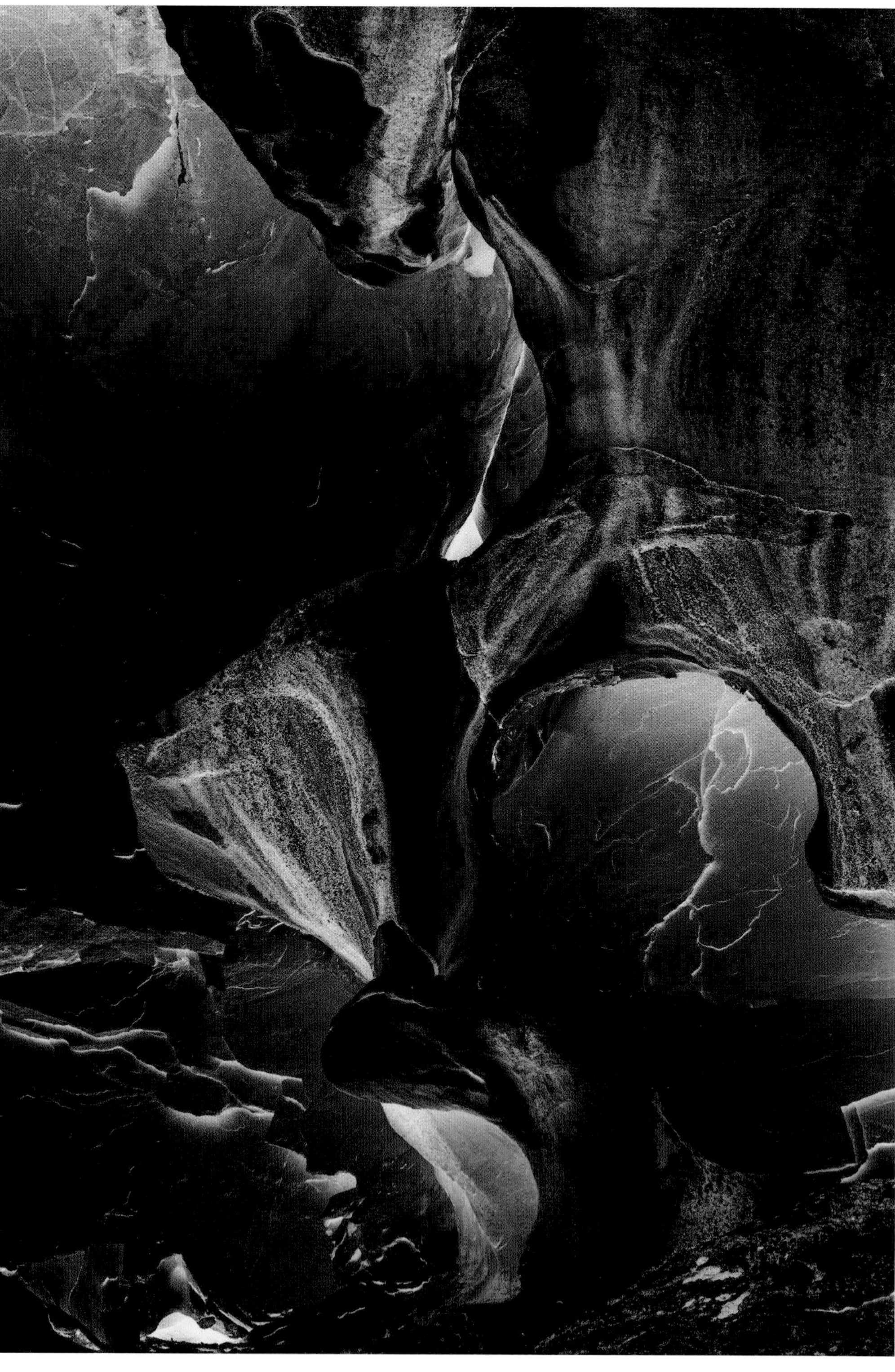

of challenge and an intensity of concentration that demands all of one's attention, leaving no attention for anything other than the task at hand. It is this latter qualification that likely prevents most artists (in any medium) from experiencing flow.

In his book, Csikszentmihalyi described the cognitive state conducive to optimal experience as feeling like "a person's body or mind is stretched to its limits in a voluntary effort to accomplish something difficult and worthwhile." Do you feel like that when practicing your art? My sense is that few photographers push themselves this hard, and many look for easier paths to some form of "success" (whether popularity, productivity, sales, winning honors, or other). Alas, if your goal is to maximize the quality of your experiences, pursuit of success may not be your best strategy. As Csikszentmihalyi explained, "After each success it becomes clearer that money, power, status, and possessions do not, by themselves, necessarily add one iota to the quality of life."

Our industry and culture in many ways lure us away from effort by offering photographers a plethora of quick and easy recipes for success: "art" filters, step-by-step guidelines, automation, directions to certain locations and the "best times" to photograph them, and so on. In our social interactions and contests, we often congratulate each other on accomplishing visually attractive photographs, even if these photographs are obviously derivative or formulaic and their making required no significant investment of effort.

For photography to be challenging and to command one's complete attention—the conditions for flow—it's not enough to strive for beautiful photographs. Odd as it may sound, because photography is relatively easy in its technical aspects, we must deliberately make our work more difficult and time-consuming if we hope to gain the most from it.

Besides adopting habits and mindsets that are conducive to flow, it is also useful to understand things that may inhibit or hinder flow. Two such inhibiting factors identified by Csikszentmihalyi are self-consciousness and self-centeredness. Many photographers today feel self-conscious because of the culture of social media and its pressures to conform and to win popularity. Many feel self-conscious because of competition or because so many "purists" seek to impose arbitrary limitations on the use of some techniques in photography. In contrast, consider this admonition by Csikszentmihalyi: "A person who is constantly worried about how others will perceive her, who is afraid of creating the wrong impression, or of doing something inappropriate, is . . . condemned to permanent exclusion from enjoyment."

One needs only to think about our age's "influencer" culture of narcissistic self-promotion, and of so many self-appointed business/marketing experts focused on sales, likes, "winning," or other aspects of photography, that upon closer scrutiny, have nothing at all to do with artistic expression, to understand how the internet age is helping promote self-centeredness.

Ultimately, it is up to you to decide which of these points of view to accept or to reject. While self-consciousness and self-centeredness may damage your experience, self-expression may well have the opposite effect. Therefore, I suggest that deciding on what attitudes in photography are worth accepting or rejecting comes down to this: accept advice and attitudes that are conducive to self-expression, and reject those that do not. Challenge yourself—first, before anything else—to be self-expressive in your work. Then, based on what you wish to express, choose your tools and methods to match, no matter who it may appease or offend. If you give up self-expression because you feel self-conscious or self-centered, you will likely end up feeling dissatisfied and unfulfilled with your art, making the endeavor self-defeating.

In choosing your creative challenges, consider that with practice things that used to be challenging cease to be so. Your goal should be to maintain a high level of challenge, rather than to become comfortable with things that used to be challenging. This requires that you consistently "up the ante" to match your skills and sensibilities as they evolve. On a graph plotting skill level on one axis and degree of challenge on the other axis, visualize a diagonal line starting at the intersection of the axes and rising as both skill and challenge levels increase. Scattered closely around this line is the area where the degree of challenge you tackle is within your skills at a point in time. Csikszentmihalyi referred to this area as the "flow channel."

Above the flow channel, challenges may be too great for your skills, leading to anxiety. Below the flow channel, your skill easily exceeds what's needed for a given challenge, leading to boredom. Given that technical skills in photography are generally not difficult to learn, photographers who wish to stay within the flow channel must push their "soft" (i.e., nontechnical) skills, such as expressive visual composition and divergent thinking, to maintain a sufficient level of challenge.

Anxiety, which may result from being above the flow channel (i.e., where challenges seem too great for your skill level), comes from having unrealistic expectations, or from feeling like you will never be good enough to accomplish the kind of work you wish to do. Anxiety is also an outcome of a trait that is regrettably common among photographers: impatience. Rather than taking the time to evolve one's creativity, voice, and expressive powers—by experimentation, practice, discipline, failure, and grit—many seek instead to avoid challenge altogether: to go after guaranteed, beautiful, popular results, without waiting, without taking the time to build and mature skills, and without overcoming challenges of any great magnitude.

Boredom, which may result from being below the flow channel (i.e., where your skill level is more than enough to tackle a given challenge without great effort), comes from pursuing photographs that are well within your abilities and experience, without pushing your proverbial "envelope." In the age of social media, there is another nefarious force at play that may sidetrack photographers from achieving flow: avoiding boredom, not by way of taking on greater creative challenges but by socializing about photography—debating minutiae of equipment, analyzing technical qualities of photographs, trading location information, competing for popularity, and so on. These distractions not only relieve the natural and useful boredom that may ensue from lack of challenge but also divert the discussion (and the work) away from artistic merits and challenges, away from creativity, and regrettably, away from flow.

There is no doubt in my mind that practicing photography with the attitudes and conditions conducive to flow—making it deliberately difficult, challenging, stretching one's abilities and imagination, requiring prolonged focused engagement, and consuming as much attention as one can muster—can make photography as rewarding to an artist as any other artistic pursuit, irrespective of medium. As such, at least from the perspective of an artist, there is no special reason, other than perhaps aesthetic preference or commercial considerations, to favor one medium over another. Certainly, in terms of personal satisfaction, photographers who experience flow in their work are much better off than painters (or other artists) who do not. More important, it is foolish to think that one's choice of any medium guarantees finding value and meaning in artistic work. Value, in terms of inner experience, does not come from any medium but from the difficulty, creativity, and seriousness with which one uses the medium.

This train of thought has led me to conclude that, so long as I maintain a high degree of creative and expressive challenges for myself, I am no worse off in terms of my experience as an artist than those working in other media. This still leaves open what in my opinion is the lesser question of whether one type of creation—a photograph, a painting, a symphony, a butter sculpture, or a novel—is inherently worthier as a work of art from the perspective of audiences and critics. Certainly, it is a discussion worth having, but be reminded that worrying about the expectations and judgments of others is a sure way to self-consciousness, which is one of the hindrances to flow. I argue that to sacrifice the potential to experience flow—as much and as often as one can—for such considerations as sales or popularity is a Faustian bargain.

Spirituality, Sensuality, and Mechanics

> Those who have only a superficial knowledge of the possibilities of our art contend that the photographer is a mere mechanical realist without power to add anything of himself to his production. Yet some of our critics inconsistently commit themselves to the statement that some of our pictures are nothing like nature. This is giving themselves away, for if we can add untruth we can idealise. But we go further and contend that we can add truth to bare facts.
> —Henry Peach Robinson

Art, by most formal definitions, is an expression of human skill and creativity. Representational photography—photography aiming literally to re-present appearances as a random person would likely see them—may seem on its face to come up short on both counts, relying on relatively easy-to-learn skills and requiring little or no creativity. However, when it comes to art in photography, we must consider that not all representation is necessarily objective or uncreative representation. Representational photographs, despite being constructed of objective appearances, can still be both creative and subjective, and as such, art. Put another way, regardless of the degree of post-exposure manipulation a photographer chose to apply, even so-called "straight" photographs may still portray objects and scenes in ways that a random person would likely *not* see them were it not for the photographer's skill and creative imagination.

The key to art in photography is not necessarily whether, or to what extent, a photograph "departs from reality" (to borrow a term used by Ansel Adams), but whether, and to what extent, a photograph is creative (i.e., a novel product of the

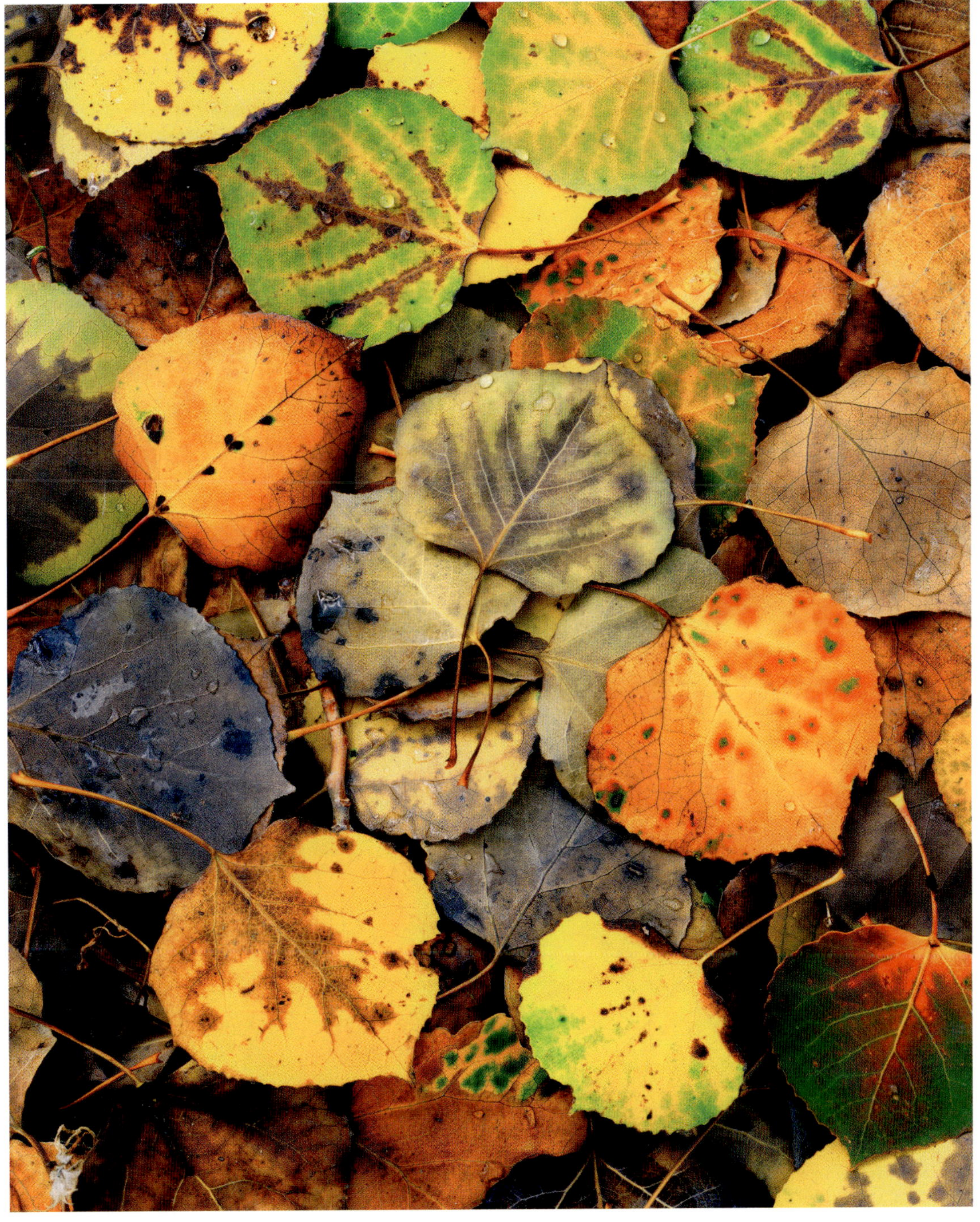

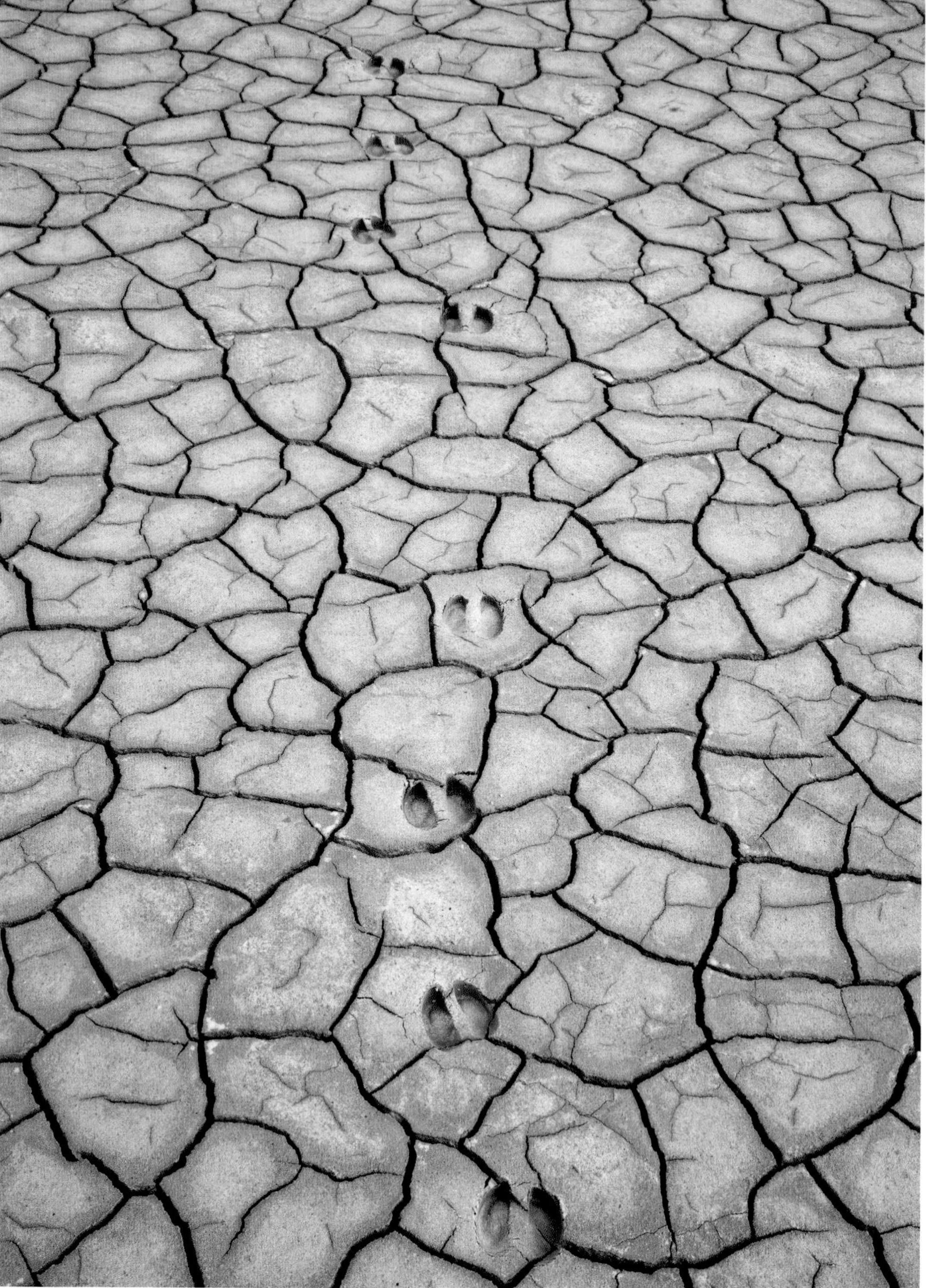

photographer's imagination) and expressive (i.e., conveying primarily a subjective mood or emotion, rather than an objective view). In this characterization, the opposite of art in photography is not representation, but *objective* representation: portraying objects or scenes in the way that any random person would likely see them without any creative intervention by the photographer.

Of course, this is not to say that artistic photographs are necessarily superior to objective photographs or vice versa. Both art and objective representation may yield good or bad photographs, useful or useless photographs, important or meaningless photographs, satisfying or banal photographs.

Sometimes, the path to truthful answers requires asking the right questions. In the simplest case, a person who sees a photograph may ask, "Is this what I would have seen if I were there?" If the answer is yes, the photograph may be considered an objective representation—perhaps one of great documentary and journalistic importance but not a work of art. If the answer is no, the photograph may be considered creative (novelty being a requisite for creativity), even artistic, being a product of the photographer's mind, rather than a mechanical reproduction. Despite being a subjective creation that a random person would likely not have seen, such a photograph may still be representational in the sense of rendering accurate details and colors. This can be made clear by changing the question to this: "Is this what I would have seen if I had looked through your viewfinder?"

Among the most powerful creative tools available to photographers (and to artistic creators in other visual media) is composition: the deliberate arrangement of elements within the frame so that they arouse a desired effect in the viewer. A good way to refer to this desired effect is as the photographer's expressive intent. A creative composition can (and, if the goal is artistic expression, should) transcend or even repudiate what John Szarkowski termed "habitual seeing"—the way that a random person may perceive an object or scene.

Creatively composed photographs may still be representational in the technical sense—accurate depictions of qualities of light reflecting off physical objects. At the same time, such photographs may also be novel and unexpected, and therefore creative. Such photographs may be considered expressions of human skill and creativity and thus meet the definition for art without need for further manipulation. Of course, a creative composition is itself a form of manipulation of the photographer's materials toward an expressive end. (This is not to say that there's anything wrong with other forms of manipulation when the photographer's goal is artistic expression, rather than objective representation.)

Creativity and expression are useful terms in assessing the artistic merits of any human-made product. This is because the terms *creativity* and *expression* can be characterized as measurable qualities. Creativity is measured by such qualities as novelty, usefulness, and unexpectedness. Expression is measured by the degree to which a product possesses subjective, rather than objective, meaning. It's worth highlighting that most current definitions of art do not extend to products of machines (including products of so-called artificial intelligence), nor to naturally occurring objects.

When it comes to art, relying on measurable qualities and clear-cut distinctions may not sit well with some. This was not lost on German poet, critic, and polymath Johann Wolfgang von Goethe. In 1798, Goethe penned a brilliant introduction for the periodical *Die Propyläen* (which he cofounded with Johann Heinrich Meyer). In the introduction, Goethe wrote:

> *A theme [for art] having been happily found or invented, it is subjected to treatment which we would divide into the spiritual, the sensuous, and the mechanical. The spiritual develops the subject according to its inner relations . . . The sensuous treatment we should define as that through which the work becomes thoroughly comprehensible to the senses, agreeable, delightful, and irresistible through its gentle charm. The mechanical treatment, finally, is that which works upon given material through any bodily organ, and thus brings the work into existence and gives it reality.*

Thinking of artistic themes in terms of spiritual, sensuous, and mechanical qualities, while eminently compatible with today's academic definitions of creativity and expression, may be more palatable to those who prefer to think of art in terms of emotional or sensory experiences.

Mapping Goethe's terms to present-day terminology, the "mechanics" of artistic creation correspond to the tools, materials, and skills of the artist. "Sensuous" (or sensory) experiences are the sights, sounds, scents, tastes, and tactile sensations associated with a work of art. "Spirituality" may mean different things to different people, but all forms of spirituality have this in common: they relate to a person's inner (emotional, cognitive) experience, distinct from physical experiences.

While the mechanics of making artistic photographs are largely the same as the mechanics of making objective photographs (if perhaps applied in different measures), the sensory and spiritual dimensions differ considerably between the two. The difference is in where these qualities originate—whether they are qualities inherent in the objects portrayed, or products of the artist's mind.

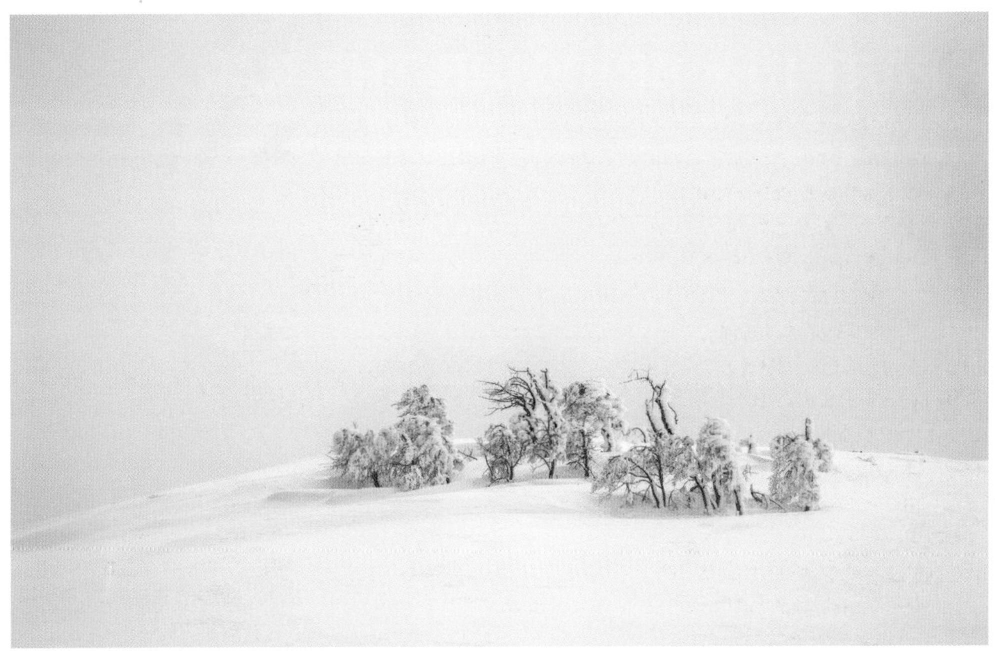

Note that the previous paragraph makes no distinction between representational photographs and photographs manipulated post-exposure to depart from realistic appearances. A representational photograph may still express a subjective—manufactured—meaning that would not have been obvious at the scene to anyone other than the photographer. Such a photograph may absolutely meet the criteria for art. More importantly, when a person asks about such a (representational yet subjective) photograph, "Is this what I would have seen if I were there?" the answer is almost certainly a decisive "no," even if the answer to "Is this what I would have seen if I had looked through your finder?" may well be "yes."

I would be remiss if I didn't state clearly that the designation of art is merely an indication of subjectivity in meaning, and not necessarily a measure of quality, importance, or value. There is no shortage of bad art, perplexing art, or banal art. "Art" is not in itself a badge of honor. Similarly, "realism" is not in itself a measure of importance or truthfulness. We must also distinguish art from beauty. Not all art is beautiful, and not all beautiful things are art. Making beautiful photographs requires relatively little skill and thus is no indication of artistic merit. As Wassily Kandinsky put it (in terms compatible with Goethe's), "External beauty is one element of a spiritual atmosphere. But beyond this positive fact (that what is beautiful is good), it has the weakness of a talent not used to the full."

The business of making a photograph may be said in simple terms to consist of three elements: the objective world (whose permanent condition is change and disorder), the sheet of paper on which the picture will be realized, and the experience which brings them together.
—Aaron Siskind

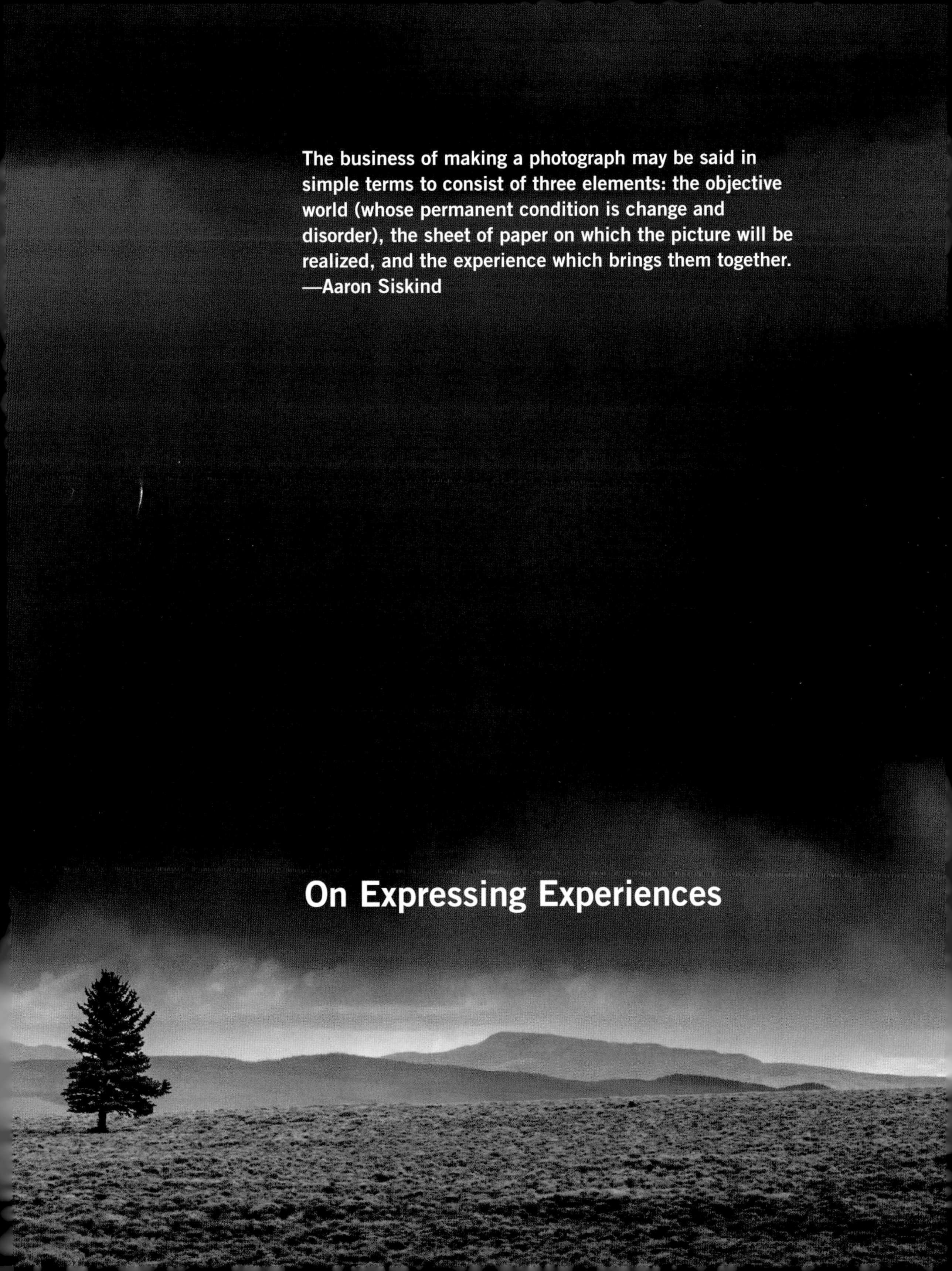

On Expressing Experiences

15 Moments of Grace

On a recent winter hike, I arrived at the rocky summit of a small desert mountain—one not even impressive enough to merit its own name but that still afforded a grand view of a little-visited portion of the Mojave Desert. I'd made the long drive here a couple of days earlier, feeling stressed and emotionally depleted, as much by recent personal setbacks as by the dispiriting effects of the long, cold winter.

The view before me was vast: undulating hills stained in beautiful pastel hues, stratified cliffs, endlessly branching alluvial washes, broad plains covered sparsely in desert brush and large boulders, all glowing in the low winter sun, stretching as far as I could see. With temperatures dropping below freezing each night, and no significant winds in the preceding days, the air was almost completely free of haze. Everything, from the small plants at my feet to the distant mesas on the horizon, appeared crisp and as detailed as my eyes could resolve. Far below me, I could hear a wild burro braying. I had seen him on occasion on each of the previous afternoons, arriving in the vicinity of my campsite just before sunset to bed among the creosote bushes.

I removed my pack, made myself comfortable, and retrieved the lunch I prepared earlier, before leaving camp. It didn't take long for a pair of curious ravens to approach. I watched them circling me, cawing on occasion, their gaze fixed on me, likely deciding if it would be worth waiting for my departure to see what morsels I may leave for them to feast on. Every few moments, one of the birds would flip upside down midair for no obvious reason other than just to have fun.

Sweaty and huffing from my scramble, I removed my jacket and sat with my back against one of the larger rocks, savoring the pleasant midday warmth. After eating my sandwich and sipping some water, I scooted a bit to make myself more comfortable, closed my eyes, and turned my face toward the sun. Suddenly, I felt a familiar sensation, as if I had woken up from a prolonged anxious dream that, up to that point, I did not realize was a dream. A great emotional burden I had carried with me in the prior weeks immediately ceased for no reason I could point to. At

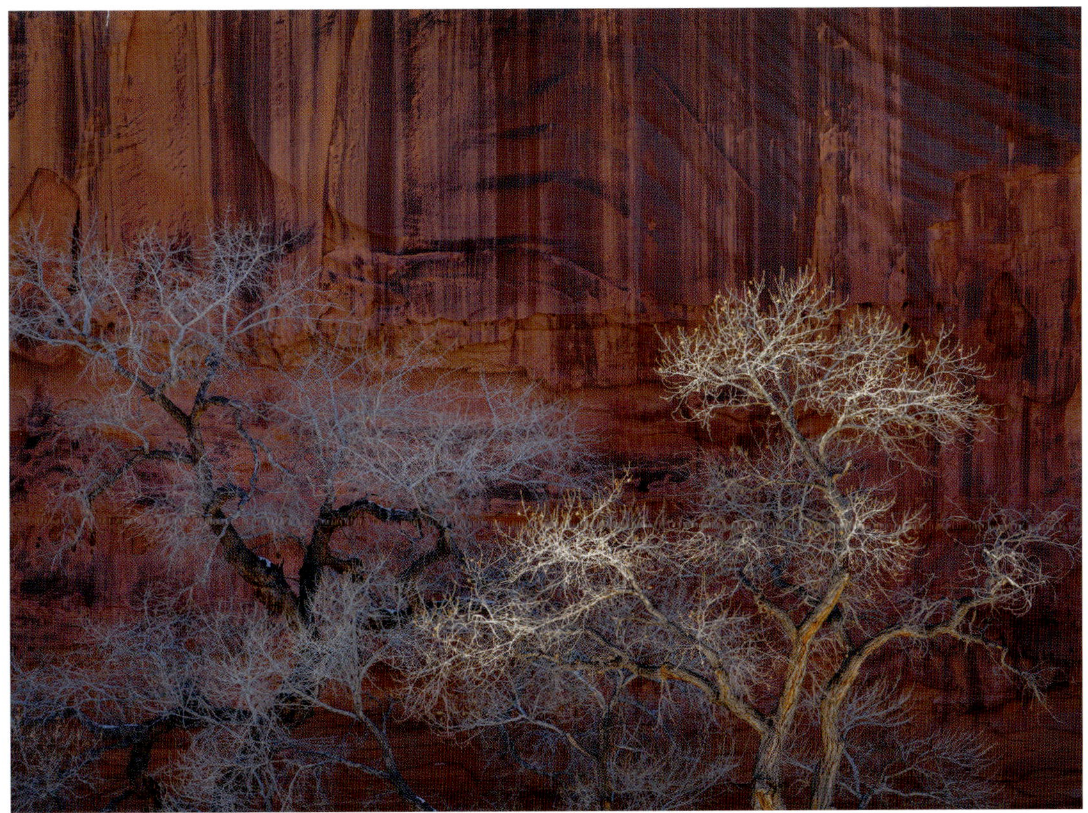

once, everything around me seemed more beautiful and peaceful—a familiar and welcome state I remembered vividly from prior occasions but that I had not felt—or remembered I could feel—in a long time.

Admittedly, I am not one prone to flowery prose. Terms like "grace," at least when used in certain contexts, often bring out the cynic in me. But perhaps this is as good a reason as any that someone like me—a philosophical materialist and obsessively analytic thinker—should attempt to reclaim, at least in part, the idea of grace in the name of fellow platitude-averse, softhearted curmudgeons who may likewise find value in it. There is a reason, after all, that despite our prickly exteriors, dry humor, and stoic dispositions, we still revere art and spend much of our time in pursuit of inspiration, beauty, and experiences such as I've had on that lonesome desert peak: moments of grace.

In photography, as in many other activities, many place great importance on productivity, often without regard for other forms of reward to be found in our experiences, in the pursuit of photographs, in striving to engage with the world in meaningful ways. This is a common sensibility among photographers: "I've invested time and effort; I'd better have something to show for it—a photograph, a piece of writing, a tangible artifact." The more, or the more popular, products we create, the more we feel that the time, labor, and expenses needed to produce these products are justified and worthwhile.

This attitude, when it becomes innate and implicit, comes with the risk of becoming the dominant—or only—way we experience the world. We begin to measure the value of our experiences in terms of the quality or popularity of the photographs we make, sometimes not realizing when the balance had tipped—when we begin to favor photographs to qualities, depth, and richness of experiences. Photographs become the only worthwhile outcome of any trip we make, the justification for money spent on expensive gadgets, the "proof" that we are "serious," the indisputable evidence that we have not "wasted" our time. It is only when a moment of grace presents itself unexpectedly that we are reminded and become aware of how much poorer a life is that does not also reward in intangible, emotional, inward-directed ways. It is in such moments that we realize, jarringly and vividly, how much more ennobling and profound such feelings as gratitude and calmness—as well as freedom from distractions and anxieties—are than any photograph or other material creation on its own can be.

Dictionaries define grace in terms like elegance, refinement, poise, and finesse—qualities that, at least in the realm of art, can be thought of as antithetical to qualities such as triteness, banality, dullness, and gaudiness. To be sure, the judgment of these qualities is primarily a matter of personal taste, for each of us to consider in our own work and life, by our own sensibilities. I mention them not as objective measures of artistic or photographic merit but as things worth considering consciously, in the ways we experience and engage with the world, and in the ways we approach making photographs. In this sense, aspiring to feel and to express grace in our photographic work stands in contrast with some common attitudes toward photography, such as trophy-hunting, preconception, competition, imitation, or striving for no higher goal than just to "get the shot."

The experience I refer to as a moment of grace is perhaps best described as a jarring realization of finding oneself unexpectedly in an unusually elevated state of being—a state in which troubling and mundane considerations, if they are not entirely absent, seem of lesser importance and become easier to set aside in favor of worthier feelings, loftier ideas, deeper thoughts, intensified emotions, and greater clarity of mind. A useful way to define such experiences is in contrast with some better-defined states, such as awe, sublimity, flow, and mindfulness.

Awe is commonly defined as the experience of profound reverence mixed with a sense of fear. Likewise, the sublime is characterized as an encounter with something astonishingly grand and at the same time mortally dangerous. Grace, by contrast, while possessing the same elements of encounter with great beauty and power, does not involve fear of dying, but rather, the comfort and promise of deeper, richer living-ness. I believe it is the feeling Fyodor Dostoevsky referred to in *The Possessed* when he wrote, "There are seconds—they come five or six at a time—when you suddenly feel the presence of the eternal harmony perfectly attained . . . This feeling is clear and unmistakable; it's as though you apprehend all nature and suddenly say, 'Yes, that's right.'"

Compared with other elevated states, like flow and mindfulness—which involve one's attention being overwhelmingly consumed for a time when immersed in some prolonged experience—moments of grace make one acutely aware of the importance of a singular, present moment. Among the defining characteristics of a moment of grace is surprise: the sudden realization of how long it has been since the last time one felt such a moment; how much time has been spent up to that point in lesser preoccupations, more tedious concerns, duller and less inspired feelings, more prosaic thoughts.

Another defining characteristic of a moment of grace is a sense of immense gratitude for the reminder that there is more to life than mundane frustrations, more than anxiety, more than cynical wit, more than dissatisfaction with other people, more than discontentment with whatever petty or unfortunate events may

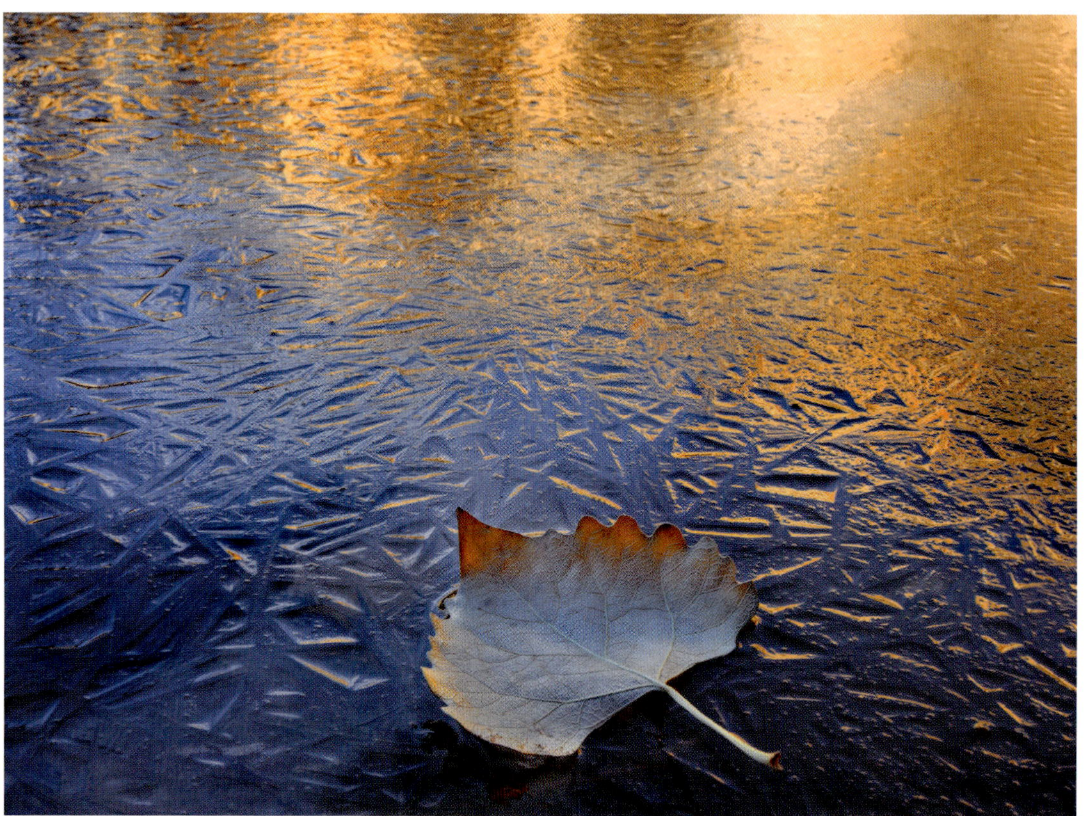

be unfolding in the world or in one's life beyond the present moment, more than concern for producing some tangible artifact to "prove" to others that one has been working—gratitude for the affirmation that one is capable also of loftier, nobler, more exalted, and more beautiful feelings, and that these feelings are worthwhile in themselves even if no one other than you knows that you've experienced them.

A moment of grace is not necessarily a moment of creative epiphany. In a moment of grace, one does not necessarily feel compelled to any action—creative or other—but rather, to appreciation, to satisfaction, to hope, and to acceptance. However, when a moment of grace does happen to coincide with a creative idea, it can rightly be considered a moment of inspiration—a moment when one not only feels grateful and elevated, but also is moved to express these feelings artistically, to render them in some aesthetic way by use of some medium so that others may also share in, and be moved by, them. I believe that one of photography's greatest powers as a medium for expressive art comes to the fore precisely in such moments.

Photography's immediacy and availability to be employed with no elaborate preparations, and with little reliance on materials requiring specialized skills and conditions, narrows the gap between inspiration and expression more than any other artistic medium.

In a moment of inspiration, photography allows a creative artist not only to visualize or to conceptualize a work of expressive art, but also to engage instantly in the production of it—to accomplish at least a considerable portion of it while still in the throes of grace, with the raw emotions still vivid and visceral, rather than recalled later from the few anecdotes one retains in one's imperfect memory. There is no need to stretch a canvas, no need to mix pigments, no need to scribble words or musical notes, no need to hammer away for hours at a chunk of rock before it begins to resemble a finished piece. The work begins to take form immediately.

Of course, not all works of creative artistic expression ensue from moments of inspiration—from the fortuitous convergence of grace and creative epiphany. (Indeed, some notable artists have expressed outright disdain for the idea of inspiration as a necessary precursor to artistic expression.) With some exceptions, independent of any other merits (which may be impressive and important in their own right), and conceding this to be an entirely subjective judgment, I admit I generally find such works to be aptly characterized as graceless.

Beyond momentary rewards, states of grace also have a wonderful dynamic: they self-replicate. Every such experience shapes one's attitude, makes the mind more attuned and predisposed to seeking and striving for them. One becomes more sensitive to circumstances and nuances that may yield more such experiences and that may go unnoticed by more distracted, cynical, or productivity-driven minds. I think Minor White was describing this effect when he commented in an interview, "Watching the way the current moves a blade of grass—sometimes I've seen that happen and it has just turned me inside out."

16 Us of the Minority

**Being in a minority, even a minority of one, did not make you
mad. There was truth and there was untruth, and if you clung to
the truth even against the whole world, you were not mad.
—George Orwell**

I spent most of the past three weeks in my beloved desert, savoring with mixed
emotions the onset of autumn after a brutally hot and dry summer season. Casual
visitors to these parts are easily overwhelmed by the natural beauty, but to one who
spends a lot of time among these canyons, mountains, and high plateaus, the effects
of the changing climate are undeniable and sometimes difficult to witness. Among
the deciduous varieties now in brilliant autumn displays and the evergreens still
dominating the high slopes are many skeletons of trees I remember being alive and
vibrant until just recently. Sagebrush plains and forest floors that would normally
be thriving this time of year, after the summer monsoon rains, are instead brown
and barren as the now-years-long drought continues. In the highlands, some lakes
have been reduced to dry or muddy basins, and some former creeks are now just dry
channels meandering among the trees.

Terms like *inspiration* and *creativity* are often bandied about with exuberant
enthusiasm despite sometimes being rooted in complex, even dark, moods. Products
of creative thought are not all uplifting or benevolent. Likewise, inspiration—that
elevated state of mind driving people to create—is not always the outcome of pleasant circumstances. To wit, my time among the beauties and tragedies of this season
has been unusually productive, not because of some benign sense of joy, not for
denying the grim reality before my eyes, but because I find beauty and grace in the
ways the natural world adapts, even surrenders, to change, good or bad: new life

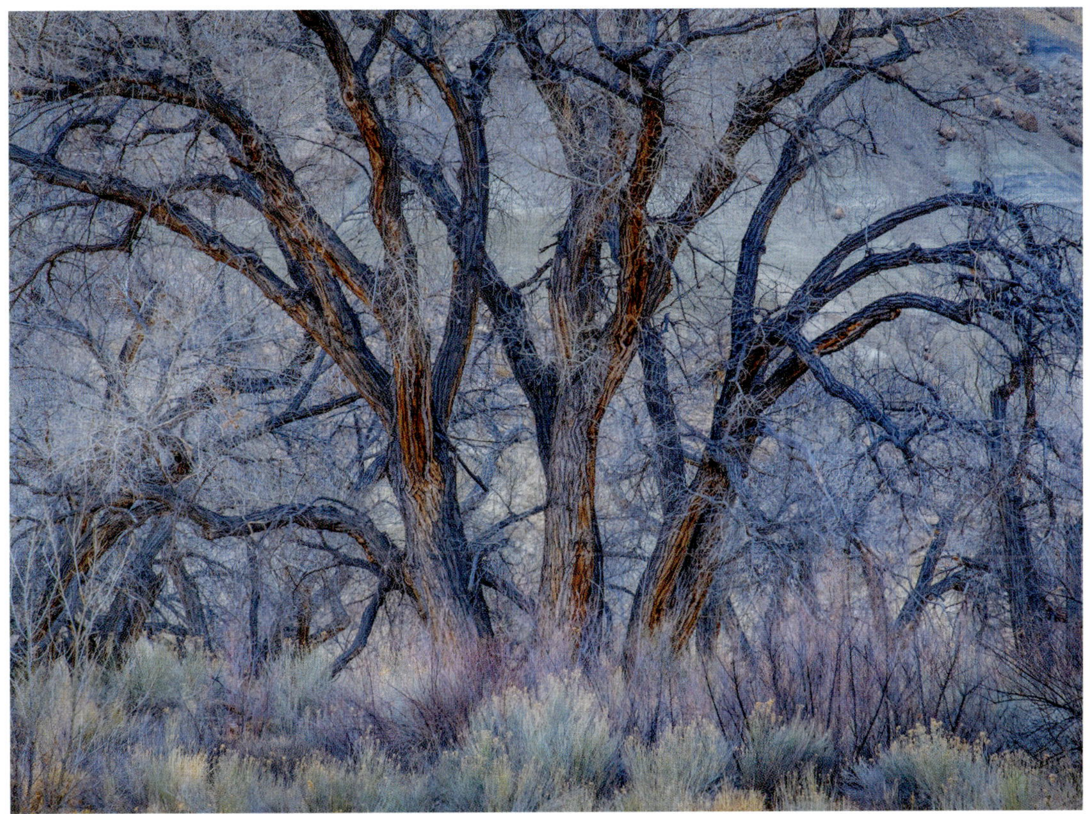

asserting itself despite hardship, the playfulness of young animals in moments of bliss despite facing existential threats, the vibrant displays of dying leaves. Such revelations, both sweet and painful at times, always seem to me in stark contrast with the pervasive jadedness, cynicism, and indifference of so many animals of my own species to such beauty, making me feel grateful for these respites of wildness among the numbness, pettiness, sarcasm, and violence so pervasive in our human made worlds.

In teaching photography, my greatest challenge is not to explain technical concepts but to instill in my students an attitude conducive to creative expression—an attitude of being constantly and defiantly inspired to create, despite ever-present distractions, mundane concerns, and sometimes-unavoidable difficulties. This I must do, at least in part, by countering so many trends and incentives pointing photographers in the opposite direction.

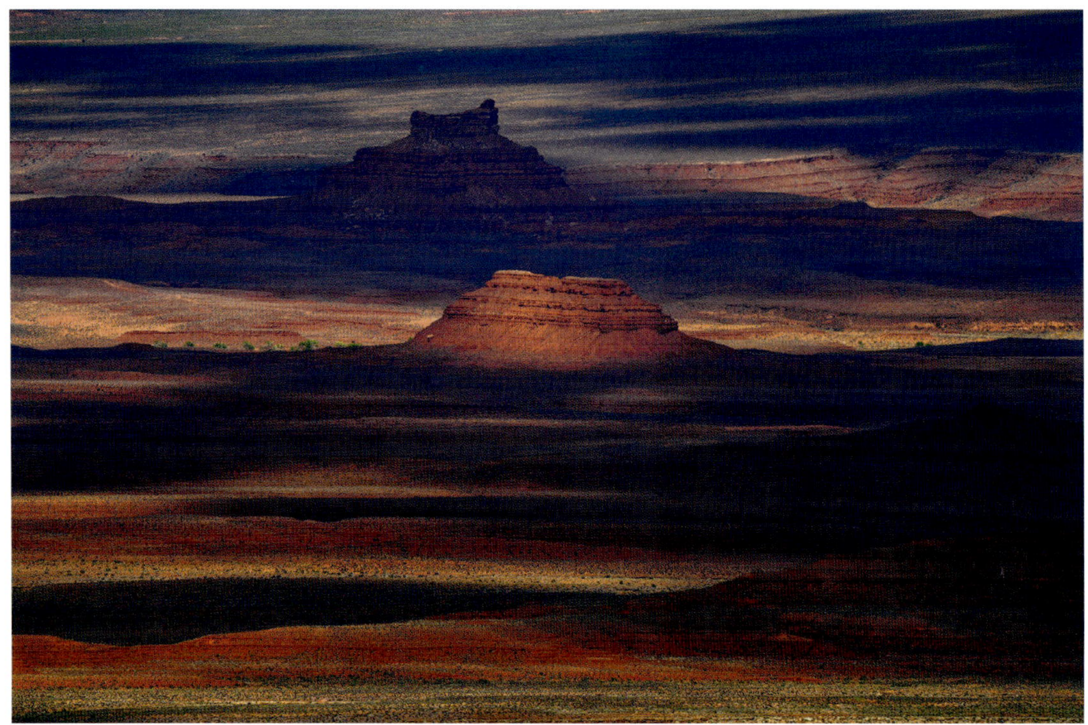

The photographic industry has given rise to an endless torrent of recipes, tips, and other shortcuts to aesthetic appeal, often at the expense of experience, creativity, and self-expression. Manufacturers tout how much their products can do by use of advanced technology, with little effort or skill needed from a photographer. Software makers advertise proudly how their products can generate attractive visual effects without need to visualize, to experiment, to compose, to imagine. Marketing mavens pontificate about the virtues of mastering search algorithms, using hashtags, and building large followings of mindless likers/sharers/subscribers by way of photographs that are popular, formulaic, overly hyped, easily digestible, requiring no depth of engagement to understand and appreciate. Why "waste" time seeking novelty, relating emotionally to one's experience, marveling unproductively at the beauty and complexity of existence, exploring beyond what's already known, challenging one's creative imagination, and risking photographic failure (or worse: unpopularity)?

"Photographers want a formula for everything," wrote Henry Peach Robinson in 1896. More than 120 years later, this still holds true for most, but not all, photographers. A minority of which I am a proud member cares little for formulas when it comes to the creative and expressive aspects of our work. We of the minority strive to give visual expression to notions of our own minds and to complex emotions arising from our own experiences, rather than seek short and easy paths to commonly popular aesthetics. "For the achievement of this," wrote Paul Strand (referring to photographs that express personal meaning), "there are no short cuts, no formulae, no rules except those of your own living. There is necessary, however, the sharpest kind of self-criticism, courage, and hard work."

Aldo Leopold's pioneering and influential book, *A Sand County Almanac*, has inspired me and many fellow naturalists and conservationists. Like so many creative and expressive photographers, so do many conservationists sometimes feel themselves in a minority: isolated, misunderstood, even tempted to give up. Leopold was no stranger to such feelings and acknowledged them in the very first page of his book. "For us of the minority," he wrote, "the opportunity to see geese is more important than television, and the chance to find a pasque-flower is a right as inalienable as free speech."

When feeling myself at odds with a majority opinion, I sometimes find it empowering to define to myself the minority I feel a part of—to write my own "for us of the minority" statement, to articulate, if only to myself, my reasons for being in this minority: the things I will not be tempted to compromise on even while most others don't share the same priorities.

I am a naturalist first, a creative and self-expressive photographer second.

For us of the minority, the opportunity to witness and to participate in wild beauty is more important than any camera technique, any piece of gear or software, any "must-see" attraction, any so-called rules, any tradition, and any measure of popularity, recognition, even legacy.

For us of the minority, the welfare of our subjects is more important than photographing them.

For us of the minority, the rewards of engaging in creative work are more important than impressing others with our photographs.

For us of the minority, why we make our photographs is more important than how we make our photographs.

17 Solace in Interesting Times

The expression "may you live in interesting times," despite being of unknown origin,
is considered by some a tongue-in-cheek Chinese curse. I've always thought of it as a
benediction. Take away the sarcasm and you are left with this simple, if profound, question: Is an easy and uneventful life preferable to a challenging but interesting life?

*   *   *

Winters are long in the high desert of the Colorado Plateau, and more so in the
highlands of my home, near the top of the series of great cliffs known as the Grand
Staircase. Having had enough of the cold and starkness of winter, I've decided to
head south to greet the first signs of spring and to deepen my acquaintance with the
lower, warmer, neighboring deserts where the northern reaches of the Mojave border
the southernmost parts of the Great Basin.

After some hours of driving, I set up camp in a small clearing among large rocks, surrounded by patches of soft, verdant grasses. After weeks of frozen silence, I am acutely aware of the presence of songbirds. Some early bloomers are already in flower: phacelia, chicory, desert dandelion, and wild geranium. After seeing almost no green plants for several months, the scents of fresh foliage and damp earth are so intoxicating that I find myself stopping every so often just to close my eyes and savor the air, a fragrant lungful at a time. On occasion, during brief lapses in mindfulness, I become aware also of the stark contrast between my immediate experience and the grim realities of the changing climate and the spreading coronavirus pandemic. When I become conscious that such thoughts have entered my mind, I dismiss them outright. Not because they are unimportant in other places and times, but because right here, right now, they don't matter.

*   *   *

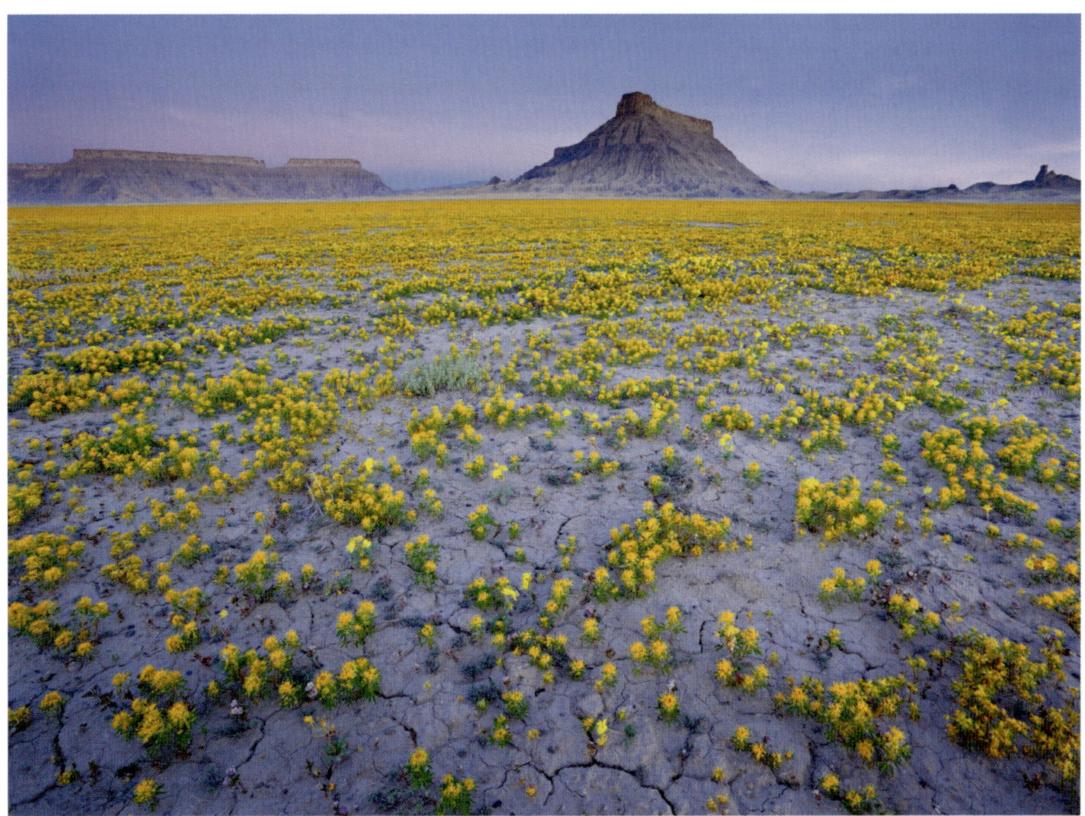

To those who feel comfortable out of doors, removed from human-made worlds and from so many odd rituals of human animals, the visceral immediacy of sensations giving rise to related emotions, perceptions, and thoughts is a defining characteristic of wild experiences. It's regrettable that for many who are not accustomed to such direct parity between experiences and feelings, the reverse is sometimes true: whatever "baggage" they bring with them to wild places from other worlds distracts or prevents them from fully experiencing life as it happens. Nagging concerns claim a portion of their attention away from their immediate experience, and they become anxious or worried about things they can do nothing about. As a result, much of the brain circuitry that may otherwise be applied to noticing, exploring, discovering, feeling, and contemplating aspects of their present experience becomes preoccupied with futile and unproductive ruminations, resulting inevitably in a lesser experience: seeing less, noticing less, appreciating less.

You can never escape the things you insist on carrying with you—the things you refuse to, are afraid to, or don't realize you can, let go of. In the (pompously translated) words of Seneca, "Your faults will follow you whithersoever you travel." Most unfortunate are those unpleasant thoughts one feels obligated to be concerned with because others have deemed them "important" or because one feels guilty setting them aside for a period, even when they serve no useful purpose—even if they may hinder and diminish worthier experiences.

Rumination is among the modes of the human mind most implicated in causing and exacerbating feelings such as anxiety, depression, guilt, anger, and dissatisfaction. Regrettably, rumination has become common and pervasive in industrialized societies. Trapped for many hours in unsatisfying jobs and various self-imposed obligations, many seek to dissociate from their immediate experience, wishing instead to be in places other than where they are, doing things other than what they do. Such dissociation is often not voluntary and may arguably be considered a defense mechanism against the demoralizing effects of tedium and boredom. Rumination often occurs when one is not consciously paying attention to some aspect of one's immediate experience. In such dissociated times, the brain's "default mode network"[1] becomes active and the mind drifts, often to anxious and self-critical thoughts. Conversely, when one engages by choice in some meaningful activity, even if difficult, rumination becomes less likely, making one less anxious and more mindful. An interesting life is rewarding, at least in part, because it is rich in opportunities for such meaningful engagements.

*　*　*

---

[1] A network of brain regions believed to be responsible for self-reflection, among other functions.

Comfortable in my camp, I begin to cook dinner as I look out over many miles of spectacular desert, now glowing and vibrant in the fast-fading afternoon light—a vast landscape of sprawling rocks, colorful earth, cacti, large yucca plants, creosote bushes rising from carpets of soft grasses, and a great open sky above it all. Around me, several mountain ranges stretch in succession toward distant horizons, fading into lighter and lighter bands of blue. I recognize some of them but can't name others. I take some pleasure in the fact that my all-knowing phone app shows no names for them, either. Some I know are inaccessible by any road, separated from the territories of human tribes by many miles of wild desert; and some summits may never have been visited by a human (or any other simian). Shortly before sunset, I notice a flock of large migrating birds flying so high that I can't identify them without the aid of binoculars. Given the direction of their travel, I have some idea of the body of water they are headed toward, and I take pleasure in imagining their view.

*   *   *

Flowery writings about the healing powers of nature may be (justly) considered platitudes by some. Still, in recent years much scientific evidence of the beneficial effects of spending time in natural settings has come to light (to no surprise of naturalists). Perhaps less obvious is how wildness as a way of life may not only heal one's spirit but also serve to make one more resilient, in some ways even immune to the ill effects that others may experience in "interesting" times.

*   *   *

Right here, right now, the world feels as peaceful, beautiful, and alive as anything I can imagine. Except for my own belongings and the rutted two-track road I drove in on, there is no other person or evidence of the existence of other people as far as I can see. The nearest highway is just shy of fifty miles away as the pelican flies (crows rarely fly in straight lines for very long).

*   *   *

A concerned friend, wearied by world news, confessed to wishing someone would just say that everything will be alright. Of course, everything will be alright. Everything is already alright. Looking back at so much beauty and meaning, so much knowledge and understanding, so many moments of awe and amazement, experienced in such circumstances, in solitude or in the notable company of some humans and other beings, even if my existence comes to an abrupt end right now, this life—all of it—will have been alright, regardless of how the universe may continue to unfold, regardless of the trials and fates of the human (or any other) species.

*   *   *

Night has fallen, and I stare into a vast sky dotted with celestial lights. Some of the photons meeting my retinas now have traveled a thousand years or more to reach me in this improbable place at this random time. I stand and stare into the vastness above me, imagining Walt Whitman whispering, "Let your soul stand cool and composed before a million universes."

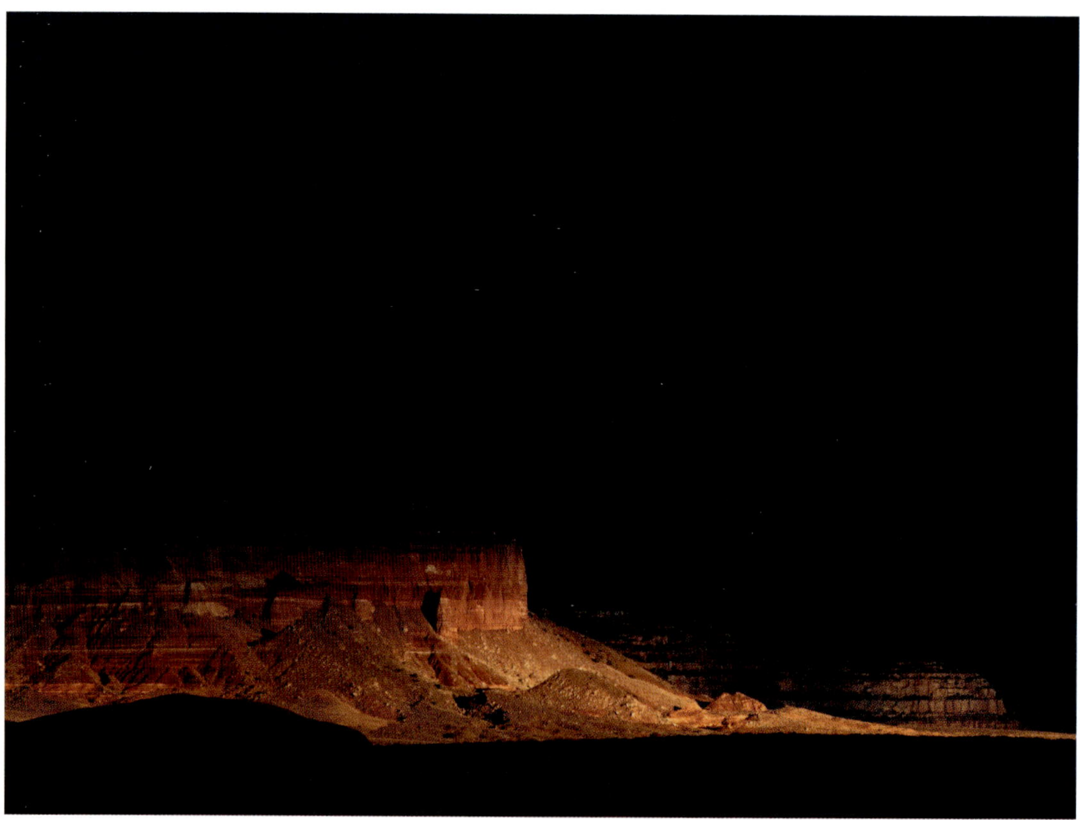

Describe your sorrows and desires, your passing thoughts and
your faith in some kind of beauty—describe it all with heartfelt,
silent, humble sincerity and use it to express yourself, the things
that surround you, the images of your dreams, and the objects
of your memory.
—Rainer Maria Rilke

In his master work, *Thinking, Fast and Slow*, Nobel laureate Daniel Kahneman draws
a distinction between a person's "experiencing self" and "remembering self": the perceptual gap between measurable qualities of an experience and how people remember the experience. The difference in perception between reality and memory raises
this interesting question: Which is more important, the qualities of a real experience
(which we may not remember) or the memory of an experience (which may be at
odds with how we felt while having the experience)?

Kahneman seems to favor the latter. He believes that, in choosing our experiences, we should favor those that may leave better memories, rather than those that
may feel better (or less unpleasant) as they happen. Our memories, after all, are our
life's stories—what remains after other aspects of our experiences fade away beyond
recall. When assessing how content we are with our lives, we rely on memories, not
on objective records. We also rely on memories to guide our decisions and interpretations. Things we forgot, or did not commit to memory to begin with, seemingly
play no role in our general sense of happiness, our hopes, our wisdom, our outlook.

Kahneman's experiments show that our memory of an experience comes primarily from the intensity of feelings (good or bad) we experience at the peak and
at the ending of the experience, not from such things as duration or richness of an

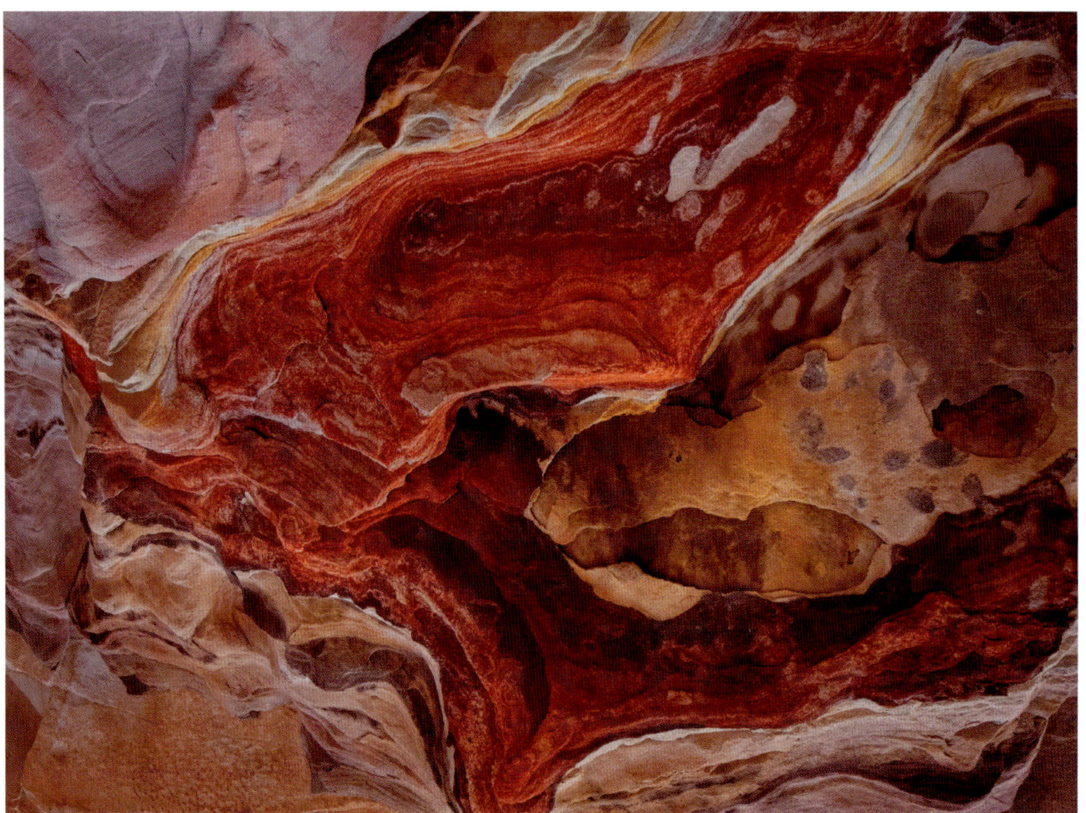

experience. Kahneman believes that most people will favor experiences involving prolonged but mild suffering over experiences involving brief but intense suffering. By the same rationale, we should favor experiences involving short episodes of intense pleasure, even if separated by prolonged periods of boredom or dissatisfaction, over drawn-out periods of mild and sustained contentment. (This, by the way, is in contradiction to some Eastern philosophies, as well as the teachings of Aristotle and others, contending that one should avoid extreme, intense emotions.)

The experiencing self has a cumulative sense of how good or bad an experience is as it happens (and thus cares not only about anecdotal peaks but also about the duration and richness of an experience). In contrast, the remembering self only cares about the intensity of short-lived pinnacles of an experience and excludes from its judgment other aspects that were relevant to the experiencing self.

With some trepidation, I propose that Kahneman's model of the two selves, although eminently useful in understanding some behaviors and perceptions, is

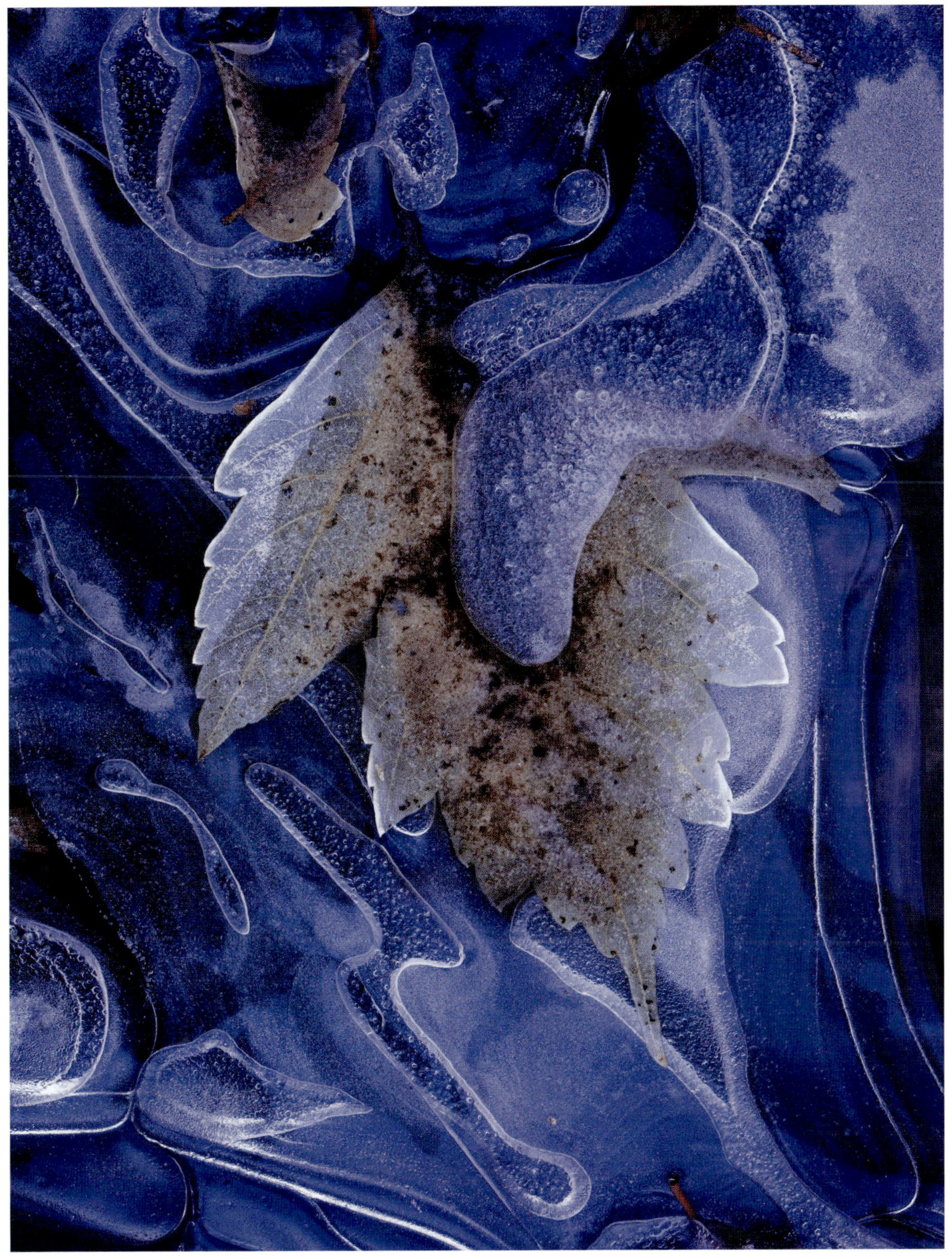

incomplete. The model assumes that the workings of the experiencing self and the remembering self are automatic and inevitable (perhaps in Kahneman's own terms: these two selves are perceptions generated by the brain's "System 1"[2]), which may be a fair assumption in most cases, but not all. I think there is a third self that has the power to affect, even supersede, both the experiencing and the remembering selves: the describing self.

The describing self is a conscious self (in Kahneman's terms, a perception generated by the brain's "System 2"[3]), having the power to shape the perceptions of both the experiencing self and the remembering self. The describing self can, by conscious choice, narrow the gap between the perceptions of the experiencing and remembering selves, having the capacity to make the former more satisfying (or tolerable) and the latter more detailed. The describing self may be dormant in most people in most situations, but it can be trained by such practices as meditation and mindfulness to a point where a person evolves the capacity to choose consciously the meaning and quality of experiences as they happen, as well as how experiences will be remembered.

A clue to the existence and the power of the describing self can be found in the writings of Mihaly Csikszentmihalyi. In his book *Flow: The Psychology of Optimal Experience*, Csikszentmihalyi compared attention to a form of energy we may train ourselves to control and to exert consciously. He wrote, "We create ourselves by how we invest this energy. Memories, thoughts, and feelings are all shaped by how we use it. And it is an energy under our control, to do with as we please; hence, attention is our most important tool in the task of improving the quality of experience."

The describing self has the power to harness attention consciously and, as the saying goes, to take control of the narrative—the story of an experience. Rather than relegating the arcs of our life stories to subconscious "ghost writers" in our brain, the describing self can, if it so chooses, assert itself as the author—at least in theory, and with proper training.

Mindfulness training provides the triggers and the skills needed by the describing self to recognize perceptions as they form, to detach itself from these perceptions if it deems them undesirable, and to narrate the story of an experience from the perspective of an outside observer rather than from the perspective of an unwitting character. In this way, the describing self may affect the perceptions of the experiencing self.

The describing self may also decide, by use of repetition and by emphasizing consciously specific aspects of an experience, to create and strengthen memories (this is

---

[2]In Kahneman's characterization, "System 1" refers to brain functions that operate "automatically and quickly, with little or no effort and no sense of voluntary control."

[3]In Kahneman's characterization, "System 2" refers to brain functions that allocate attention consciously, and that are "often associated with the subjective experience of agency, choice, and concentration."

the mechanism underlying such strategies as constructing a "memory palace"). In this way, the describing self may affect the perceptions of the remembering self.

Having the power to influence the perceptions of both the experiencing self and the remembering self, the describing self may narrow or even reconcile the discrepancies between their default and often disparate (or even contradicting) perceptions.

Photographs can be powerful tools for the describing self. Beyond just recording objective appearances, in practiced hands photographs can also be means for subjective expression. Expressive photographs are those that venture beyond just recording what there was. By use of consciously chosen composition and processing decisions, expressive photographs may hint at subjective aspects of an experience—things that an observant, mindful, and sensitive photographer found meaningful and worthy of commemoration, that may not be obvious to another person, and that may otherwise not "make the cut" to be committed to long-term memory.

Similarly, journal entries—as subjective interpretations of true experiences—may serve the describing self by articulating and recording not only factual information but also aspects of an experience considered important and meaningful by the experiencing self, and thus guide the formation and contents of memories. Even if these journals are never revisited, the acts of conceiving, narrating, and writing likely will influence our perception of our experiences and how they are encoded in memory.

Expressive photographs and journal entries commemorate not only anecdotal pinnacles of experience—the default shorthand used by the remembering self—but also rich details and progression in time, which make up the reality of the experiencing self but that may otherwise be lost when the experience is over.

By taking conscious control of the emotional content of our experiences, we can elevate the quality of our experiences as they happen (the experiencing self). We can also consciously shape our judgment of experiences in hindsight (the remembering self).

19 The Finger and the Moon

**It is a pity that our medium, photography, which is practiced by
so many, is understood by so very few.**
—Ernst Haas

The Śūraṅgama Sūtra tells the story of the Buddha attempting to explain to his
cousin, Ananda, why clinging to common thinking patterns may obscure for most
people the true nature of things: the Dharma-nature. A person attempting to point
others in the direction of higher meaning, according to the Buddha, "is like a man
pointing a finger at the moon to show it to others who should follow the direction of
the finger to look at the moon. If they look at the finger and mistake it for the moon,
they lose both the moon and the finger."

The finger in Buddha's example is just a means to an end: a way of leading
another person to some important knowledge or meaning (the moon). In the language of semioticians, looking at the pointing finger rather than at what the finger is
pointing at can be considered failing to understand the difference between a *signifier*
(a sign) and the thing *signified* (the intended interpretation or meaning implied by
the sign).

Failing to distinguish between signifier and signified is regrettably pervasive in
attitudes toward expressive photography. Rather than focus on what a photographer
wishes to express, many—both photographers and viewers—instead become mired
in technical considerations of the photographic process or in qualities of the objects
portrayed (which, in the case of expressive photography, may be irrelevant to, if not
outright distract from, what the photographer intended to express). They focus on
the finger, miss the moon, and gain no enlightenment from either.

The purpose of expressive photography is no different from that of any expressive art: to signify meanings—moods, emotions, and other states of mind—not to report on the existence of some objects, not to testify to the occurrence of some event, and certainly not to belabor the trivial details of photographic technology. To an expressive photographer, meaning is the moon, and photography, the finger. A means to an end. A way of pointing.

Only after the function of an image is first established should we apply further criteria in our evaluation of its meaning and merit. Certainly, for some applications of photography, considerations of the tools or techniques used, or whether the things portrayed really looked "like that," are important. In expressive photography,

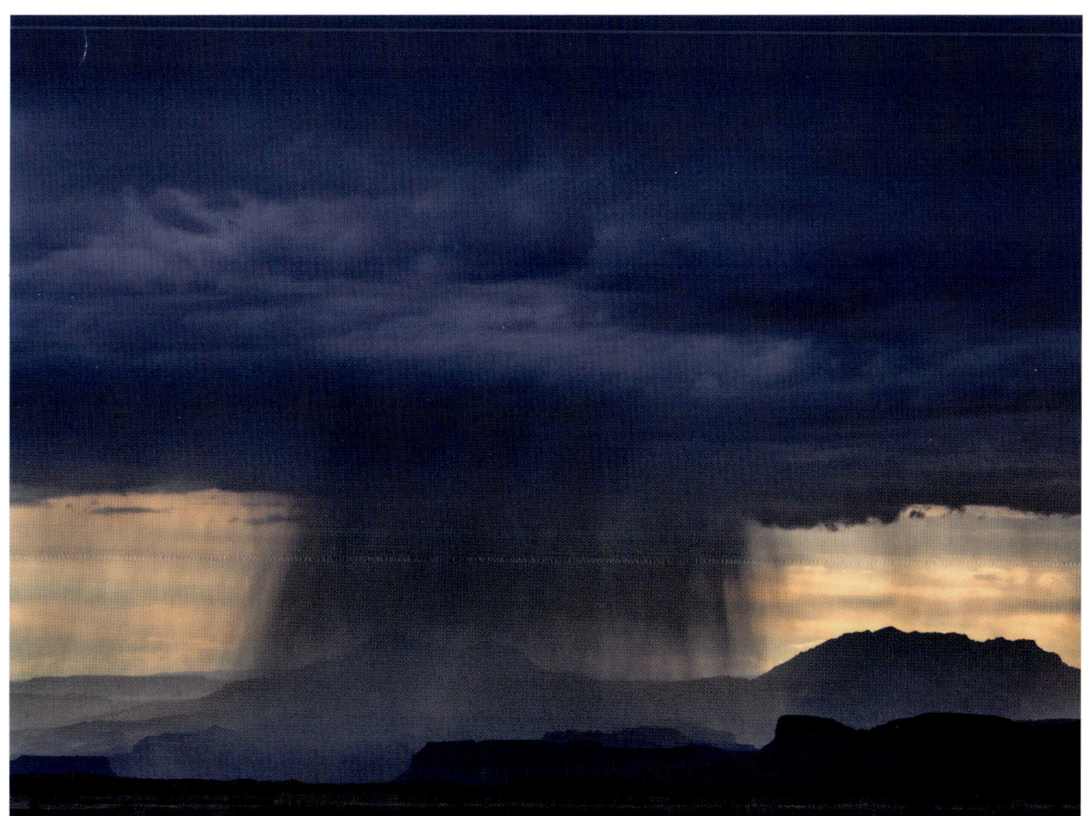

they are not. In expressive photography what matters—the moon—is the concept. The concept for an image is the idea or feeling expressed: the thing the image is *about*, not the thing the image is *of*.

Beyond perhaps considerations of general curiosity, all factors related to the production of an expressive photograph, by comparison, matter less than the concept—or not at all. "Photography would have been a settled fine art long ago," observed Henry Peach Robinson, "if we had not, in more ways than one, gone so much into detail. We have always been too proud of the detail of our work, and the ordinary details of our processes."

In a conversation with her teacher Ludwig Wittgenstein, philosopher Elizabeth Anscombe once commented that it's understandable why, for many years, people thought the sun revolved around the Earth because that's how it looked to them. True to his famous knack for pointing out logical errors in thinking, Wittgenstein responded, "And what would it have looked like if the Earth revolved around the sun?" Likewise, most people assume that all photographs are documentary, objective, factual records because that's what it looks like to them. An expressive photograph may look like a true representation of reality, but its truth is, in fact, of a different nature. To understand the truth of an expressive photograph, viewers must first question their default impressions and allow for the possibility that what they think they see is not what the photograph is about.

So many times, when presenting my work, I realize that viewers, clinging to common preconceptions about the nature of photography, are more concerned with the finger—the camera, the process, qualities of the subject—and miss the moon, the photograph's expressive intent. I confess, it is somewhat deflating when presenting a photograph as expressive art to be met with questions or comments regarding gear, technique, subject, location, or processing choices.

I often wonder whether, if people like my work, I should care if they fail to understand it. A part of me wishes I didn't, but I do. The remedy, at least in part, is to remind myself of why I photograph: my time in nature, my joy in thinking creatively, the elevated and intensified feelings I experience and hope to express—and the knowledge that I will not want to give these things up, even if nobody but me could understand or relate to them.

I see the moon. I point my finger. That is my part. What you see is up to you.

**Photography, if practiced with high seriousness, is a contest
between a photographer and the presumptions of approximate
and habitual seeing.
—John Szarkowski**

In his seminal work, *The World as Will and Representation*, philosopher Arthur
Schopenhauer proposed this thought experiment: "Let us transport ourselves to a
very lonely region of boundless horizons, under a perfectly cloudless sky, trees and
plants in the perfectly motionless air, no animals, no human beings, no moving
masses of water, the profoundest silence. Such surroundings are as it were a summons to seriousness, to contemplation, with complete emancipation from all willing
and its cravings."

Being in such a setting, Schopenhauer suggested, has the power to liberate one's
mind from its default state of constant striving for some goal and to assume instead
a state of pure contemplation. "Whoever is incapable of this [state of seriousness
and pure contemplation without striving]," he warned, "is abandoned with shame-
ful ignominy to the emptiness of unoccupied will, to the torture and misery of
boredom."

Although photographers may differ in where we feel most at ease and most
inspired to photograph, when we find ourselves in such circumstances, instead of
rushing to "get the shot," we may instead choose to consider such times a "summons
to seriousness."

Seriousness manifests both in how we pursue our own work and in how we consider the works of others. We may consider seriously the importance we give art in
the greater scheme of our lives. We may take seriously such things as the sincerity

and courage with which we experience and express our thoughts, views, and feelings. It is likely that most, perhaps all, of those we consider "the greats" (in any context) have taken their work as more than just a casual pastime—as something in which to invest serious thought and effort. I propose that it is seriousness, what Paul Strand described as "the sharpest kind of self-criticism, courage, and hard work," and not just fortuitous circumstances—commercial success, celebrity, or virtuosity of skill—that is the true essence of greatness.

It's fair to say that some pursue photography more seriously than others: that photography plays a greater and more consequential role in some people's lives than in others', that some invest more thought and effort than others in creating and presenting their work. For some, photography is just an enjoyable hobby, for

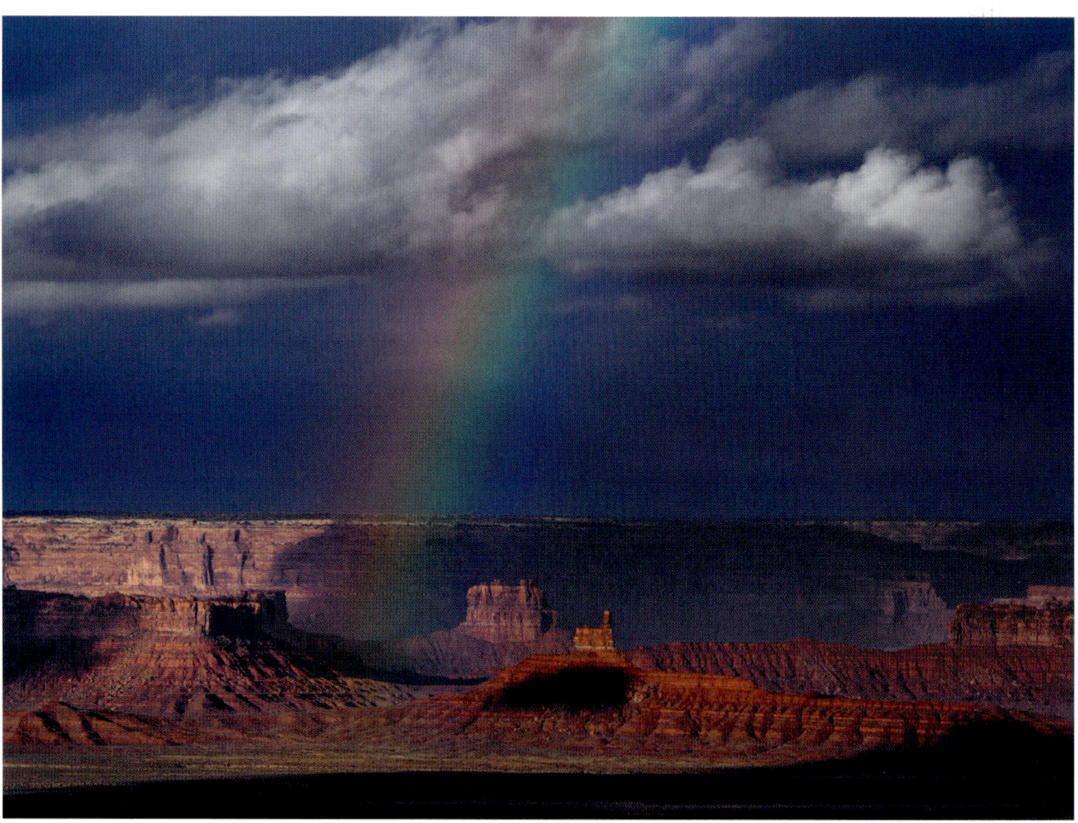

others a profession. For some, photography is a common interest they share with others whose primary value is in fostering friendships and social interactions, for others a means of creative expression, rewarding in its own right. No matter what photography is to you, I propose that its potential rewards will be greater the more seriously you consider it. By this I mean that I believe there is a correlation between what you put into photography and what you get from it.

Seriousness involves difficulty, but not in the negative sense. This kind of difficulty is rooted in voluntary (not imposed) effort, driven by a desire to excel and to overcome challenges rather than to seek quick and easy solutions. The difficulties involved in serious pursuits are of the sort psychologist Robert A. Bjork termed "desirable difficulties"—challenges that, while requiring effort and perhaps the need to overcome some frustrations in the short-term, pay dividends in the long-term. In our ease-obsessed world, seriousness is among the most challenging "desirable difficulties" for artists to maintain. It requires transcending cynicism and jadedness, resisting the temptation to please or to entertain others, maintaining independence of thought and creativity against pressure to conform, eschewing the seduction of "easy wins."

Henri Matisse claimed that creativity takes courage, but I think that in a greater sense it is, in fact, seriousness that takes courage. Creativity without seriousness is common and doesn't necessarily take courage. Such creativity—sometimes termed "small c" creativity—yields simple solutions to simple problems, or, in the realm of art, simple and emotionally benign creations. Seriousness is a precondition for revolutionary ideas and departures from norms—so-called "big C" creativity.

How does seriousness manifest in photographs? In his book *Beauty in Photography*, Robert Adams proposed that "a serious landscape picture is a metaphor," suggesting that in order for photographs to express more than just superficial appearances and pleasing aesthetics, photographers must also give (conscious, serious) thought to, as Minor White put it, "what else" things are. White himself, responding to irate critics of nontraditional work featured in *Aperture Magazine* (which he cofounded and edited) mentioned seriousness as a quality people need to evolve, not only to make expressive photographs but also to fully appreciate such photographs. He wrote, "One has to earn the innocence of vision—by hard effort, by serious and deliberate search for meanings in photographs."

Having the ability to produce beautiful photographs with little effort or cognitive investment by simply recording found beauty, photographers are especially at risk of falling prey to the fallacy that beautiful photographs are the highest accomplishments to aspire to in photography. Many photographers miss entirely the realm of inner experiences that may arise, not from any photograph but from paying prolonged focused attention to experience and process, from trying new things at the risk of failure, from breaking with norms in pursuit of discoveries and revelations, from transcending what Szarkowski referred to as "habitual seeing," from rising to creative challenges, from philosophical contemplation; in short, from approaching their work as a serious and worthy endeavor.

Hermann Hesse described the trap of limiting one's work to just beautiful formulas. Being a poet, he used poems as examples, writing:

> *Here, then, is the beginning of a vicious circle. Because "beautiful" poems make the poet beloved, a great quantity of poems come into the world that attempt nothing except to be beautiful, that pay no heed to the original primitive, holy, innocent function of poetry.*

The consequence, according to Hesse, is that such poems "are no longer dreams or dance steps or outcries of the soul, reactions to experience, stammered wish-images or magic formulas, gestures of a wise man or grimaces of a madman—they are simply planned productions, fabrications, pralines for the public. . . . One does not have to project oneself seriously and lovingly into such poems, one is not tormented or shaken by them, rather one sways comfortably and pleasurably in time to their pretty, regular rhythms."

Among the reasons I prefer to work alone is that I find it difficult to invest serious time, serious thought, and serious effort in creative work when people around me are in different states of mind. Like any person who undertakes a demanding challenge, who rises to a noble calling, or who seeks profound meaning, I need to set aside times when I can make such things the primary focus of my attention, and to exclude from these times people who may distract me from serious work. Beyond just avoiding interruptions, in my serious times I also need to feel comfortable setting down my shields, to allow my emotions to overwhelm me without concern for judgment or ridicule, to contemplate deep and complex ideas, to consider possibilities beyond the obvious without concern for any tradition or for anyone else's sensibilities or dogmas, to work in the most meticulous and disciplined way I can, no matter how long it takes or how much effort may be involved.

A turning point in my photographic journey was when I realized that instead of being concerned with improving the quality of my photographs, I stand to gain more from striving to improve the quality of my photographic experiences. Contrary to so many tips, shortcuts, and nonsensical marketing claims, I found that my

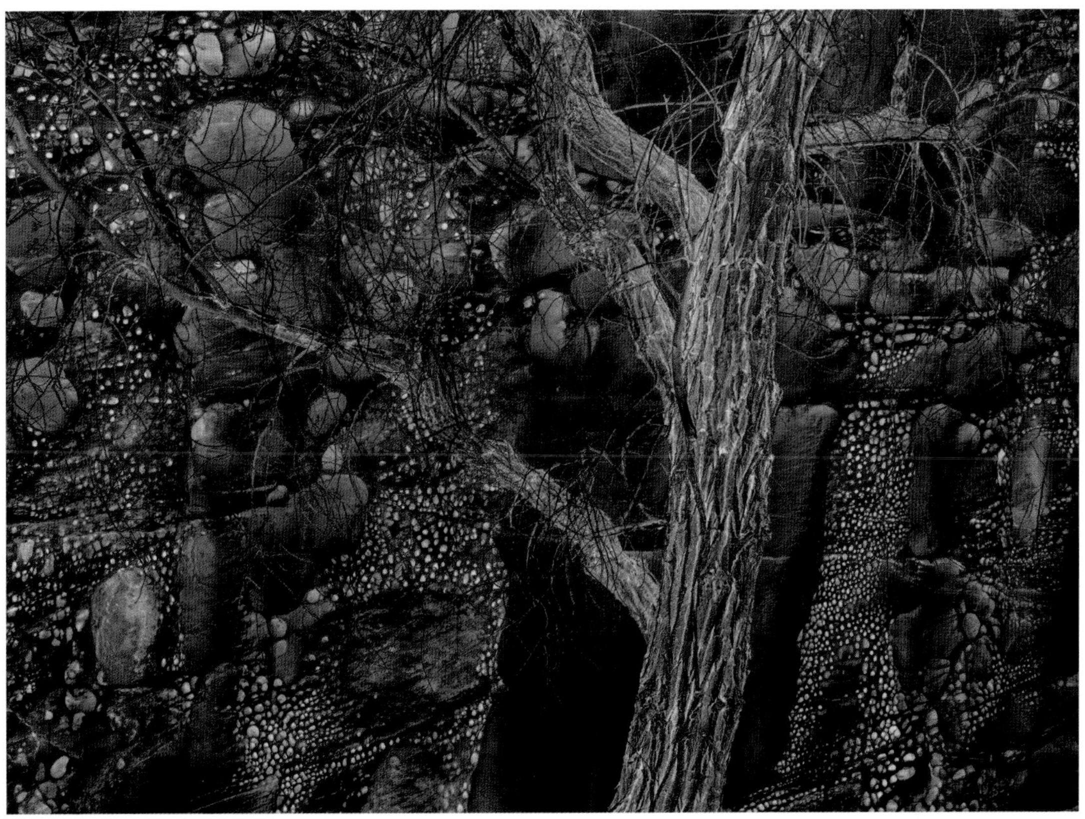

photographic experiences become deeper, richer, and more personally meaningful, not when they are easy, automated, and predictable but when they are difficult, challenging, uncertain, and prone to failure; not when serendipitous opportunities present themselves at random or when following prescribed directions but when I approach my work seriously, openly, and with all the maturity of thought and depth of feeling I have gained in the course of decades. At the same time, I recognize that I must do so with a beginner's mind: with the attitude of always striving to learn more, to discover more, and to understand more—to treat photography not just as a fun pastime but as an eminently important endeavor.

21 On Equivalence, Expression, and Art

Equivalency is the ability to use the visual world as the plastic material for the photographer's expressive purposes.
—Minor White

Following an exhibit of his photographic portraits, Alfred Stieglitz was jarred when a critic suggested that the power of the photographs came from a hypnotic power Stieglitz exerted over his models. Recognizing he did not actually have such powers, Stieglitz nonetheless wished to understand where the "hypnotizing" effect came from: What quality in his photographs made them express more than just the likenesses of recognizable subjects and allowed them also to express ulterior, subjective meanings such as emotions, moods, and ideas. To test his theory, Stieglitz wanted to see if he could use this quality, which he later dubbed "equivalence," to communicate emotions to viewers independently of any suggestive qualities of the objects he portrayed, and not relying on privileged access to uncommon subject matter. Toward that end, he decided to photograph clouds, explaining:

> *I wanted to photograph clouds to find out what I had learned in 40 years about photography. Through clouds to put down my philosophy of life—to show that my photographs were not due to subject matter—not to special trees, or faces, or interiors, to special privileges, clouds were there for everyone—no tax as yet on them—free.*

Explaining the idea of equivalence, Stieglitz wrote, "My cloud photographs are equivalents of my most profound life experience, my basic philosophy of life." More specifically, he claimed that the test of an equivalent photograph is "to hold the moment, to record something so completely that those who see it will relive an experience of what had been expressed" (i.e., that viewers not just see what the photographer has seen but also feel what the photographer intended them to feel).

In equivalence, Stieglitz had a creative—novel and useful—idea, but like many creative people, he was quick to move on to other things[4]. Beyond his portfolio of clouds, Stieglitz did not make many other photographs he claimed as equivalent. Indeed, in his later years, despite still writing and corresponding vigorously about photography, Stieglitz did not make many photographs at all. Still, he discussed the concept of equivalence extensively with his closest followers. Among these followers were the likes of Minor White and Ansel Adams, who became great believers in equivalence. In an article about equivalence published in a 1973 edition of *Popular Photography*, Adams proclaimed:

> *I'm a total believer in the concept of the equivalent—a concept promoted by Stieglitz. I can paraphrase what he told me, not too inaccurately; he said, "I perceive the world around me as an experience of emotional and spiritual substance. I record this with my camera. I present the photograph as an equivalent of my response to this world which I wish to share with the spectator." But, I might add, only if it means anything to him. I hope it will mean something to him, but not necessarily just what it means to me.*

Beyond merely explaining the idea of equivalence as taught to him by Stieglitz, Adams also pointed out that equivalence is of primary importance to the photographer's own experience, and in no way guarantees that others who view the photographs will experience the effect in the same way. This explains the apprehension of photographers who aspire to make expressive photographs but are concerned that viewers may not understand what they wished to express. Adams was correct that visual expression is ambiguous by nature. As artists we must accept this ambiguity and create according to our own sensibilities, even if some viewers may not quite understand what we wish to express.

Minor White offered a similar thought to Adams's ten years earlier in an article titled, "Equivalence: The Perennial Trend," published in *PSA Journal*: "When any photograph functions for a given person as an Equivalent we can say that at that moment and for that person the photograph acts as a symbol or plays the role of a metaphor for something that is beyond the subject photographed." Put another way, photographs may have the effect of equivalence only for some given persons or only in some given times and circumstances, but perhaps not universally.

---

[4]The personality trait conducive to developing an idea in structured and disciplined ways is called "conscientiousness." Artists generally score lower on conscientiousness tests compared with the general population.

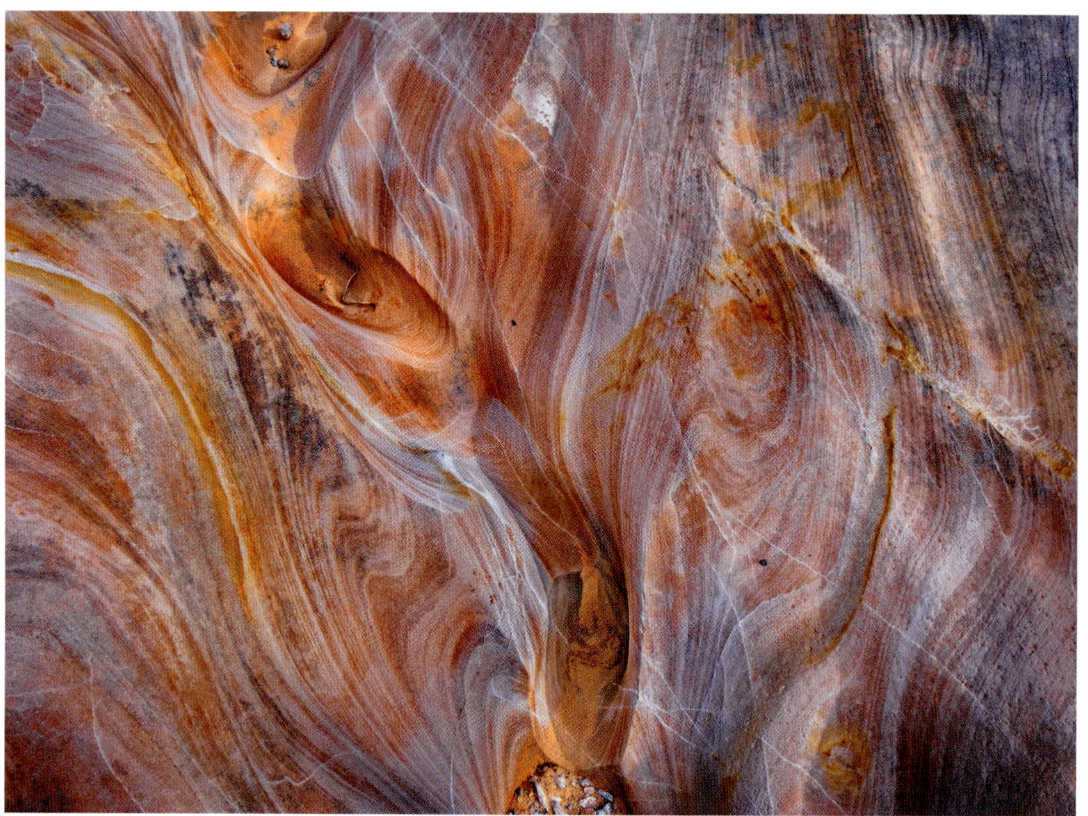

In truth, Stieglitz did not discover anything not already known to artists working in other media. He just coined a name for the effect and proved that it may exist in photographs, not just in paintings or other artistic creations. Before Stieglitz was even born, painter Caspar David Friedrich described how he accomplished a similar effect in his paintings. He wrote: "Close your bodily eye, so that you may see your picture first with the spiritual eye. Then bring to the light of day that which you have seen in the darkness so that it may react upon others from the outside inwards. A picture must not be invented but felt."

Paul Cézanne, likely without knowing it, also referred to the same effect that Stieglitz called equivalence and to its importance in artistic expression. He wrote: "Make others feel the same way about it. Without their realizing it! That's the meaning of art."

Ralph Waldo Emerson, also likely without knowing it, referred to the effect of equivalence and to its importance in inspiring people to become artists. Emerson

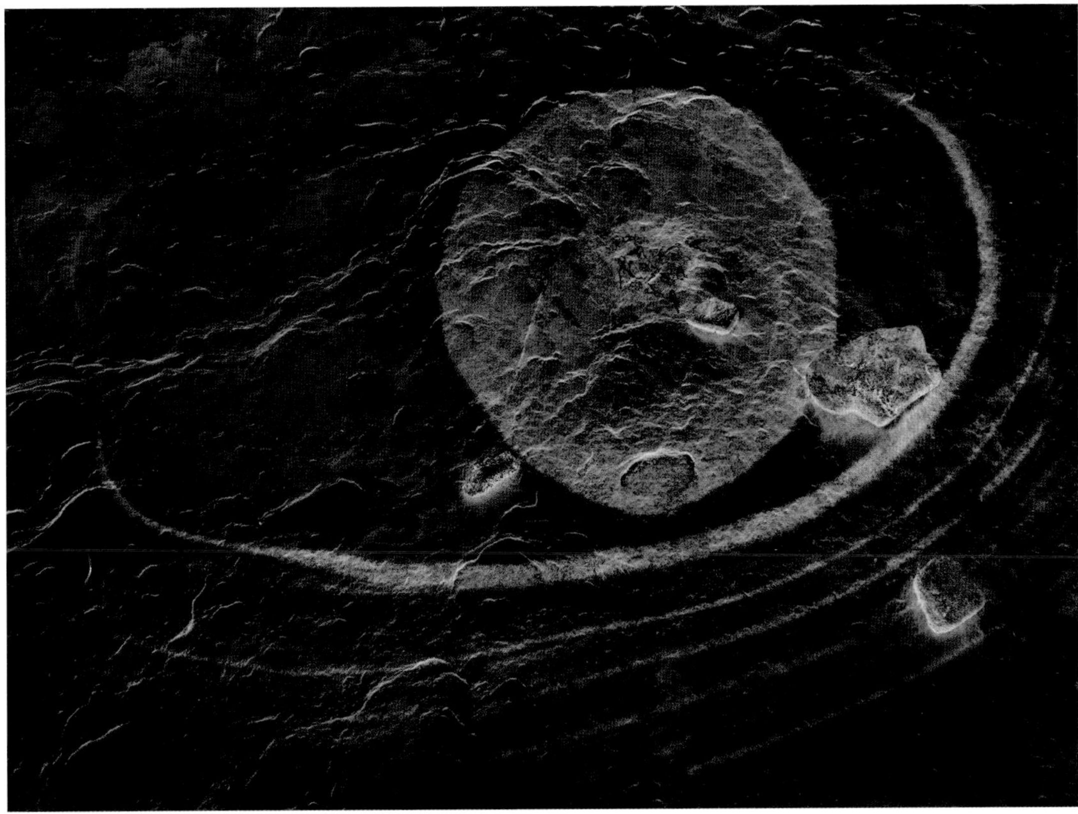

wrote, "Art should exhilarate, and throw down the walls of circumstance on every side, awakening in the beholder the same sense of universal relation and power which the work evinced in the artist, and its highest effect is to make new artists."

In common among all characterizations of equivalence is the idea that a work of art may impart to viewers feelings equivalent to an artist's inner experience and not just represent objectively the appearances of objects or scenes. Implied in the idea of equivalence is that an artist must strive for parity between experience and expression, leading to a constant striving to experience things worthy of expression, having the effect of elevating both art and life. The parity also suggests that art and life may, if the artist aspires to be self-expressive, elevate each other reciprocally. Gustav Mahler expressed this sentiment succinctly, writing: "Only when I experience do I compose—only when I compose do I experience."

Since there is no guarantee viewers will understand what a photographer intended to express in an equivalent photograph, equivalence is of greatest benefit to photographers who are motivated *intrinsically* to find value in artistic expression for its beneficial effects on their own psyche and on the quality of their experiences. Such photographers are also likely to be more creative than those motivated primarily by *extrinsic* rewards—popularity, awards, sales, social interaction. As creativity researcher Teresa Amabile noted, "People will be more creative when they are motivated primarily by the interest, enjoyment, satisfaction, and challenge of the work itself—and not by extrinsic motivators or constraints."[5] This explains why some don't value creativity in photography as much as others and may be satisfied with uncreative, unoriginal, even plagiarized work so long as this work garners extrinsic rewards—praise, "likes," awards, celebrity.

Beyond loss of creativity, another great threat of our technological age related to artistic expression now comes from so-called artificial intelligence (AI). More and more these days we see works of "art" generated by computerized algorithms capable of analyzing great quantities of data to determine what most people may like or are likely to purchase. Although such works may elicit emotional responses—the illusion of equivalence—these works obviously are not equivalent to any inner experience of any artist.

Computers may soon be able to produce more popular "art" than humans can, faster than humans can, and more prolifically than humans can. When that day comes, intrinsic motivations—the desire to create art because it is interesting, engaging, challenging, and elevating to the artist—may remain as the only reason for a living person to pursue artistic creation. Admittedly, I'm conflicted when trying to characterize this outcome as good or bad. On one hand, a proliferation of machine-made artlike creations may devastate art as a profession. On the other hand, whatever human-made art remains is likely to be profoundly more creative and more rewarding than most photographic art made today.

Although our industry has changed much in the last couple of decades in terms of the power and abundance of extrinsic motivations (maximizing profitability, pursuing popularity and influence, winning contests), my own enjoyment in creating personally expressive photographs rather than chasing after "easy wins" has only increased during this period. Leave it to machines to do what they can now do as well, or better than, human artists: generate large numbers of generic, uncreative "pretty pictures." Machines can't enjoy or suffer. Machines can't feel flow, pride, or awe. Machines can't make equivalent photographs—they can't express any inner experience because they can't have any inner experience. As a consumer of art, I want to relate to the experiences, expressive powers, and creative genius of a fellow human. As an artist, I want to elevate my own living by engaging in artistic creation.

[5]Teresa Amabile, "Creativity and the Labor of Love." The Nature of Human Creativity, edited by Robert J. Sternberg and James C. Kaufman, Cambridge University Press, Cambridge, United Kingdom, 2018.

The pursuit of equivalence in photography ultimately amounts to this: seeking inner experiences worthy of artistic expression and finding creative ways to express these inner experiences in photographs. Machines can at best simulate, but not do, either of these things.

It is the nature of the photographic medium that in some situations equivalence may come into contention with realism. This is because equivalence is concerned with conveying inner, subjective experiences, whereas realism is concerned with representing outer, objective appearances, and the two don't always overlap. It is a common and unfortunate notion in photography that objective representation is considered by some to be synonymous with truthfulness. It is a misplaced notion, which can easily be dispelled with this simple question: Which truth?

Certainly, there is a simplistic sense in which accurate representation is "truth" by virtue of showing people what they would have seen if present when the photograph was made. Such accurate representations, in fact, often misrepresent the experience one would likely have had in the same circumstances. For example, photographs of wild-looking landscapes may inspire a sense of awe, solitude, or remoteness, even if the photographer followed directions to an easily accessible location and stood shoulder-to-shoulder with dozens of others, excluded from the frame. Likewise, most people may assume that a photograph presented as "art" is the result of uncommon skill and creative vision, when in fact, many such photographs are repetitions and derivations that required no special talent or original thinking to make.

Rather than just objectively representing seen details, a photograph may also aim to convey—truthfully—its maker's inner experience: the mood, thoughts, or state of mind of a real person at a real moment in time. What a photographer has seen may influence their experience, but it is not the only thing, nor necessarily the most important aspect of this experience. In some cases, fidelity to appearances may even distract viewers from the truthful essence of what a photographer wished to express. Therefore, we must be diligent, both in presenting our own work and in evaluating others' works, to distinguish clearly between documentary, representational photographs; and equivalent, artistic photographs. Both can be considered real, but the reality they express is not always of the same nature; it may be objective or subjective, represented or expressed, experienced or manufactured. In the words of Hermann Hesse, "There is no reality except that which we have in ourselves. For that reason most people live so unreally, because they hold the impressions of the outside world for real, and their own world in themselves never enters into their consideration."

 # The Introvert Game

> **Are introverts misunderstood? Wildly. That, it appears, is our lot in life.**
> **—Jonathan Rauch**

According to estimates, between one third and one half of people are introverts. The ratio is likely even higher among so-called "creative types." If you're not an introvert, you probably know some introverts. It's possible that some people you may believe are extraverts are, in fact, misunderstood introverts, or introverts who may pretend to be extraverts, believing that in order to be successful, they must force themselves to be more social than they are comfortable being.

As someone on the extreme end of introversion, I spend most of my time alone, both when working in the field and when in my office. When in public, even if I enjoy my time among people, I always look forward to the peace of solitude. This may seem anathema to those who consider socializing, teamwork, or some tribal affiliation as core aspects of their lives and personalities.

In contrast to extraverts, whose primary interests are generally outside themselves and who feel energized by social interactions, introverts easily become overstimulated after spending too much time with other people ("too much" being different for each of us). Our main preoccupation is our own inner life. As the expression goes, we live inside our heads. While extraverts thrive on, and never tire of, such things as lively conversations, competition, popularity, or collaborating with others, introverts need frequent and prolonged quiet times to ourselves even if we may enjoy some of these things on occasion.

Although introversion and shyness often overlap, they are not the same thing. Introversion is a personality trait; shyness is a handicap. Introverted people can be

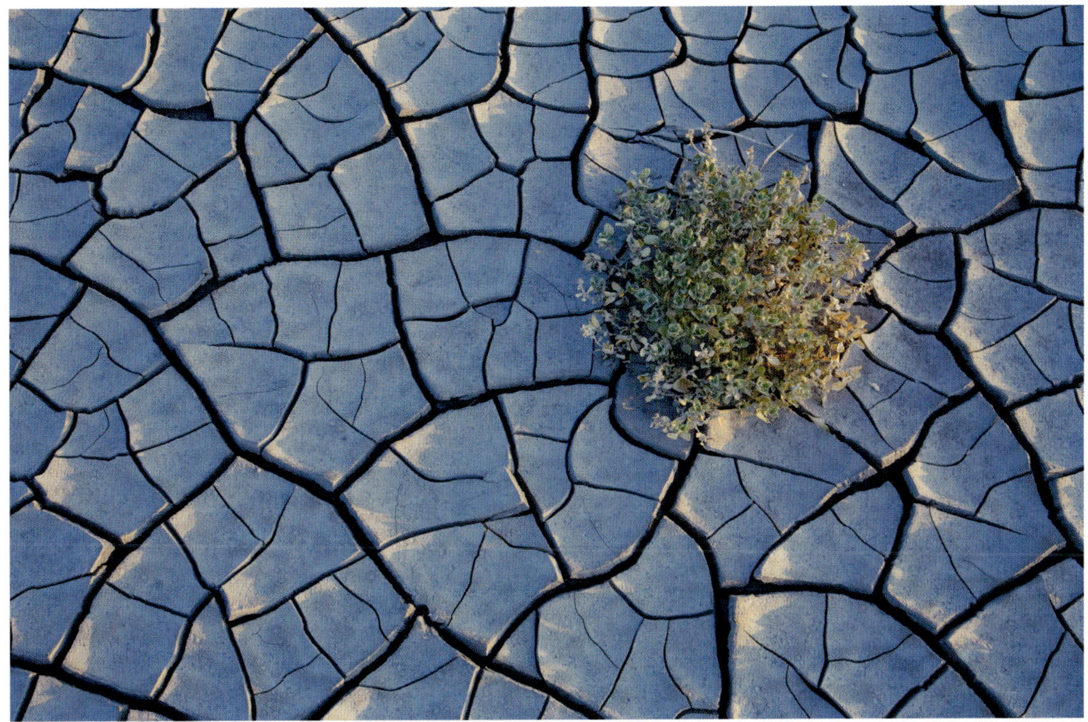

as outgoing, as talkative, and as self-confident in social situations as extraverts. It's just that at some point, no matter how good the company, we become "peopled-out," feeling emotionally depleted and in need of solitary time to recharge before we're ready to engage with people again. Shy people avoid social interaction, not necessarily because they want to be alone but for fear of judgment or disapproval. Many introverts are also shy, but not all. Although less common, extraverts can also be shy. Introverts who are not shy can be gregarious "type A" people just like most extraverts; we just can't sustain it for very long.

Introversion is one of the "Big Five" personality traits in the Five-Factor Model (FFM), which is used in many psychological studies. According to Susan Cain, author of *Quiet: The Power of Introverts in a World That Can't Stop Talking,* "The single most important aspect of personality—the 'north and south of temperament' . . . —is where we fall on the introvert-extravert spectrum. Our place on this continuum influences our choice of friends and mates, and how we make conversation, resolve differences, and show love. It affects the careers we choose and whether or not we succeed at them."

Introverts and extraverts often have a hard time understanding each other, sometimes resulting in unfortunate perceptions. Extraverts may regard introverts' penchant to withdraw from social activities as arrogant or aloof, whereas introverts may regard outgoing extraverts as vain, insensitive, or lacking in depth, as people who will do anything for attention. Extraverts tend to assume implicitly that everyone enjoys socializing, collaboration, competition, and vigorous conversation, as they do. They rarely consider the possibility that another person may not relish such activities, which seem to them intuitive and quintessentially human. Introverts, by contrast, often fail to understand why extraverts feel the incessant need to talk so much, not realizing that talking is part of the way extraverts think: throwing ideas out into the world even if not fully considered, so they can discuss them with others, argue about them, leverage them as conversation pieces. Introverts, meanwhile, tend to first consider (sometimes to overthink) their ideas carefully before expressing them to others.

Just as extraverts may find it difficult to understand how introverts can spend most of their time alone in quiet contemplation, introverts may find it hard to believe the results of a 2014 study[6] in which one-quarter of women and two-thirds of men (on the extreme end of extraversion), preferred receiving electric shocks to spending even just a few minutes alone with their thoughts. The reverse is almost certainly also true: some introverts would likely prefer electric shocks to excessive socializing.

There's plentiful evidence that Western societies are generally biased in favor of extraverts. Studies show that people who are more talkative generally are perceived by others as smarter, more interesting, more likeable, more effective as leaders, and even better-looking than less gregarious people. Extraverts also tend to be generally happier than introverts (introverts' tendency to ruminate and to overthink, while giving us an advantage in such areas as creativity and academic achievement, comes at a cost in terms of emotional well-being).

Social media culture seems to exacerbate the discrepancy between introverts and extraverts. Social media rewards and popularizes such things as celebrity, influence, competition, self-promotion, and favoring volume over depth, even creating the appearance that these things are essential to being "successful." Those who spend considerable time on social platforms may end up losing sight of the plethora of opportunities for profoundly rewarding activities that may only exist outside of these virtual, addictive-by-design worlds. Understandably, such perceptions may cause great anxiety to an introvert who may believe them, or who feels obligated to yield to peer pressure.

---

[6]Led by Timothy Wilson of the University of Virginia.

A word of advice to introverts: it's futile for you to attempt to compete with extraverts in areas such as popularity and self-promotion. Extraverts have an innate home-court advantage in these activities and often take great pleasure in them, putting you at a competitive disadvantage. Even if you do manage to compete successfully, the experience will likely not be enjoyable to you and may lead to frustration and anxiety. Rest assured, there are many of us introverts who are doing just fine, both as professionals and as hobbyists, both in the social media world and outside of it, without compromising our need for prolonged solitary times. The key to finding fulfillment in any endeavor is, as the saying goes, to play for the love of the game. But we don't all have to play the same game.

Extraverts thrive on attention and competition. They play to "win," meaning they are focused on the end result: how popular their work makes them and how they measure up to others based on public opinion. Give extraverts a copious dose of social media likes, awards, "epic" compositions, or tips on how to make their images more impactful, more popular; quicker and easier to capture, to process, and to share; and they can be entirely satisfied. In photography, this means that the ideal "game" for extraverts is competing for attention—making photographs that are popular and eye-catching, striving to win awards and recognition, and engaging in prolonged exchanges with fellow photographers.

Notably, an extravert who is motivated primarily by external rewards may not consider such qualities as creativity and expression very important. Striving for creative originality may make a photographer less productive. Striving for subjective self-expression may result in photographs that appeal only to limited audiences.

Introverts prefer solitude and quiet contemplation and therefore tend to value not only the end results of our work but also the quality of our inner experience when working. Give us a stretch of time in a beautiful place, a quiet private setting to process our work in—slowly and meticulously, perhaps while listening to music or savoring a glass of wine—and we can spend hours consumed in our experiences without even realizing how much time has passed (a characteristic of being in a state of flow). Our images may ultimately be less impactful to casual viewers, perhaps even esoteric, but that's because we value them based not only on how others may respond to them but also on how creative, intimate, personal, unique, or expressive they are; how challenging they were to make; and the blissful memories they may later evoke. While we enjoy positive feedback from others, we don't crave it enough to be worth sacrificing our deeper, slower, more contemplative experiences.

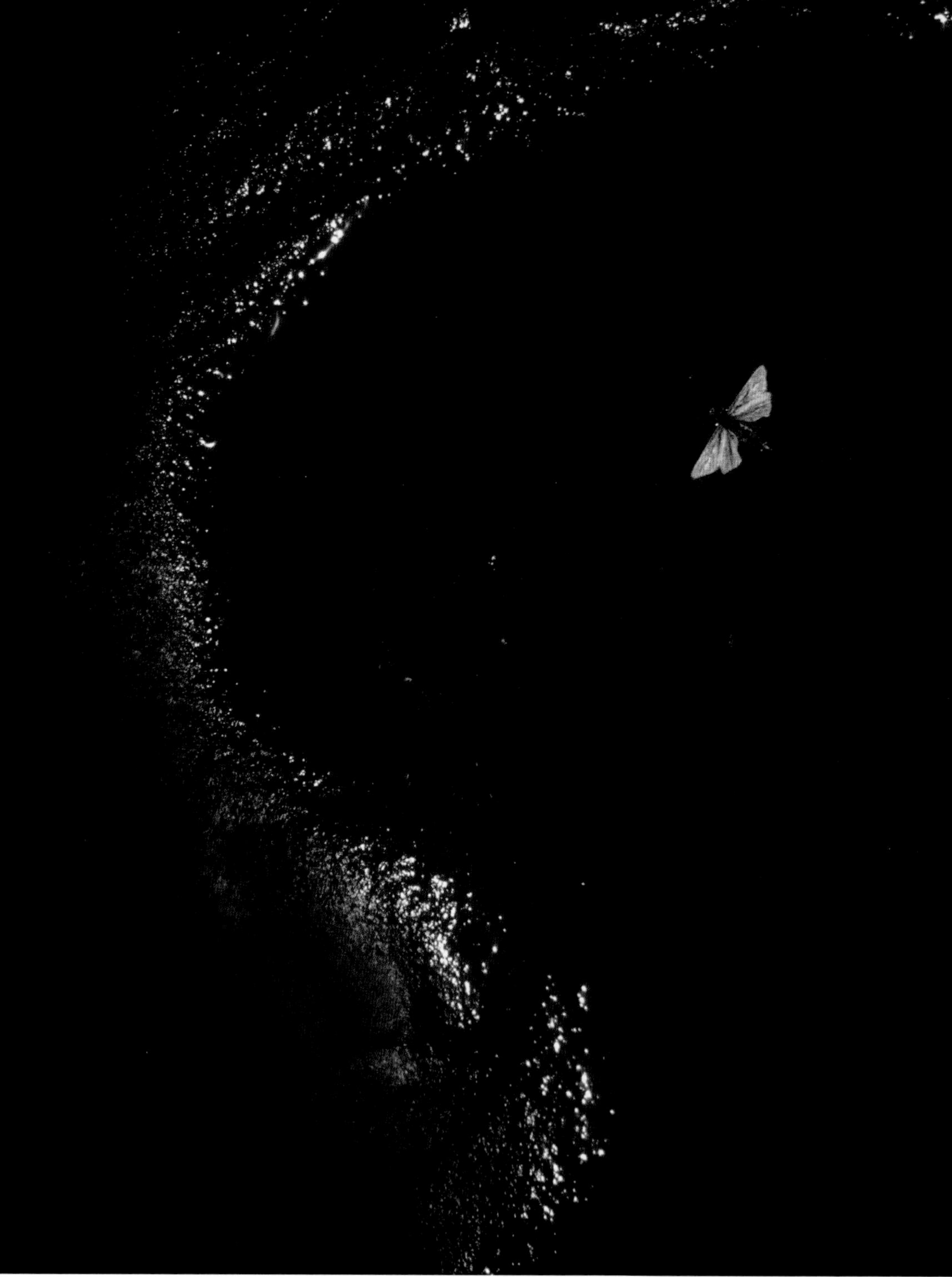

In photography, the ideal "game" for an introvert is striving to maximize joy in the process—rather than the outcome—of making photographs. To an introvert, striving for creative self-expression, even at the risk of lowering our productivity or limiting our potential audience, may pay enormous dividends in terms of qualities of inner experience.

To an extravert, a missed photo opportunity may seem like a net loss—wasted time and effort with nothing to show for it. An introvert, by contrast, may still have a wonderful, richly rewarding time experimenting, tinkering, and contemplating photographic possibilities, even if nobody knows what we were up to, and even if ultimately unsuccessful. To an introvert, a popular or even award-winning photograph may seem like a hollow victory if the experience of making the photograph was not memorable and intellectually stimulating.

Chatty extraverts who enjoy socializing for its own sake may talk your ear off about the latest, greatest, rootinest, tootinest, shootinest camera, lens, drone, or other piece of gear. Don't bother them with such pointless questions as whether they have any demonstrable need for such items, and don't bother pointing out that there may be more practical and rewarding ways to spend time and money than buying expensive gadgets or belaboring their technical specifications. It's something to talk about, to socialize about, to brag about, to proselytize about, to compete about, to argue about. Indulge them.

For us quiet introverts, however, just give us a camera system capable of producing images meeting our practical needs, regardless of brand, price tag, age, or any other technical trivia, and leave us alone to commune with nature, to contemplate ways of expressing our thoughts and emotions in creative compositions, to experiment, to savor our experiences in peace, and to forget for a while that other people even exist. To an extravert, a good photograph is the goal no matter how it is produced. To an introvert, a good photograph is, before anything else, the byproduct of a good photographic experience.

Whether you are introverted or extraverted, pretending, or convincing yourself, that you must try to play the "other team's game," aiming for a goal that does not accord with your personality is a sure path to frustration. An introvert trying to compete for attention or volume at the cost of giving up their quiet time likely will become anxious. An extravert trying to force themselves to find deep meaning in prolonged solitary time will likely become bored. To get the best of both worlds, remember that while you may enjoy playing one game, you can still enjoy being a spectator in the other. Introverts may benefit from social dynamics made possible by extraverts, and extraverts may benefit from complex and innovative creations that may not be possible without an introvert's prolonged solitary contemplation.

Photography offers many "games" to choose from, and one game is not necessarily more "right" than another just because it happens to be more popular or glamorous. We are each free to practice photography in a manner that best fits our own individual personality, for whatever reasons and rewards are most meaningful to us. Certainly, there are also broad areas of overlapping interests among introverted and extraverted photographers. Undoubtedly, many of us share a love for certain places and things we feature in our work, at least a degree of interest in photographic technology, and an appreciation for beauty. Most of us find value in sharing our work, albeit perhaps not to the same extent. Just because many of us refer to ourselves as landscape photographers, wildlife photographers, or any other kind of photographers doesn't mean that in adopting a label we cease to be unique—and often different—individuals. All of us photograph because we love something about the photographic endeavor, but that something doesn't have to be the same for everyone.

Gear talk, popularity, even sales, are just some of the games of photography, but if you don't enjoy them, you don't have to play them. If you're a social butterfly, you may thrive on drawing attention and winning accolades; if you're a reader, you may enjoy studying the history of the medium, the philosophies of great photographers, or the science and art of visual expression. If you're a writer, you may find your niche in authoring articles or books; if you're an avid hiker, the camera can enrich and be a faithful companion on your explorations. You can be a celebrity, a teacher, a scholar, or an artist, if such things fit your temperament, but you don't have to be any of these to find at least some aspects of photography deeply satisfying.

Competition is one of the more common games in photography. If you're an extravert who thrives on "winning," by all means compete. But if you're an introvert who doesn't enjoy competition, then don't bother with it. You'll be no worse for it. In his book *Flow: The Psychology of Optimal Experience*, Csikszentmihalyi explained, "The challenges of competition can be stimulating and enjoyable. But when beating the opponent takes precedence in the mind over performing as well as possible, enjoyment tends to disappear. Competition is enjoyable only when it is a means to perfect one's skills; when it becomes an end in itself, it ceases to be fun." For me, competition is not fun and doesn't motivate me. I am not—and feel no need to present myself as—an "award-winning" photographer. Likewise, the knowledge that a photographer may have won an award is not a criterion by which I evaluate a photographer's work.

As an introvert, the game of photography has always appealed to me in great part because photography doesn't have to be a team sport, or any kind of sport. Photography is appealing to me because it is something I can do by myself, in places and times of my choosing, and for no other reason than to satisfy my own sensibilities. I don't feel myself in competition with other photographers. In many cases, I don't even feel we're playing the same game. Some photographers approach their work as a trophy hunt, some as a game of strategy, some as a crossword puzzle. Some want to beat an opponent, some want to improve their personal bests, and some just want to spend their time and attention in personally rewarding ways.

No doubt you've heard from extraverted influencers about the importance (to them) of playing the popularity game: being vocal, visible, and busy. If those things make you anxious, or just don't fit your personality, rest assured you are not alone. Allow me, if you will, to share with you my game. Being introverted and reclusive, I find more reward in the challenges of making creative work than in how many people may like my work. The time that other people may invest in building their online following I spend outside in my favorite places, doing my favorite things. If I return from an outing with no photographs, I still cherish my experiences and never feel my time outdoors was wasted. The way I've structured my business and the time I spend thinking, hiking, camping, studying, reading, and writing about photography are more profitable to me—literally and figuratively—than any photograph I might make.

There is more than one game in town, and you are free to explore and to find your own, even to create one for yourself.

 The Art of Transcending Seeing

> The medium of photography can record not only what the eyes
> see, but that which the mind's eye sees as well. The camera
> is not only an extension of the eye, but of the brain. It can see
> sharper, farther, nearer, slower, faster than the eye. It can see
> by invisible light. It can see in the past, present, and future.
> Instead of using the camera only to reproduce objects, I wanted
> to use it to make what is invisible to the eye, visible.
> —Wynn Bullock

Photographers often wander the world filled with the false confidence that if
something worth photographing enters their field of vision, it would be obvious and
impossible to miss. Perhaps this is the reason that some photographers sabotage
their own efforts, believing that photography is "the art of seeing." It is not. Unless
we force ourselves to be mindful—to pay deliberate conscious attention to the
things around us, to the exclusion of other distractions—we, in fact, are not conscious of much of what happens before our eyes. Also, there is much more we can
express in photographs than just what we see.

The expression "art of seeing" is a contradiction in terms. Seeing in the literal
sense cannot be an art. We see only what already exists in the world. Making art
is creating new things that don't yet exist—things we artists bring into the world.
Photographic art, then, is not so much an art of seeing as an art of doing something
with what we see.

Ansel Adams defined visualization as "the entire emotional-mental process
of creating a photograph . . . the ability to anticipate a finished image before making the exposure." Implied in the definition is that a visualized image—an image

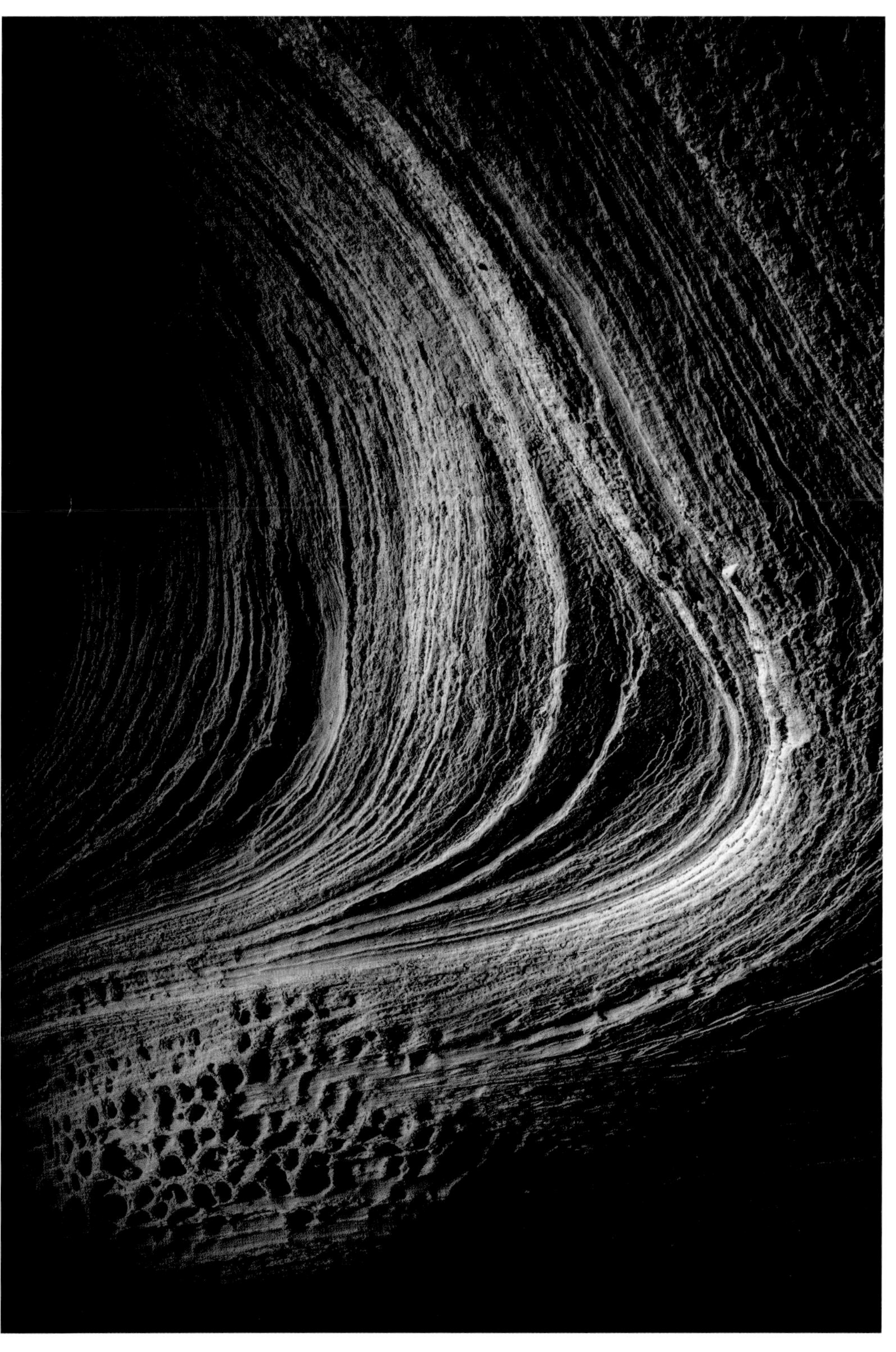

anticipated in some future time—must be different from what we see (otherwise, there would be no need for us to visualize). In this sense, photographic art may be considered not an art of seeing but an art of visualization—an art of imagining possibilities, rather than an art of recording what exists; an art of evaluating a range of possible compositions, the effects of capture techniques, the processing and printing options available to us—and then choosing the most effective outcome from among all the possibilities.

It's a common misperception that we see with our eyes. The eyes are just one source of information for the visual system in our brain. Indeed, our visual system is capable of conjuring images even without input from the eyes, such as when we dream or hallucinate—or visualize. What we see, even when our eyes are open, is in truth just an approximation of what's really "there"—an approximation based in part on impressions of light on our retinas, but not entirely.

If someone could figure out a way to place a camera behind the eyes and capture a video stream of the information sent to the brain's visual cortex by way of the optic nerve, it would look nothing at all like our perception of seeing. Our eyes are never at rest; they constantly scan and shift. These constant movements of the eyes are called saccades. Our brains omit information coming from the eyes during each saccade, so we are not aware of information seen during these erratic movements. Our eyes also constantly adjust to lighting conditions and constantly shift focus, so our visual system performs the equivalent of constant frame-stitching and HDR-blending to give us the illusion of a singular, stable, well-focused, and well-exposed view.

Before we become conscious of what we see, our brain gathers information from all sensory organs to give us a sense of our environment. Combining this information takes the brain about half a second, so in fact, what we think we see really happens about half a second before we see it. When we expose a photographic frame with a shutter speed faster than half a second, the camera captures an image before we see it. Even after sensory information is aggregated, it is not presented to our conscious mind as-is but is corrected and averaged based on readings occurring over a period of about 15 seconds. Nothing we see is ever a true representation of what is happening in real time.

Our visual system evolved to help us survive in the world, not to see everything in the world. Then came art, which we evolved ourselves to transcend and to enrich our aesthetic experiences beyond just what we find in the world. Then came photography, offering at first a means of emulating what we see. Today, we are well into the age of art photography, having photographic technology capable of doing much more than just emulate vision: a technology allowing us to transcend what we see and to create aesthetic experiences of our own. The question for photographers today is, as Edward Weston put it, "Why limit yourself to what your eyes see when you have such an opportunity to extend your vision?"

The art world has become mired in confusing philosophical distractions beyond just considerations of aesthetics (for proof, or entertainment, try asking an art maven to explain postmodernism). An important role for art today is to serve, according to Marshall McLuhan, as "a distant early warning system that can always be relied on to tell the old culture what is beginning to happen." I think it's worth considering—without prejudice, and in light of what we are seeing in the photographic world today (rather than romanticized obsolete notions of what photography should be)—where photography is headed as an art form.

Representing reality (at least in a practical sense) likely will always remain one of photography's most important uses. But for a long time now, representation has not been photography's only use. Despite so much resistance from traditionalists and purists, photography continues to make inroads as a medium for art and to evolve beyond the tenets and sensibilities of past movements, such as pictorialism and "straight" photography. With the rapid evolution in the quality and capabilities of our tools, the next revolution in photographic art is likely not too far ahead.

Much photographic art of recent years is decidedly not representational, not "slices of life," not captured in single exposures, and not resulting from chasing after "decisive moments" or "epic" conditions. Photographic technology has largely liberated us from many former limitations of the medium that bound us to certain subjects and styles. We are now free, and it is in the nature of art to thrive and to evolve in new directions in times of freedom.

Certainly, realism in photography is still as important as it ever was in applications such as photojournalism, law enforcement, and scientific research. But when it comes to art—an endeavor intended to transcend and to enrich reality—the words of Rumi come to mind: "Why do you stay in prison when the door is so wide open?"

24 Photographer! Beware…

Photography's rise in popularity in recent years, paralleling to a significant degree the rise of the Internet, has resulted not only in an unprecedented plethora of photographs but also in great volumes of online discussions, comments, critiques, and other interactions among photographers. Alas, it is the nature of such interactions that they often become so focused on such things as equipment, techniques, ethics, and so on that they become detached from the ostensible purpose of photography: to make photographs (presumably with some purpose in mind other than as pretext to online bantering). In reading such prolonged accounts, one may sometimes come to suspect that for some people the primary purpose of making photographs is to exercise the mechanics of the medium, rather than the other way around.

Opening his poem "How to Be a Poet," Wendell Berry noted parenthetically, "to remind myself." In the poem, Berry warns, "stay away from screens. / Stay away from anything / that obscures the place it is in." You might think that a poet, of all people, wouldn't need such reminders, but Berry is not alone among poets in recognizing the risk of becoming too mired in mundane minutiae of life and work as to miss the greater purpose of poetic expression. In a similar note to himself, Walt Whitman admonished, "Poet! beware lest your poems are made in the spirit that comes from the study of pictures of things—and not from the spirit that comes from the contact with real things themselves." As photographers, perhaps we should be even more wary than poets of becoming so mired in pictures that we lose our affinity for the real things themselves. By this I'm not referring only to the real things we aim our cameras at but also to the real—visceral, and emotional—experiences out of which we make photographs.

In practical terms I see the loss of connection with real things as a confusion of ends and means. I see landscape photographers arriving at some viewpoints at some prescribed time, making a couple of exposures, and leaving, having taken no time to appreciate the natural wonders of the place they were in beyond its potential to yield pleasing photographs. I see street photographers and travel photographers become so obsessed with the hunt for some serendipitous "decisive moment" or some visual anecdote that they become oblivious to the lives of the people they photograph, or to the social and historical significance of some places and rituals. Ironically, so many photographs today, created implicitly for the sake of social sharing after the fact—for attention, for competition, for bragging rights, rather than as means of engaging with the things photographed as they happen—may end up arousing greater empathy and interest in the viewers seeing them as finished pieces than they did in the photographers who were present at the scene.

Social interaction, as well as fascination with the mechanics of photography, are powerful motivations to engage in discussions with other photographers, but we should be mindful lest our interest in debating about photography supersedes our interest in practicing the very things we debate about.

Ask photographers, "Why do you photograph?" and odds are their responses will have something to do with affinity toward certain subjects; perhaps a desire to share with others some qualities of cherished places, things, or experiences; a love for beauty; a means of creative expression; and so on. Whatever your own reasons, it's worthwhile to pause every so often and articulate them to yourself, to remind yourself of your own *why*, even if you assume you already know, even if you are a consummate artist or journalist, a seasoned expert, or a poet of the highest degree. None of us is immune from becoming mired in distractions on occasion.

> *Photographer! beware lest your photographs are made in the spirit that comes from the study of pictures and technicalities—and not from the spirit that comes from the contact with real things themselves.*

25 Mindfulness with a Twist

Sitting alone near my camp on the edge of a high-desert mesa, I watch as a large haboob (sandstorm) sweeps over the valley floor several hundred feet below me. An unpleasant electronic chirp emanating from my phone jars me out of a moment of flow, but my annoyance is short-lived. A message from a friend appears on the screen. He has just arrived at the summit of a remote peak in the Mojave Desert, hundreds of miles away from me, and has shared a snapshot of his impressive, hard-won view. I describe to him the spectacle I just witnessed and add jokingly, "Should we be fearing what we may be missing out on?" I'm referring to the unfortunate phenomenon known as "fear of missing out" (FOMO), which has become prevalent in our age of so-called-social media.

Such exchanges, few and far between, and only with close, like-minded friends, are the extent I'm willing to allow mobile technologies to interrupt my outdoor experiences. On the occasion that I even have a good enough cellular signal to access the internet, I may check my email messages every few hours to make sure no emergencies require my attention. Otherwise, the gadget stays in my pocket or in my pack, and I reserve—diligently and defiantly—my attention for events, sensations, thoughts, and emotions making up my immediate experience. All else can wait until I re-enter the manufactured worlds of humanity. Things I can do nothing about and that may diminish my immediate experience are set aside until (and if) I deem them worthy of attention.

Although I have practiced mindfulness—the deliberate focusing of attention on events happening in the present moment—for many years, the practice is still (likely always will be, by its nature) not completely intuitive to me. I must constantly remind myself to take conscious charge of my attention, to direct my attention where it is most profitable, and to prevent my thoughts from being hijacked toward distractions: things that are irrelevant to my current experience, even if they may be important in some other times and contexts. The rationale for mindfulness is simple: anything I can do nothing about right now should not diminish the quality of my experience right now. Simple in theory, but not quite so simple in practice. Contrary to common belief, humans are not rational beings; we are beings capable of rationality. Thinking rationally is one thing; acting rationally sometimes requires great effort and trained skill, at times even enduring discomfort and inner conflict.

One prospective hijacker of attention toward unproductive thoughts is a gang of brain areas known collectively as the "default mode network" (DMN). This gang

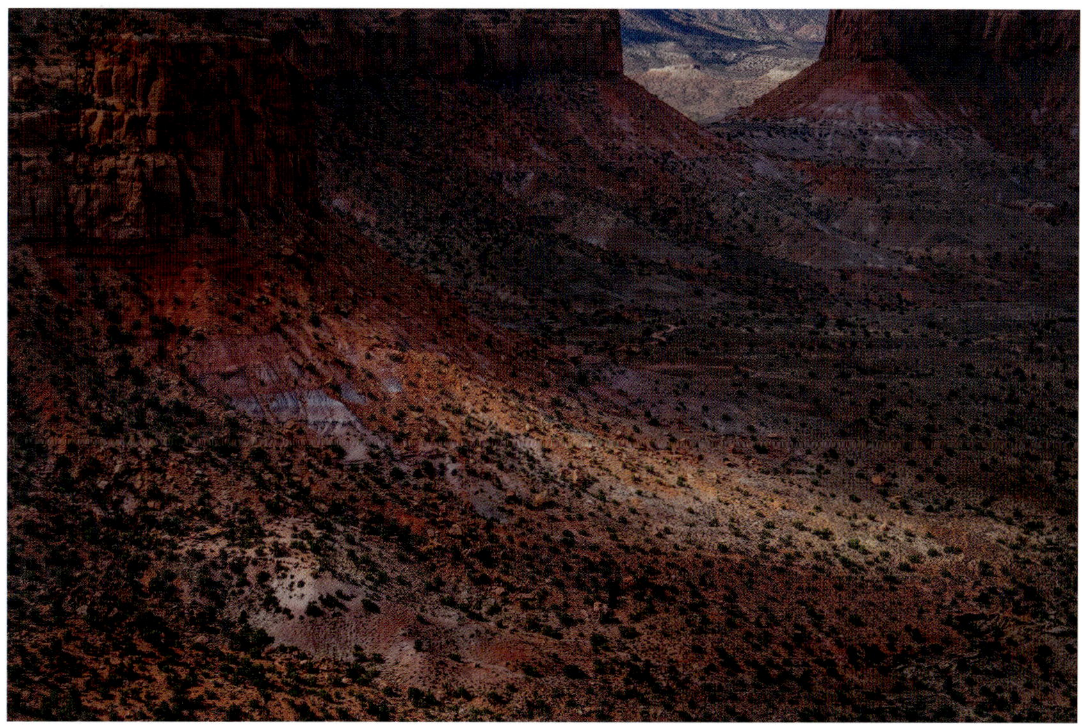

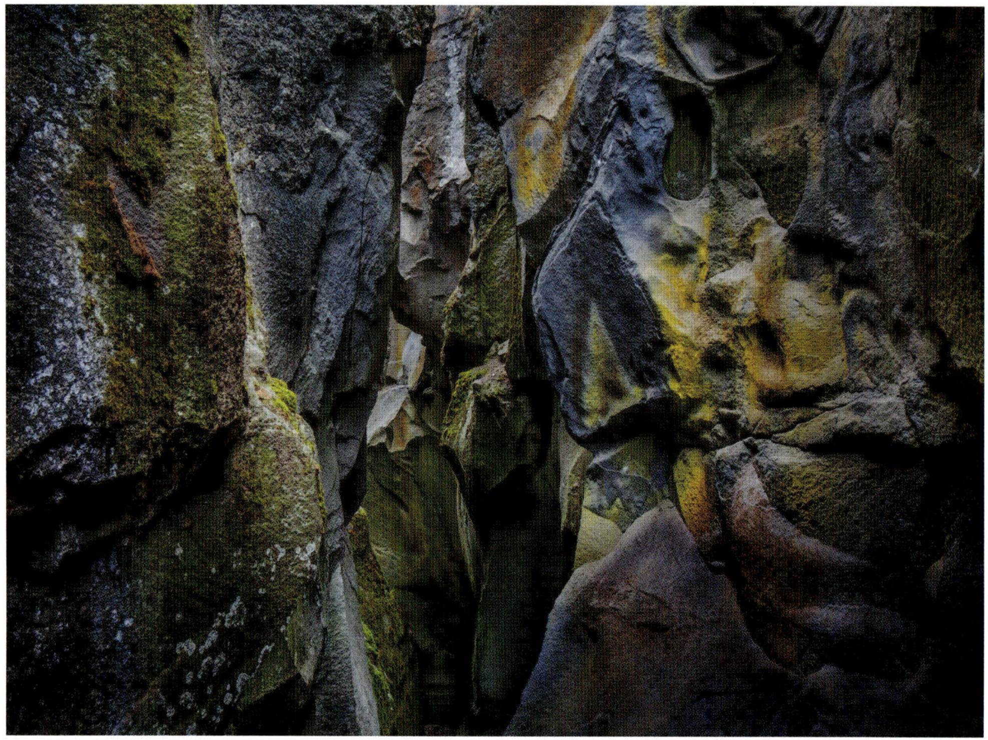

springs into action and becomes active as soon as the brain stops paying conscious focused attention to some activity. Although the DMN plays an important (albeit not entirely understood) role as the author and narrator of our life stories, perhaps even as the generator of our sense of self, when left to its own devices DMN activity may also result in self-defeating ruminations and give rise to unnecessary or overly exaggerated anxiety, worry, helplessness, guilt, depression, anger, or dissatisfaction.

To be mindful is to take charge of attention and to direct it at will. This has the effect, among others, of silencing the DMN. It is no surprise, therefore, that studies show mindfulness to be correlated with improvements in general mood, and with increased ability to generate creative ideas. This may seem at odds with the common belief that creative ideas often appear when the mind is distracted, rather than when the mind is focused on a task.

The apparent paradox of creativity being associated both with a distracted mind (daydreaming, incubation) and with a focused mind (mindfulness) seems to be related to the timing and difficulty of the distraction. A 2014 study[7] found that creative ideas are more likely to arise when the mind is engaged in undemanding

---

[7]Benjamin Baird et al., "Inspired by Distraction: Mind Wandering Facilitates Creative Incubation," *Psychological Science* 23, no. 10 (August 2012): 1117–1122, https://doi.org/10.1177/0956797612446024.

tasks, rather than in complex or difficult tasks. A different study[8] narrows things further, suggesting specifically that "trait DMN activity" (a term referring to the mind wandering when in a restful state, as opposed to just being distracted in some other context) is detrimental to creativity and mood, but perhaps other kinds of DMN activity may not have this effect. Although speculative, the upshot seems to be that creative ideas are more likely to arise when the mind is distracted with relatively easy and benign activities, but not when grappling with difficult or troubling ones.

Regardless of specific brain mechanisms, the correlation between mindfulness and improved creativity (specifically the process of generating creative ideas, known as divergent thinking) is well-established in scientific research. Conversely, the general lack of mindfulness in most people's lives today is likely responsible for what has been dubbed the "creativity crisis" in many industrial societies. As photographers this should not come as a surprise to us. The prevalence of similar, if not identical-looking, photographs in so many photographers' portfolios today is convincing evidence that creativity is greatly lacking, and perhaps broadly underappreciated, in our discipline. It's also likely that social technology is largely to blame, as the dynamics of social media are known to promote conformity and constant distraction, and to exacerbate such neuroses as FOMO, mentioned earlier. Beyond the obvious benefit of improving overall emotional well-being, especially in our age of technology-induced angst, evidence suggests that mindfulness can also help one become more creative.

It seems self-evident that mindfulness is worth investing time and effort in. What may not be as obvious, however, is how to go about it. Most experts recommend meditation as a good way of achieving mindfulness. Meditation is, in a nutshell, a way of training the brain to focus attention consciously—both toward desirable thoughts and away from undesirable ones. Contrary to intuition, this is not an easy thing to do beyond random short-lived episodes. It requires training and practice. Our brains want to drift and to ruminate as soon as we stop paying conscious attention to specific things or activities. Our challenge is to first recognize when thoughts bubble up in our minds, then to examine these thoughts consciously, keep the thoughts worth keeping, and—much harder—let go of thoughts deemed undesirable, along with the negative emotions associated with these thoughts.

Usually, by the time we realize our thoughts had wandered to negative self-defeating territory, it is already too late to reverse their emotional effect. The trick (and the skill trained by meditation) is to recognize when our thoughts and feelings begin to drift right when they start to, so we can refocus them consciously before they get too far and affect our mood irrevocably. Here, we run into another apparent

---

[8]Aviva Berkovich-Ohana et al., "Creativity Is Enhanced by Long-Term Mindfulness Training and Is Negatively Correlated with Trait Default-Mode-Related Low-Gamma Inter-Hemispheric Connectivity." *Mindfulness* 8 (2017), 717–727, https://doi.org/10.1007/s12671-016-0649-y.

paradox between mindfulness and creativity, which is this: If, in meditating, we may choose to focus our thoughts on specific things (e.g., our breaths, as some meditation teachers suggest), and if we do so repeatedly according to a prescribed schedule or ritual, then how (and when) can we expect our minds to come up spontaneously with novel ideas (i.e., to think creatively)?

Unlike other forms of meditation, mindfulness meditation involves focusing attention not on benign things like counting breaths or repeating mantras but on becoming hyper-aware of things happening in the present moment: on sensations (sensory perceptions originating outside of us) and feelings (emotions arising within us). By their nature, sensations and feelings are not always the same, and are not predictable (especially if we practice mindfulness in natural, uncontrolled settings or when engaged in uncommon experiences). This allows for novel, creative ideas to emerge spontaneously. It's only after we become conscious of these random ideas that we can decide which are worth keeping, and perhaps developing further.

Some traditional meditation techniques are founded in the belief that powerful emotions are all, and always, detrimental. Avoiding powerful emotions, both positive and negative, is considered a form of enlightenment. If all your feelings are benign and equanimous, if you don't care about anything too passionately, you will not suffer emotionally. As one predisposed to powerful emotions, both elevated and miserable, I disagree with this premise wholeheartedly. Intense suffering, as well as intense joy, have been great sources of and catalysts to finding meaning in my life. Indeed, scientific studies suggest that people may experience a greater sense of meaning in life by overcoming misfortune and suffering, not by avoiding them. Certainly, we all know of the well-founded link between powerful emotions and artistic creativity.

This is the twist I refer to in the title of this essay: when I practice mindfulness, I don't aspire to rid myself completely of powerful emotions, as some traditions suggest. My goal instead is to examine these emotions as I experience them, so I can keep those that are most useful, elevating, and beautiful, even if painful or difficult to endure. No doubt joyous states are always welcome, but when I experience difficult feelings, the practice of mindfulness helps me accept the pain and, when appropriate, to draw meaning from it—to distinguish useful suffering from useless suffering.

As an expressive artist, my goal is to have my work express my life—my experiences, my personality. Being mindful of all the dimensions—both external and internal—of my experience as it happens gives me a rich inventory of materials and concepts I may channel into my work.

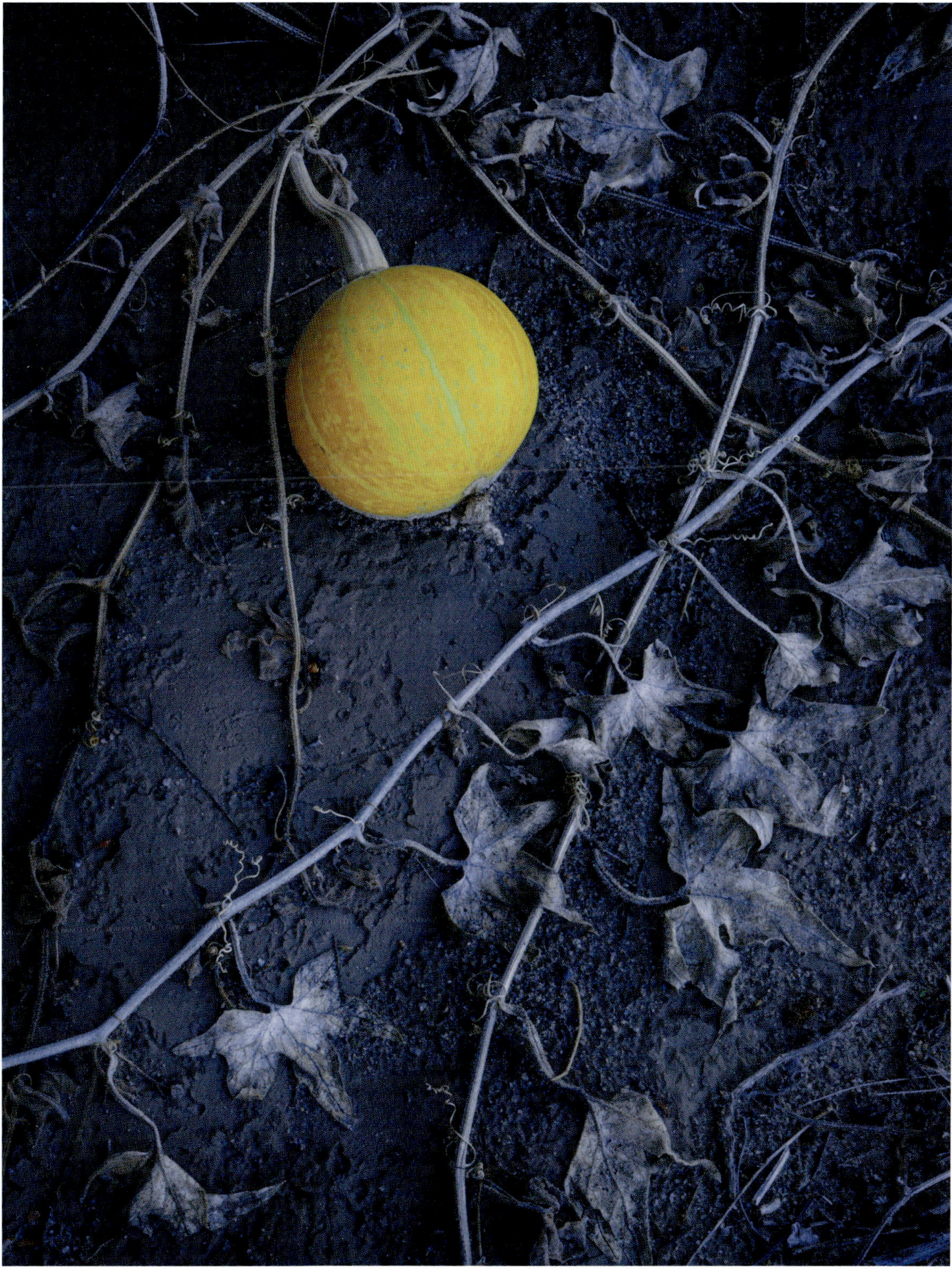

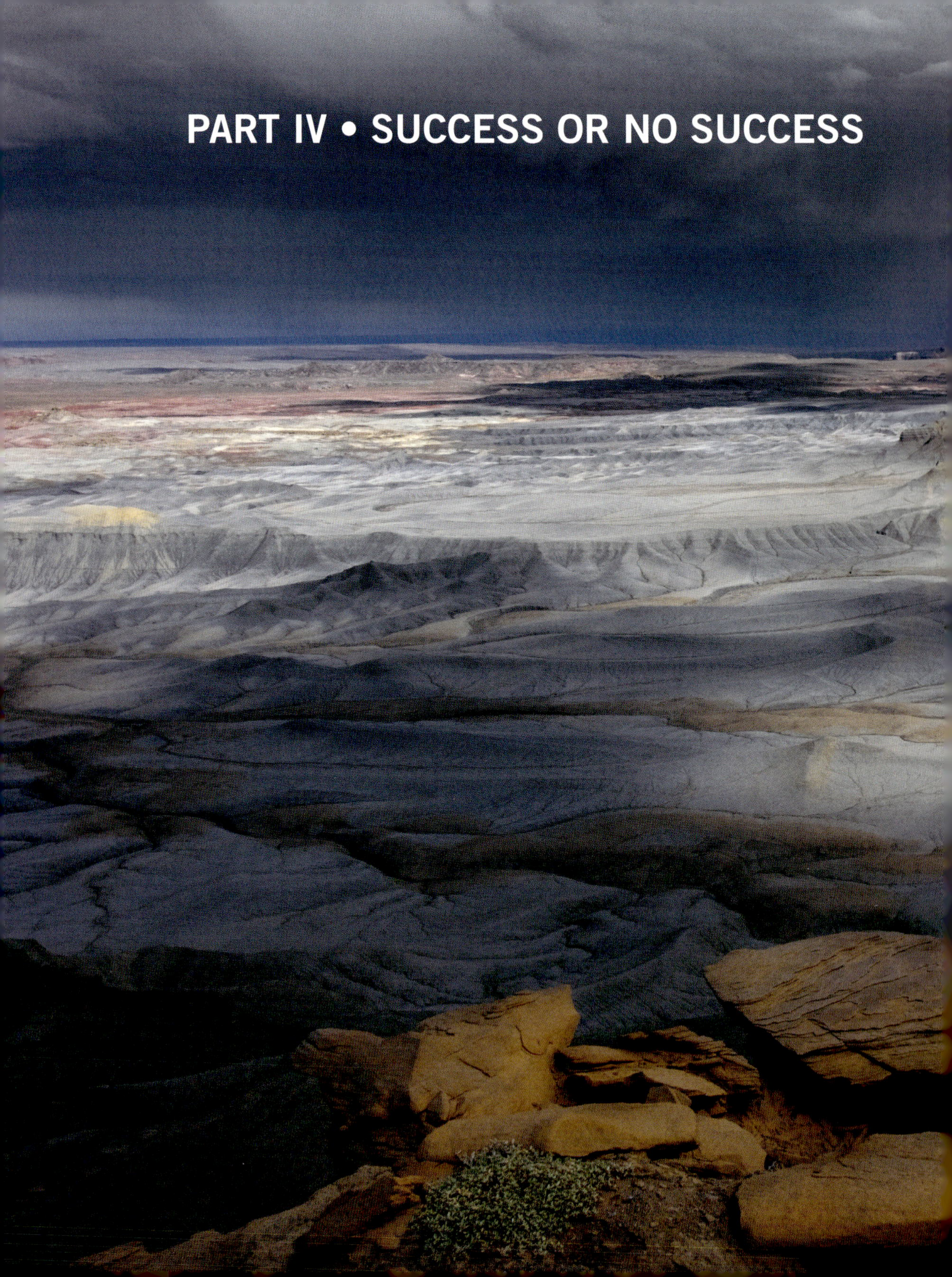

PART IV • SUCCESS OR NO SUCCESS

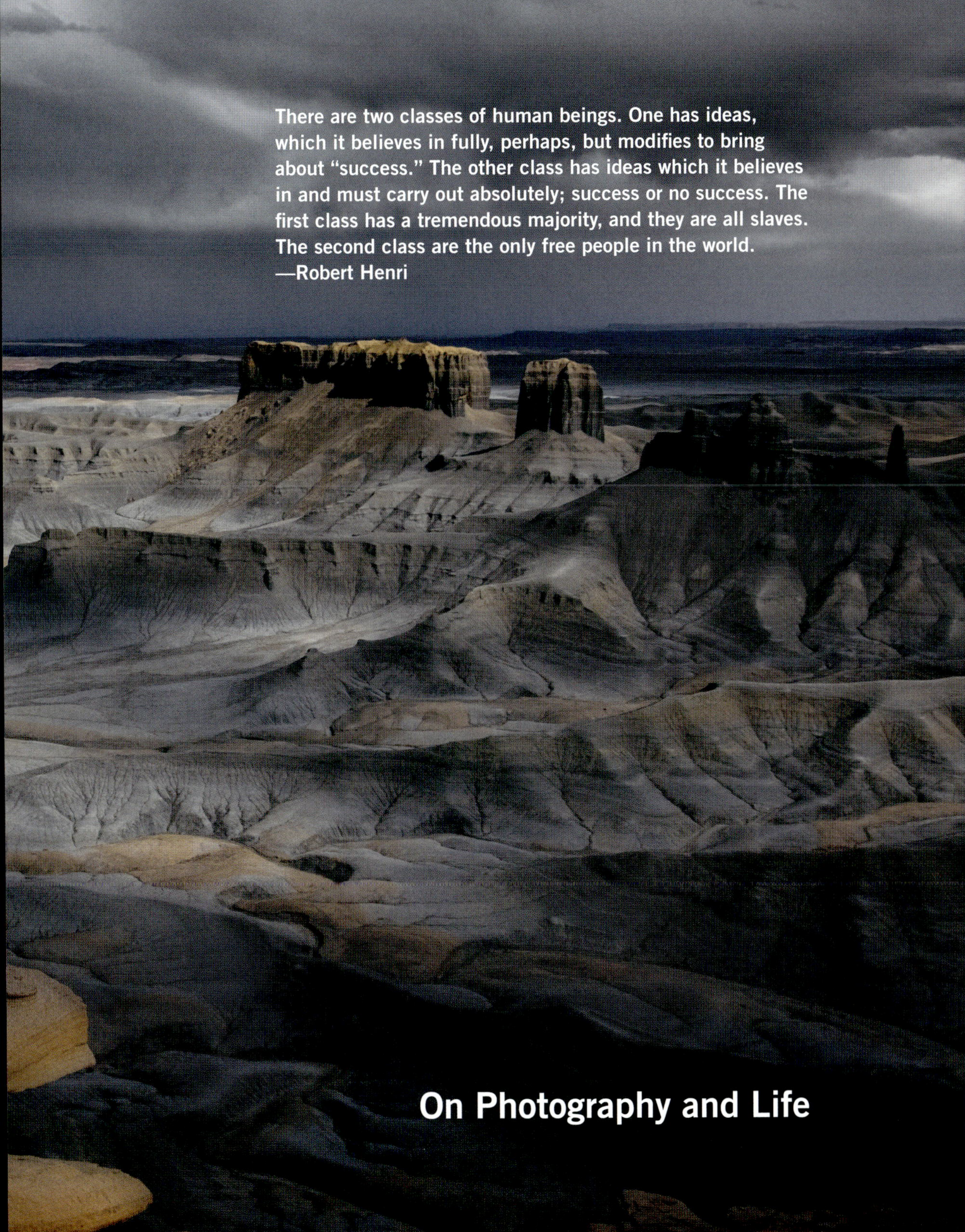There are two classes of human beings. One has ideas,
which it believes in fully, perhaps, but modifies to bring
about "success." The other class has ideas which it believes
in and must carry out absolutely; success or no success. The
first class has a tremendous majority, and they are all slaves.
The second class are the only free people in the world.
—Robert Henri

On Photography and Life

26 The Art and the Artist

> **There are two approaches, maybe three, to any art: you can
> make it a real business first of all, in which case "Art" could,
> probably would, be killed; or you can live for your art, and
> maybe grow lean in the living, or try to combine the two
> approaches. In trying to achieve the latter, I have learned that
> you can't make a lot of money, get rich, out of your own hide, no
> less than the corner grocer.**
> **—Edward Weston, in a letter to his son, Cole**

There are those who refer to themselves as artists by virtue of being skilled at producing artistic creations. There are also those who refer to themselves as artists by their conviction, beyond just producing art, to live as artists. To the former, the highest purpose of being an artist is to make art, often alongside or in deliberate contrast to less-artistic aspects of life. To the latter, the opposite is true: the highest purpose of making art is to sustain an artistic life by occasionally giving tangible form to certain experiences that ensue naturally out of such a life.

Although it is likely that those who choose to live as artists may be more inclined than others to choose art as their profession, this is not necessarily the case. The decision to live as an artist is primarily one of attitude. The decision to become a professional artist is primarily one of pragmatism. There are many who live their lives as artists but earn a living in other professions (or perhaps are fortunate to not have to earn a living at all), and there are also many professional artists for whom art is primarily a means of earning income rather than an expression of intensified living.

The dichotomy explains some otherwise seemingly incompatible views among artists. It explains why some preach the virtue of paying no attention to public opinion, whereas others strive to align themselves with the zeitgeist. It also explains why some, even those who may otherwise be progressive in their views, adhere conservatively to strict traditions, whereas others feel free, if not outright compelled, to defy traditions when traditions prove incompatible with personal expression. It explains why some are satisfied producing works that are largely derivative or outright plagiarized so long as these works are beautiful and popular, whereas others consider such works anathemas. It explains why some are more preoccupied than others with the mechanics of their chosen media, whereas others may consider media—mechanics and all—as just means to expressive ends.

To me, living as an artist means living, to the extent that one is free and driven to do so, according to one's creative urges, striving to elevate the quality—the depth, richness, and intensity—of one's inner experiences by engaging in artistic activities. For this reason, one may not conclude by any measurable qualities of a person's work whether this person lives as an artist. Conversely, no degree of similarity in methods, subjects, or styles among any two persons is reliable evidence that both live as artists, which is to say that both aspire to the same inner rewards—the same profound and elevated states of mind—in pursuit of their work. More important, it is largely pointless to conjecture whether any person lives as an artist. Being that both the risks and the rewards of living as an artist may be substantial, and are primarily subjective, they must be primarily the concern of individual artists, to be accepted or avoided by whatever criteria they deem appropriate. It is for each of us to decide for ourselves whether, and to what degree, we are prepared to commit to living as artists—that is, the degree to which we may wish to venture beyond just pursuing art opportunistically alongside other priorities or to balance less enjoyable activities.

Enjoyment, to some, may be the only justification for and purpose of artistic work. However, pursuing art for enjoyment alone is not a practical possibility for those of us who are committed to living as artists. To us, enjoyment, while certainly desirable and a powerful motivator, is by necessity underscored by less pleasant, yet unavoidable, aspects of living as artists: the dispiriting effects of prolonged creative ruts, the stings of occasional misunderstanding or disapproval of our work, the insults of others receiving and accepting credit for plagiarizing us, the pangs of—or even constant—anxiety about earning sufficient income. All these and more we must not only accept and endure but on occasion transcend consciously, at least for a time, so we may also experience such things as inspiration, awe, mystery, flow, curiosity, grace, discovery, and gratitude as often and as intensely as we can endure.

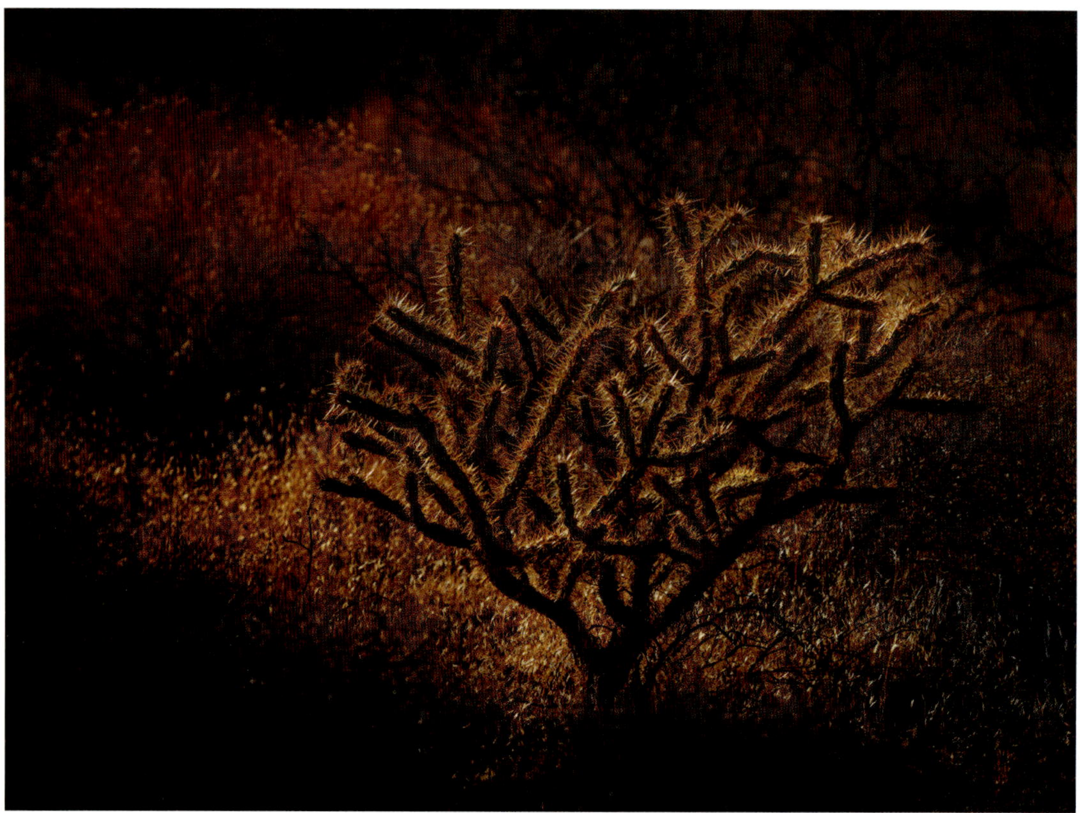

The choice to live as an artist is not necessarily a result of an abiding commitment to any art; it is the result of an abiding commitment to something—art or other—that inspires one so deeply that one's life would seem empty, perhaps not even worth living, without it. To me, this thing is the freedom to explore and to roam unhindered outside the manufactured realities where most other humans spend most of their living moments—to spend prolonged times in natural and largely unspoiled places; to witness and to commune with wildlife, geography, weather, and other phenomena that fascinate me; to saturate my senses and emotions to the farthest extent I am capable of, and to do so not only on some blissful and serendipitous occasions but as a matter of course.

When a worthy artifact—a so-called "work of art"—ensues from such experiences, this artifact, before anyone else even knows of its existence, has already served its greatest value for me: roughly speaking, the cumulative effect of all the times, experiences, thoughts, and feelings involved in its production, and all the lessons and memories that these things may yield for me in years to come. Whatever other value this artifact may later produce—income, fame, acceptance—is undoubtedly important and welcome but in a different sense. It is important in the sense that it allows me to continue doing what I do and affords me the freedom to do it even in those (not uncommon) cases when my efforts fail to yield any artifacts worth sharing, or any artifacts at all.

*　*　*

I write these words, as I often do, in a campsite in the desert. It is a beautiful and chilly winter morning. I'm enjoying my third cup of coffee, my dog at my feet, soaking in the morning sun. My body is pleasantly sore after yesterday's long hike to a remote canyon. Today is a "workday," meaning I'll stay in my camp, far away from any evidence of humanity, writing and preparing some presentation slides, perhaps go on a couple of short walks.

I feel profoundly grateful to have lived on this Earth for more than five decades now, a considerable portion of which I've been free to roam and to marvel at whatever wild beauty still remains in some parts of this world, to have abundant wild places available to me to spend my days in and to explore where few if any others have, to commune with wildlife, to discover incredible things, and to do whatever it is that I do to earn my living. (I suppose "professional fine-art photographer" is as good—and as inadequate—a term for it as "great hairless photo hunter," or "desert bum.")

I have now been here, hiking and watching the light, for three days, and have so far not made any "serious" photographs, not for lack of opportunity but because I felt more inspired to occupy my mind and my time with other things—exploring, reading, writing, listening to music, looking for interesting rocks, tracing the presence of animals by their tracks in the sand or by their yelps and howls in the evening hours.

All of it, to me, is living as an artist, only a portion of which directly involves making art. I am not a "landscape photographer" because I love photographing "the landscape." I'm a landscape photographer because I love photographing and living in *this* landscape. Because this landscape inspires me to think, to feel, to experience intensely, and on occasion also to make photographs in the hope that they express some of these things.

27 Out of the Woods

**Nourish yourself with grand and austere ideas of beauty that
feed the soul. You are always being lured away by foolish
distractions. Seek solitude.**
—Eugène Delacroix

Shortly before the Christmas holiday, I arrived at my campsite in a remote region
where the Mojave Desert transitions into the now-frigid highlands of the Colorado
Plateau. It is early afternoon. I have just enough time to set up camp and to make
myself comfortable before the sun sets. With that done, I feel a strange elation sitting
outside comfortably—the temperature hovering just above freezing—a luxury I won't
have in the desert of my home until spring arrives, perhaps four months from now.

Although the season's holidays never played a significant role in my life, these
days around the winter solstice still feel uniquely festive and restful to me. The sun
hanging low in the sky, the soft golden light filtering through trees and shrubs all
throughout the day, and the intense silence all lend an uncommon peacefulness and
dignity to these desert places otherwise prone to extremes. Like most wild beings, I
take great comfort in the notable absence of people and their noisy trappings. I have
not seen or heard another vehicle since leaving the highway about three hours ago,
and I don't expect to until I leave again in a few days.

I settle into my chair with a glass of tequila and the stub of a cigar I've been
working my way through for the last couple of days. Millie the dog is sniffing happily among the grass-lined creosote bushes. After hours on the road, it's now time
to corral my thoughts, to bring my mind to where my body is, to become mindful of
the silence and majesty of the place, and to savor the beauty of the fading light as it
retreats slowly from the slopes of desert mountains all around me.

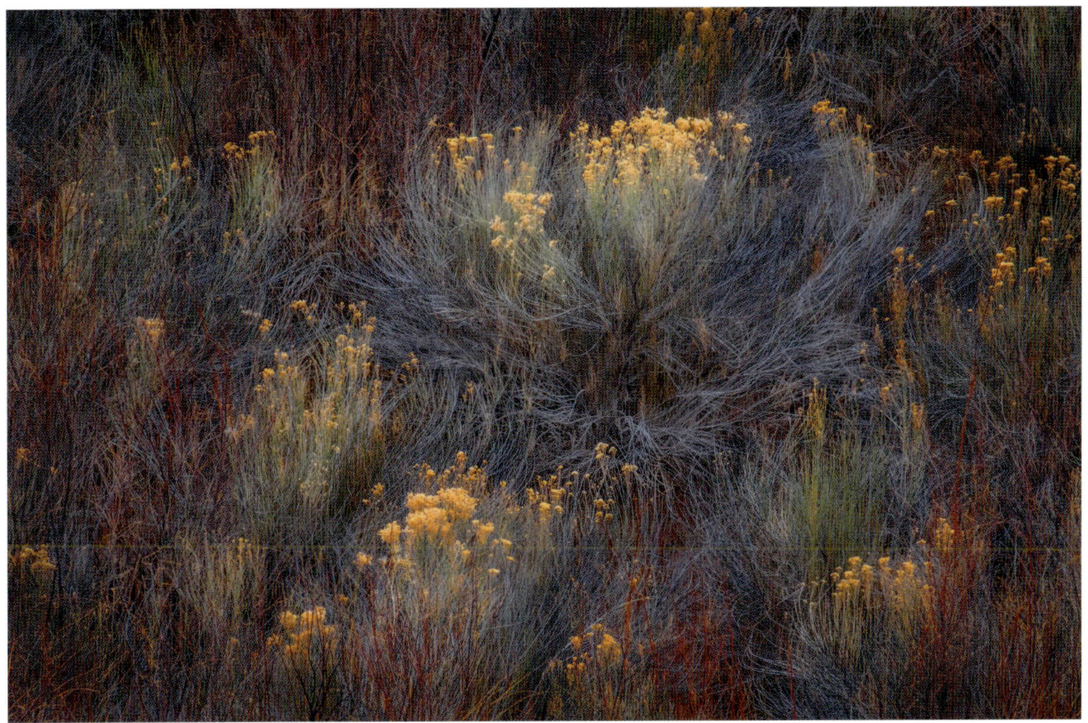

In recent weeks I've given several virtual presentations to various camera clubs, usually in the form of question-and-answer sessions. Despite my social anxiety, I find these talks rewarding to work on. Other than the enjoyable challenge of putting my thoughts into words, these sessions also offer me a glimpse into the minds and preoccupations of other photographers, allowing me to compare them with my own. Often, a question or idea will rattle around in my mind for some time even after presenting my answer. A couple such recent questions were about my approach to scouting new locations, and how I get myself into an "artist mindset."

I suspect that my answer to the first question may not have been very satisfying to the person who asked it: I don't scout; I just go to some general area that appeals to me and keep myself open to experiences and to whatever may call out to me to make a photograph. The second question is what set this train of thought in motion. The answer I gave was this: My goal is to never not be in an artist mindset. This is my life, it's what I do, it's who I am, it's always on my mind, it's my default state. When I'm distracted from this mindset, I can feel it viscerally; something just doesn't seem right.

I remember times when this was not the case—times when, encumbered by the demands of urban living and professional obligations, it was difficult and at times impossible for me to set mundane concerns aside on short excursions. Much like trying to get rid of a song stuck in my head, I couldn't get past a nagging anxiety born from knowing that shortly I'll have to go back to an uninspiring routine, that I had just this brief time to myself to "make the most of." Paradoxically, this stress prevented me from achieving the very things I wished for: inspiration, calmness, disconnectedness from petty and mundane concerns, and relief from the stresses of everyday life. Absurdly, even in such remote places, surrounded by beauty, I couldn't stop stressing . . . about stressing.

My sense is that people who are concerned with scouting locations may experience a similar kind of anxiety: stressing about making photographs, to a point of blinding themselves to the greater joys of peace, inspiration, beauty, mindfulness, presence, and creative epiphanies. For those caught in this self-defeating loop, my advice is this: convince yourself (hard as it is) that it's OK to return with no photographs, that it's OK to do nothing at all, to have nothing material to show for your time outside, to not even have enviable stories to tell others, to just let go, to just be. Then again, it's really not OK . . . in the sense that it's not just OK. It's one of the most powerful and life-affirming things you can do: absolutely nothing, except feel, sense, notice; without striving, without expectations, without any concern for what may come after. It's the only way to extend an invitation to the muses, to put yourself in the path of opportunity, to experience the kind of profound peace that is only possible in the absence of stress, guilt, or any concern for "productivity."

In his essay "Walking," Henry David Thoreau mused about the futility of being distracted when out in nature:

> *I am alarmed when it happens that I have walked a mile into the woods bodily, without getting there in spirit. In my afternoon walk I would fain forget all my morning occupations and my obligations to Society. But it sometimes happens that I cannot easily shake off the village. The thought of some work will run in my head and I am not where my body is—I am out of my senses. In my walks I would fain return to my senses. What business have I in the woods, if I am thinking of something out of the woods?*

At times, when I find myself distracted by mundane concerns, I have adapted Thoreau's advice, asking myself, what business have I in the . . . woods, desert, mountains . . . if I am thinking of something outside of where I am? Simply answering this may not be enough. In these instances, tools such as mindfulness, meditation, and immersion in some creative challenge can be helpful in getting myself back into the artist mindset.

I don't know of any sure way to get into an artist mindset, but I do know many ways to prevent myself from getting into it. One of these sure ways is to focus my attention on the singular goal of making photographs, to the exclusion of all other rewards that to me are the greater part of "making the most" of any experience. Photographs are most rewarding not as goals in themselves but as outcomes and byproducts of mindful and elevated states. And these states, whether they yield any photograph or even any experience worth telling others about, are more worthy and rewarding in themselves than any photograph that is not the fruit of true inspiration.

⁂   ⁂   ⁂

The sun has set, and the world looks calmer still in the twilight. The resident Western screech-owl is calling from among the rocks behind me. Stars begin to appear, and I know there will not be as many of them visible this time of year. I proceed to a favorite pastime: identifying the farthest celestial body I can see. It never fails to amaze me when I think about it, the astonishing scale of existence, the spectacular randomness of it all, me being here, being me, thinking these thoughts with whatever knowledge is available to me, and the immensity of the mysteries all around me: the staggering extents of my ignorance. And then, the cathartic moment occurs when all I can think and experience collapses into this most blissful, singular state: acceptance.

Sadness, anxiety, dissatisfaction, stress—these are all feelings that accompany any thought or circumstance that shatters the delusion of having control, of being anything other than a feeble being, limited in mind and body, making the most of my very temporary existence on a speck of dust floating in a fathomless immensity.

I remind myself happily that all else—all that I can do nothing about at this moment and in the coming days—is not worth an iota of concern. I'm safe and warm. I have the makings of an excellent dinner waiting. I am in a place of great beauty. I'm not here to solve any problem, not to arrive at any destination, not even to make any photographs. I'm here, first and foremost, to camp and hike with my dog, in solitude, in terra incognita, in the beautiful light of the winter solstice. And that is as much as I can ask for.

May you stay in your woods.

28 Perspective and Meaning

When you're in the desert, you look into infinity. It's no wonder that nearly all the great founders of religion came out of the desert. It makes you feel terribly small, and also in a strange way, quite big.
—David Lean

It's a chilly autumn morning in the desert. I am still in my sleeping bag, leaning against a large rock, sipping fresh coffee as I savor the first rays of sunlight, looking down a beautiful canyon through the sheltering arc of a large alcove that has been my home for the last three days. The air is perfectly still. Not even a single leaf in the old cottonwood trees lining the creek below me is so much as trembling. The only sounds are the soft gurgle of flowing water, reverberating off the stone walls, and the occasional chirping of juncos among the grasses and shrubs.

Evidence of the presence of now-long-gone Neolithic people is all around me, but no person has lived in this canyon in at least two hundred years. I suspect that only a handful of people make the long hike here in any given year. Although I can't know this for sure, I take some pride in the not-unlikely possibility that I may have spent more time in this canyon in the last two decades than perhaps any other human currently alive. The alcove I now occupy has likely been used for social or ceremonial purposes for several centuries, evident by the presence of many petroglyphs in the rocks around me, and the absence of evidence of fires, food storage, or toolmaking.

Although I generally try to dismiss such thoughts when I become conscious of them, I take a moment to reflect on the human world I disconnected from a few days ago. Here in the canyon, I can't even tune into a radio station, let alone make a phone call or access the internet. Other than the occasional whooshing of a jetliner in the sky, I have not seen or heard any hint of the existence of other living people in three days so far.

Somewhere in the human world, momentous events are undoubtedly unfolding. Cultures rise, fall, and change; wars are lost or won (depending on whom you ask); relationships form and break; technologies are invented and retired; fortunes are made and lost; lives begin and end. "Oh well," I think, and decide that this is as much attention as I'm willing to give these matters at this time. Certainly, some of these are eminently important to some people. Some may prove to have important consequences for me too. But there's nothing I can do about them, or want to do about them, right now.

The most important thing to me right now is to savor this rare experience, to make myself conscious of as much beauty as my senses can feed into my brain, to consider my options for filling the coming hours, to come to terms with the reality of the illness that will likely shape my remaining years, and perhaps to find some meaning in it all—in my being here, in the life, light, geology, and weather surrounding me. Photography will also have to wait. To be sure, there is a lot I may photograph here. But I'm not ready to think about it just yet. Millie the dog has climbed onto my sleeping bag, flipped on her back, and needs her belly rubbed; and we both need some breakfast.

Over the years, I have learned how powerfully perspective can shape experience and meaning, and consequently, the importance of taking conscious control of my perspectives. With little effort I can probably think of a dozen or more things to be concerned about, to feel anxious about, to want to rush out to where there is cellular signal so I can learn what's "going on" in other places. But why in the world would I want to do that? Right here, right now, beauty abounds, and peace, and gratitude, but only if I am open to them, only if I am willing to set aside less profitable thoughts in their favor, only if I can muster the discipline to maintain a mindful perspective: a perspective of myself as an ephemeral being fortunate to be having a rare, ephemeral experience, here and now, while also aware that I have only so many grains remaining in the hourglass of my days—only so many opportunities remaining to have experiences such as this.

"A man who dares to waste one hour of time," wrote Charles Darwin, "has not discovered the value of life." But an hour is a long time. In an hour, the light will be different, the birds may be gone, the wind may pick up, perhaps another person might show up. How can I defend wasting so much as a second of this?

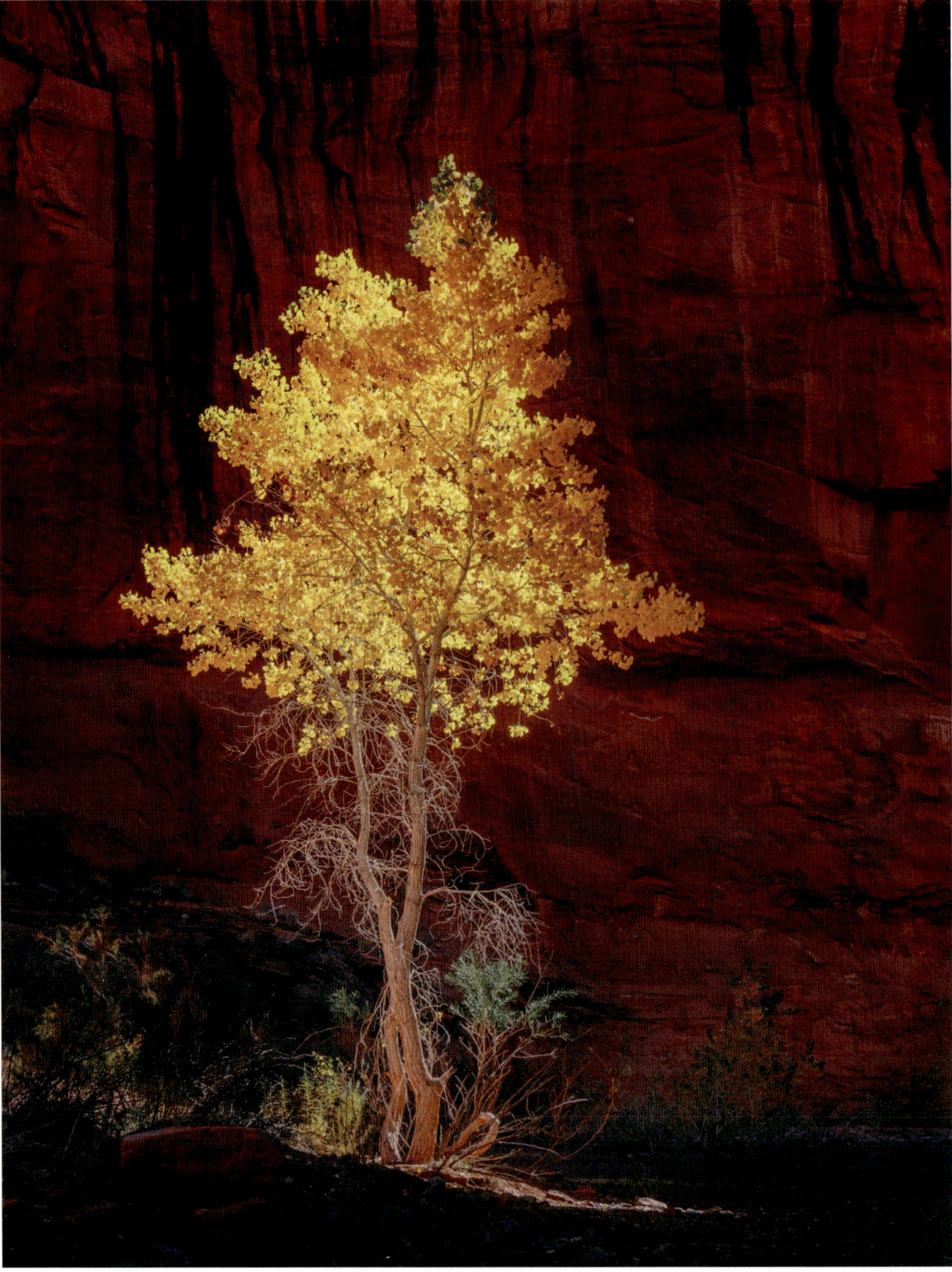

When teaching photography, I explain perspective as a quality of visual composition, along with framing and visual balance. As a photographic artist, perspective
in the literal sense is a powerful expressive tool for me. But perspective can also be
a useful metaphor. A perspective is a relationship between myself (or my camera)
and something outside of me. In photography, perspective is the spatial relationship
between my lens and an object or a scene I may wish to photograph. Metaphorically,
perspective can also mean the relationship between myself and some idea, concept,
or perception. Just as optical perspective affects the visual relationships in a photographic composition, metaphorical perspective affects the relationships between me
and other things in the world, or even between me and the entirety of all things in
the world that are not me.

I never bought into the idea of monism—the philosophy that all things are one.
Everything that makes me, me—my mind, my body, my perceptions, my senses—
seems designed explicitly to separate me from the world, to give me a sense of
agency and autonomy, and to find meaning in this separation. What I know about
the natural order also tells me that my sense of self is transient, very soon to be
gone without the possibility of recall. Of course, my sense of agency and individu-
ality may ultimately amount to an elaborate delusion, but it really doesn't matter
to what degree this separation between me and the world is "real" in any objective
sense. It matters that, by shaping my perspective according to this perceived separation, I can find value and meaning in my living experience, which, if nothing else, at
least feels real.

For me, the calmest and most rewarding of all perspectives is that in which I
find myself entirely insignificant in the immensity of the universe in which I am
little more than a coordinate harboring some arrangement of particles that by some
yet-unknown means has the capacity for a subjective (even if illusory) sensation of
consciousness and agency. This universe, spanning more than ninety billion light-
years, harbors things more numerous, more powerful, and more fantastical than I
can begin to imagine, let alone understand or even speculate on what meaning or
purpose they may have. I'm enough of a scientist to know that even this astoundingly grand universe may be only a tiny part of a much vaster existence. For cry-
ing out loud, I am looking at plants older than I am and that will almost certainly
outlive me.

There is comfort in feeling myself inconsequential—in knowing something
about the limits of my ability to know, in knowing that I cannot hold myself responsible for things beyond my limited capacities. It's only in narrowing this scope, in
treating some arbitrary portion of the world as if it's all there is, that anxiety and

discontent arise, and peace is disrupted. It's worthwhile to remind myself that such narrower scopes are contrivances: artificial designations assigned by limited minds to arbitrary concepts in a futile effort to block out inconvenient truths (curiously, sometimes replacing these truths with far less convenient myths).

Objectively, I know without a doubt that all things—myself, the place I'm in, the society and culture I'm part of, the labels on the map, this planet, this solar system, this galaxy, and ultimately all material existence in this universe—will change, come to some end, become unknown, and eventually unknowable. Subjectively, it's a different story—a different perspective. My diminishing moments of conscious living, inconsequential as they are in the grand scheme, are all I will ever get to experience. To use my tiny span of conscious existence in the most appropriate way I know how is as high a purpose as a mortal being may aspire to. As such, this knowledge must inform every choice I make, every path I travel, every story I make myself a part of.

There is no mystery about the purpose of life. The purpose of life is to be lived, to the greatest and deepest extent that one can, while one can.

I need more coffee.

*   *   *

I've come here hoping to find the penultimate and most venerated of the so-called "stages of grief": acceptance. (The ultimate, usually unmentioned, and often unachievable stage, is forgetting.) Acceptance is also a perspective: a relationship between me and things outside of me—events, objects, people, ideas, perceptions, feelings, memories—things located elsewhere in space or time, some existing only in private dimensions of inner experience.

Reality, to any person, is not made just of measurable or even quantifiable things. It is the amalgam of objective circumstances, subjective perceptions, and unverified speculations at a point in life—a set of coordinates within the multidimensioned matrix of conscious experience. Sum ergo sum, cogito or no cogito. Knowledge of existence only proves the existence of knowledge.

To be at peace is to be unperturbed by paradoxes in one's understanding of one's reality. Some may accomplish peace by cognitive dissonance or by willful ignorance. I am not so fortunate. To come closest to peace, I must examine and reconcile what I know, feel, and believe to the best of my rational abilities, and to accept whatever reality emerges.

To a person like me—a skeptic, a rationalist, an analytical thinker, a philosophical materialist—acceptance, ultimately, is an ideal to aspire to while acknowledging that, at least to a degree, it likely will forever remain beyond reach. (Damn you,

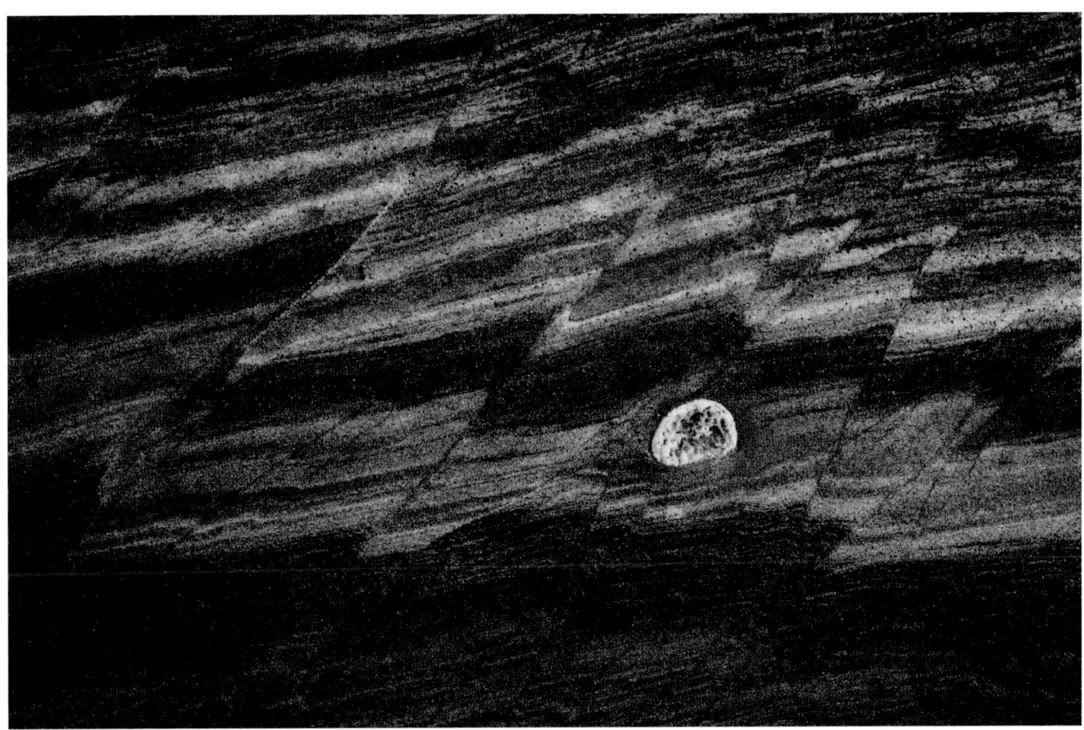

Gödel![1]) I am not wired for absolutes, no matter how much I may wish to believe in them. I must consciously reconcile rational observations with irrational emotions, things known with things felt, perceptions generated by parts of my brain capable of complex logical analysis with perceptions emerging from primal instincts. I must, in short, choose my perspective with the best knowledge I have.

This experience—being here, seeing these things, feeling these things; assimilating them into thoughts, emotions, memories; all the dimensions of my present conscious experience—is meaningful and enjoyable to me. Still, I take comfort in knowing that my existence as a conscious being is (hopefully) finite. I never understood why so many wish for immortality or reincarnation. The thought of being trapped in this game forever is terrifying to me. The universe, immense as it is, surely must offer greater possibilities than doing yet another stint as an ape on a small planet.

Knowing that meaning is subjective and having a sense of conscious control over it, if only a conscious choice of perspective, is what makes meaning and acceptance possible. If meaning were objective and unequivocal—an inherent property of things or events beyond my ability to control—acceptance would be meaningless;

[1]Philosopher and logician Kurt Friedrich Gödel, author of Gödel's incompleteness theorems.

it would be either surrender or self-deception. The hard part is to maintain this perspective amid the discomforts, conflicts, pettiness, and banalities of everyday life. But this is why I've come here, to the desert, to be away from agents of conflict, irrationality, pettiness, and banality.

Catching sight of the tripod situated next to my makeshift bed shakes me out of my train of thought. It's time to go for a walk, to experience and to make some meaning out of my experiences, perhaps even to employ that simpler idea of perspective to make some photographs.

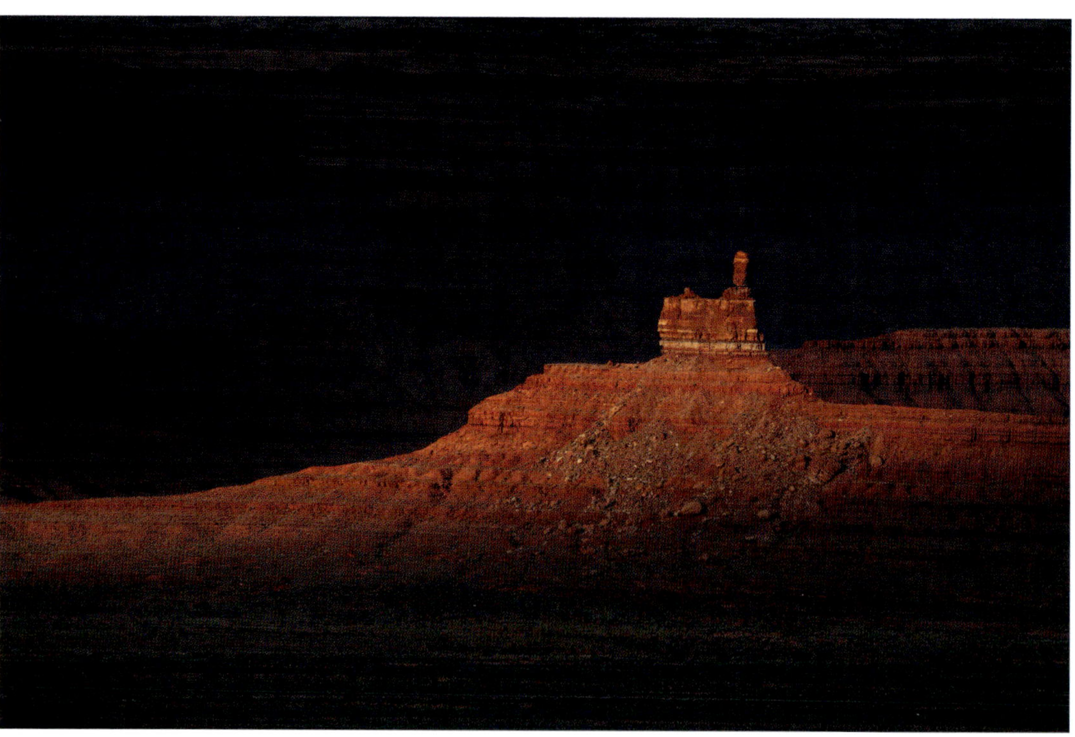

Whoever wants music instead of noise, joy instead of pleasure, soul instead of gold, creative work instead of business, passion instead of foolery, finds no home in this trivial world of ours.
—Hermann Hesse

I began using the internet in the early 1990s, before it became available as a public service. I was studying and teaching at a university in Israel at the time and had the good fortune to work with the systems administrators at the university's computer center. Little did I know how this experience would change my life and how consequential it would become to my career in (of all things) photography. Rather than pursue my original plan for a career in the academy, I instead began working in technology, which ultimately brought me to the US, where, partly thanks to my interest in photography, I fell in love with the place that is now my home. For a while I earned income in both technology and photography, but as my corporate career wore me down, photography always offered me refuge and inspiration, and I finally decided to make it my primary occupation. When I recounted this history to a photographer friend, he asked how I felt the internet had affected photography during this period, which prompted the following train of thought.

Scientists and engineers sometimes use the term "signal-to-noise ratio" to describe the proportion of desirable information to unwanted distractions and interferences. This seems to me a good metaphor to describe how I feel the internet has affected the evolution of photography. I think about my early photographic experiences, in a world where I did not know any other photographer, where I saw only other people's photographs in printed form, and where my only sources of information about photographic techniques were books. I would show my own photographs only to a handful of friends on rare occasions using an old carousel projector and had no ability to share my work with large numbers of viewers around the world. Comparing those times with today's abundance of photo-related information, discussions, and distractions, my conclusion seems self-evident: the "noise" has increased tremendously and has outpaced the growth in "signal" by a considerable margin. Certainly, the signal has improved in many ways, too, but it seems to me that today photographers like me, who turn to photography primarily for inspiration and artistic expression (rather than as a way to earn income, or as a means for social interaction) must contend with a staggeringly smaller signal-to-noise ratio than I had to in my early days as a photographer.

Beyond the constant distractions of world events, personal challenges, the ever-pervasive effects of social media, and the technical minutiae dominating so much of today's photographic zeitgeist, the landscape of photography has gotten very noisy in both the literal and figurative senses. A lot of people are photographing, a lot of people are talking about photography, and a lot of people are out in places that were formerly bastions of peace, and solitude.

I concede that much of my disdain for virtual socializing is not about the media or the social aspects of online communities, but rather, stems from the realization that the great enthusiasm I had for internet technologies in their early years has turned to disappointment with how these technologies are now applied as instruments for commerce and social engineering. One big reason I don't want to share my work on many of these platforms is the creepy feeling I get knowing that all my activity on social media sites is tracked and monitored; that there is no escaping the distractions of constant advertising; that algorithms are feeding me targeted information to influence my thoughts, to make me addicted, to hijack my attention; that data banks are profiling me in real time, recording what I see, attempting to guess what I might want to buy or how I might vote. Contrasting this typical online experience with the intimate experience of sitting quietly with a book, my attention dedicated to appreciating a beautiful photograph or other work, to feeling kinship with the photographer or author, I feel a sense of loss. To me, the typical internet experience of photographs sized so small that I can barely make out their fine details, presented alongside endless streams of inane banter and animated advertisements, feels less dignified than my encounters with fine photography before the internet age.

It's worth remembering, however, that quieter and more reverential modes of practicing and appreciating photography are still possible even in the internet age, despite no longer being the default. But we must be willing to choose these modes deliberately, to take active measures to isolate the signal and to block out the torrent of noise. I urge you, for the sake of photography, for the sake of art, and for the sake of the qualities of your own experience: make these choices! Favor visiting photographers' personal websites rather than (or in addition to) their social media feeds, or at least carve out and dedicate a slice of your online time to do so. When possible, make time to study books and prints, preferably in quiet settings. Visit galleries and exhibits. When photographers take the time to write, take the time to read.

When working on your own photography, make an effort to turn down the noise of expectations, distractions, worries, and anxieties about the crises of the day. Take deep breaths, slow down, find the courage to allow yourself to feel deeply about where you are, about who you are. Assimilate fully your experiences, thoughts, and emotions; let go of cynicism and prejudices for a time; and immerse yourself completely in the creative endeavor for its own sake, not as an extension of the game-like contest for the attention of internet viewers, club members, or anything

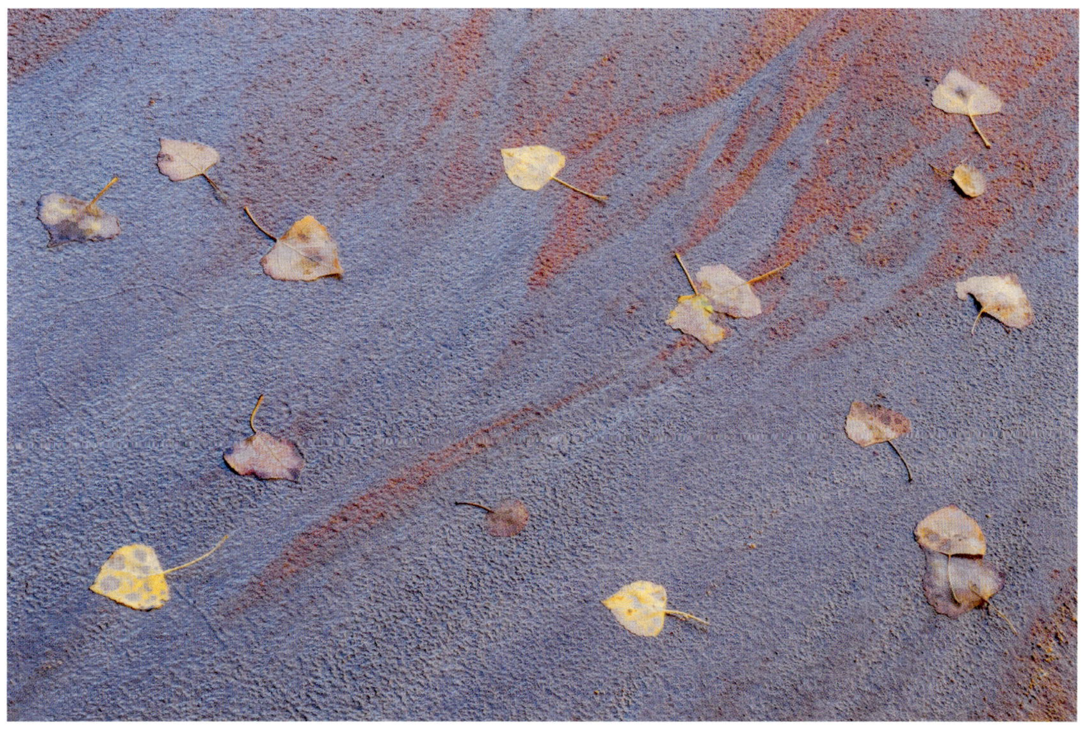

else irrelevant to making the most of your present experience. Dare to think about life, about death, about art, about the grandest and most timeless questions of existence. Set aside mundane and petty concerns for a time. Wander away from the herd, see what's behind that hill you've never scrambled, or where that road you always wondered about may lead. When you get there, search yourself for ways to express whatever new knowledge, feelings, and sensations you may find. It is within your power to tune your mind to such elevated states—to isolate the signal from the noise.

Perhaps selfishly, when I see a photograph or other work that impresses me, I wish to believe that its making involved some transcendent and extraordinary states of mind in the artist. So many times I have felt let down and jaded when all a photographer has to tell me about their work amounts to their camera techniques, what's in their bag, who their corporate sponsors are, or some puerile bragging about what it took to "get the shot." Lo, the unbearable lightness of the "epic." Where's the emotion? Where's the reverence? Where's the "what else it is"?

As noisy as our world is today, it is likely to get noisier still in the years ahead. Merchants of noise—those who profit from noise—are no longer just minor inconveniences; they are enormously powerful media machines, employing technology and psychology to make their noise ever more pervasive and inescapable, sometimes even disguise it as a signal. The skills to filter and to prioritize information, to resist and to set aside distractions, to hear the voice of your own mind uninterrupted and undistorted, and to be mindful of and to give expression to your own feelings will likewise become more and more important as our life experiences continue to become more virtual, more managed, more monitored, less private, less intimate, less sensory and visceral. Claim your own quiet space within—a space impervious to both errant and deliberate noise, a space where you get to choose and to isolate those signals you wish to tune into because they are meaningful to you, rather than those served up to you—and defend this space staunchly from all that try to invade it by force or by cunning. The future of art as a peaceful, elevating, rejuvenating, and personally meaningful experience—rather than as a social rite or a casual distraction—depends on our ability to tame, to ignore, and to escape from, the noise.

Nothing is more unbearable, once one has it, than freedom.
—James Baldwin

A young photographer wrote me recently asking if I would consider filming some of my outdoor work and making the footage available publicly. He also inquired about advice I might have for people aspiring to become professional landscape photographers like me. Admittedly, making videos is not compatible with my reclusive personality. When I work in the landscape, I am in my own world of thoughts and sensations. Solitude is indispensable to the experiences that inspire my work. The thought of other people watching me photograph feels invasive to me. Paradoxically, a camera lens pointed at me is a sure way to discourage me from pointing my own lens at anything else, and to diminish or extinguish the very reasons I live and photograph as I do.

Some may consider "fine-art landscape photographer" a profession similar to other vocations, having well-established career paths, prescribed goals and milestones, reliable revenue streams, and daily routines. For me, that is not the case. Photography for me has always been, before anything else, something I pursued intending to enrich my life, independent of how I earned a living. It is by sheer coincidence that photography became my profession. Also, I don't know anyone else who earns a living in photography in the same ways I do. I'm not even certain I could reconstruct my own career path if I had to start over again.

Whatever advice I have for those aspiring to become professional photographers in the sense that I am may not quite fit with most people's expectation to have "landscape photographer" as their formal occupation in the same way as "physician," "engineer," or "plumber." Earning a living in photography, to me, is not just a job; it is but one of several aspects of an uncommon lifestyle I have evolved organically over years, pursuing serendipitous opportunities I could not anticipate in advance, and refusing to settle for a comfortable living so long as I felt life had more to offer me than just a career. Also, for those who consider such things important: I could not practice photography in the way that I do today if I had to earn enough by it to support a family, or if I wished to live in a city, or if I could not frequently disconnect from humanity for prolonged periods.

Beyond whatever obligations I must accommodate to earn sufficient income, I choose to work alone in remote settings and to commune with natural places as often as I can. I do this not just because it offers me opportunities for appealing photographs but also because my personality and temperament are such that my emotional well-being and my sense of meaning in life depend on it. Although this may not be the case for most people, my ability to spend much of my time in solitude, in remote places, is also a precondition to feeling inspired to make photographs.

In thinking about my so-called "career" in photography, I realize how profoundly the world and photography have changed in my lifetime. I'm reminded of a scene from the movie *The Shawshank Redemption* in which longtime prisoner Brooks Hatlen, upon being released, writes back to his still-incarcerated friends, describing his struggles outside the prison walls. In a letter to his former inmates, Hatlen wrote, "The world went and got itself in a big damn hurry." The words resonated in my mind as I composed my response to the person who asked for my advice.

I was writing while sitting by my campsite on the rim of a remote desert canyon, surveying a vast view without sign of human presence, in perfect silence, awaiting the drama of an approaching thunderstorm, my dog resting at my feet. Now a couple of years into my sixth decade of life, I felt proud and grateful to be outside, savoring the peaceful pace of nature and the beauty of the place on what to many would be a regular workday, beyond the reach and relevance of troubling affairs unfolding in the human world; to still be able to live as a consummate "dirtbag" naturalist, same as (in some ways more so than) I was in my younger years.

Likely no career counselors in their right mind would advise a young person to pursue the path that had brought me here, yet I can't imagine a better life for myself. "Before dispensing advice," I wrote to the young photographer, "I urge you to first consider what matters to you beyond just photography: how much risk you are willing to live with, how much income you really need, how you may deal with failure, and what you are willing to do without."

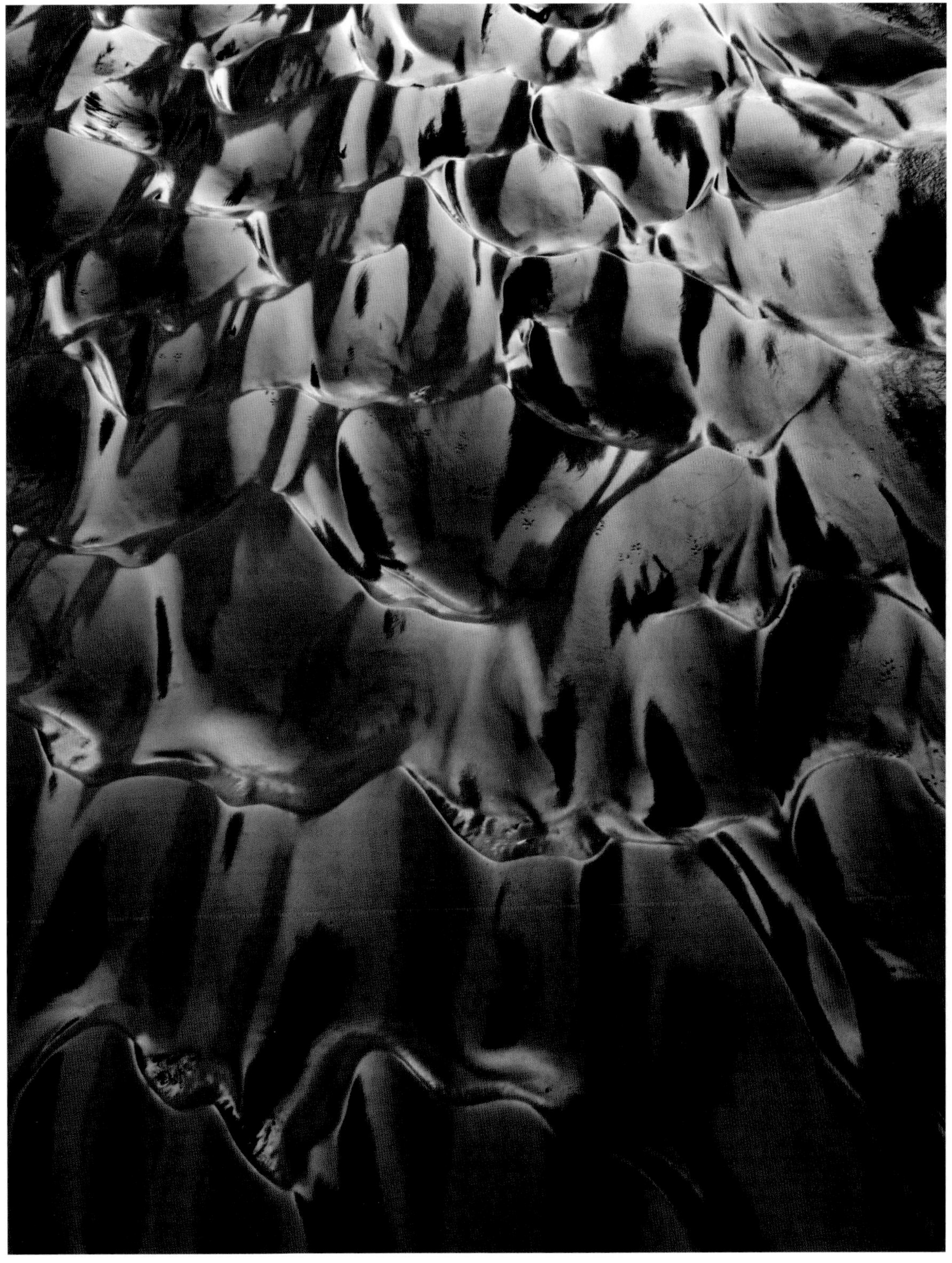

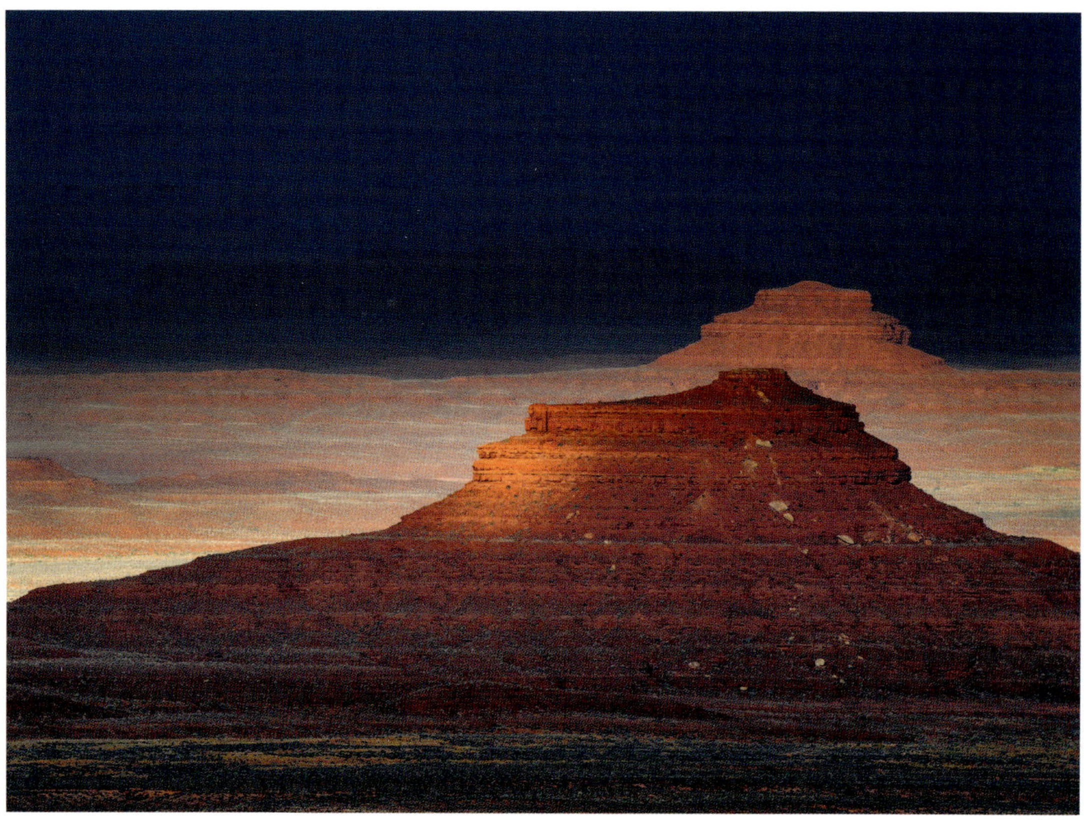

When I first picked up a camera intending to use it for "serious" work, landscape photography was largely a pursuit favored by people of my kind—introverts, social misfits, seekers, adventurers—who preferred, or at least were comfortable with, spending prolonged periods alone, disconnected from others, whether in the field, traveling in places where human presence is scarce, or isolated for hours in a dark-room with the door firmly shut. Among the things that appealed to me most about photography as a profession were that photography did not require teamwork or collaboration, answering to bosses, fitting into any corporate culture, regular office hours (or any office hours), or reliance on products or services generally found only in cities. I liked that I could mail my submissions and applications to editors and curators without having to interact directly with them, and to expect that on occasion, some of my work may be accepted for publication or exhibition without need for prolonged negotiations or long-term commitments.

Today, almost the opposite is true about photography as a profession (at least if one's impression of professional photography is derived from watching celebrity photographers on social media). "Successful" professionals today are constantly visible; always connected; and revel in sharing details of their lives and processes, travels and equipment, corporate sponsors and public speaking engagements. Once a solitary and disconnected pursuit, professional landscape photography, at least in some venues, has now become the domain of extraverts and exhibitionists. I likely would not make it as such a photographer, nor would I want to. As the tides shifted, I turned to writing and teaching for income. The alternative—to adapt my work and persona to the celebrity-influencer culture of social media—is beyond my ability and desire, and I am not the right person to offer guidance for anyone aspiring to become this kind of photographer.

Reflecting on his life as a photographer and artist, Edward Steichen wrote:

> *The most precious factor in the creative life of an artist in any medium is freedom. Totalitarian, political, or national ideologies that seek to direct or channel the arts are pernicious; they can strangle the work of individual artists and cripple their own culture. They are not, however, the only things that hamper an artist's freedom. It can also be curtailed by commercial conditions or by the theories of aesthetics ordained by various groups, cults, cliques, or "isms." But it seems to me that the most damaging restrictions on an artist's liberty are self-imposed. So often, what may have begun as fresh thinking and discovery is turned into a routine and reduced to mere habit. Habits in thinking or technique are always stultifying in the long run.*

I concede (with some pride) that routine and habitual thinking have never appealed to me. Although some people find comfort in predictability, I get bored quickly without novelty and challenge. I need mystery, variety, the constant potential for unexpected discoveries, and the occasional creative breakthrough to find value and meaning in my work and life. If I were not free to photograph what, if, how, when, and where I wanted to, if I had to treat photography merely as a means of making products for popular consumption to earn a living, if I were expected to photograph only by criteria dictated by others, I would see no point in being a photographer. More concisely, if the personal rewards I get from the creative and free pursuit of photography had to be subordinate to commercial or practical considerations, photography would not appeal to me either as a hobby or as a profession.

Freedom to work on my own terms is, in my mind, indispensable to creative work. Without such creative freedom, without the benefit of spending most of my time in solitude, in remote natural places, I may as well earn my living in some other (likely more lucrative) profession. I accept fully that such freedom comes at the cost of "leaving money on the table" (to borrow an expression from a former career that I never liked), being at peace with an inconsistent income stream, and doing without some common comforts.

Freedom alone, although alluring, is not enough to reap the most from photography. Neither is income. Photography couldn't have enriched my life as much as it has if I didn't consciously give it the power and importance in my life to have such an effect. This required taking my work seriously, becoming as educated and knowledgeable as I could about the medium and about art (including relevant peripheral knowledge in philosophy, psychology, and science), evolving a lasting and complex relationship with my tools and subjects, and on occasion being humbled by my experiences and by insights I gained from others. I would not have gained as much as I have from photography if I considered it just a hobby, or a profession, or otherwise separated it from other aspects of my life.

The camera has been part of some of my most profound, emotional, contemplative, and consequential life experiences, which would not be the case if photography served no higher purpose than just making pretty and popular images—if I did not invest hard work, creative imagination, and deep thinking in the process of making my photographs, if I did not constantly question my goals, beyond just earning an income, in making photographs, or if I did not consider the ways in which creative work may elevate and enrich my life.

For anyone who envies my being a professional photographer and my freedom to roam and to work as I do, who wishes to become a professional "like me," I suggest considering seriously this admonition by André Gide: "To know how to free oneself is nothing; the arduous thing is to know what to do with one's freedom."

As one grows older, one loves the autumn more and more, but
one fears the spring.
—Hermann Hesse

No doubt there is much to be said for so much bold, vibrant, in-your-face beauty. There is also, however, something to be said for other kinds of beauty: quiet beauty, melancholy beauty, mournful, nostalgic beauty—the beauty of fond memories, the beauty of unfolding change, the beauty of mystery, the beauty of yearning, the beauty of accepting and transcending misfortunes and imperfections.

Although for most people the arrival of spring gives rise to hopefulness, to relief from winter's drudgeries, to a sense of renewal, for some, spring is also marked by increased depression and anxiety. The condition known as seasonal affective disorder (SAD), although most often associated with winter, in some cases also arises in other seasons.

Alas, as most people constantly seek reasons to celebrate, my own mind habitually seeks reasons to contemplate and to despair. I can't help it. My sort of happiness comes not from focusing on the positive and ignoring the negative things in the world, but from reframing in meaningful ways the negative things I can't help being mindful of, finding reasons for gratitude and acceptance rather than celebration.

I don't spend as much time outdoors in the winter months as I do in other times. When March arrives in this high desert after several months of winter, temperatures are still cold, and weather can still be unstable. Sunny days are often followed by freezing nights, and the last of the winter storms may still bring snow and ice. Here and there, however, small flower buds and tufts of green begin to show, whispering to the mindful: "It won't be long now." The air is again rich with earthy

scents and the calls of birds. The sun no longer glares for hours at eye-level over
blotted white expanses, but instead, illuminates at steeper angles, defining discrete
areas of light and shade that shift noticeably throughout the day.

Although there are no prolific displays of flowers or vibrant foliage this time of
year, there is, for those who know it, a deep and quiet kind of beauty in anticipating
the imminent arrival of the abundance of spring, in finding small reminders and
reassurances that life is slowly awakening, returning from faraway places, striving to
reclaim, to thrive, and to commune again with other life.

The return of life, always beautiful, never quite the same, is in a sense both
a mirror and a prophecy—a reminder of what is and a harbinger of what is yet to
come. What is, right now, is not just the return of warmer weather but also the
relentless and accelerating march of climate change. What is to come is also—in
truth, always is—change. Watching the way the seasons transition each year, and
how each is different from previous years, points to trends and evidence-based
prognostications. Alas, if the future of this desert is bright, it is because there will be
fewer trees to offer shade, fewer shrubs and grasses to cover the sand, fewer water
pockets to emanate water vapor.

On my recent outings, despite the absence of flowers in bloom, I have found
bees: pollinators unable to feed themselves or to fulfill their age-old role in a now-
broken cycle. By the time the flowers come, they will have fewer insects visiting
them and thus a lesser chance of giving rise to future generations. Such is the ruth-
less nature of evolution by natural selection. The processes that bring about species
in time also extirpate or replace species with better-adapted ones. In this desert, the
better-adapted species, many we consider "noxious" (tumbleweed, tamarisk, Russian
olive, goathead), have already arrived and are rapidly invading new territories.

On my hikes, I've visited some once-perennial water pockets, normally fed by
rain and melted snow, deep enough to hold sufficient water year-round, sustaining
vibrant plant communities. Most are now dry, filled with sand and silt and bovine
excrement, some still surrounded by the dry remnants of reeds, sedges, willows,
even the occasional skeletons of once-mighty ponderosa pines. Soon little evidence
will remain of their former existence here. Mournfully, I still admire their delicate,
graceful beauty, even in death.

In the highland forests of this region, as in most forests in the American West,
many trees are dead or dying from drought, from beetle infestations, from fires. It
was perhaps two decades ago that scientific models began to predict the decline of
aspens and conifers, some predicting the trees' complete devastation within just a
few short decades. Theses prophesies—like most founded in disciplined scientific

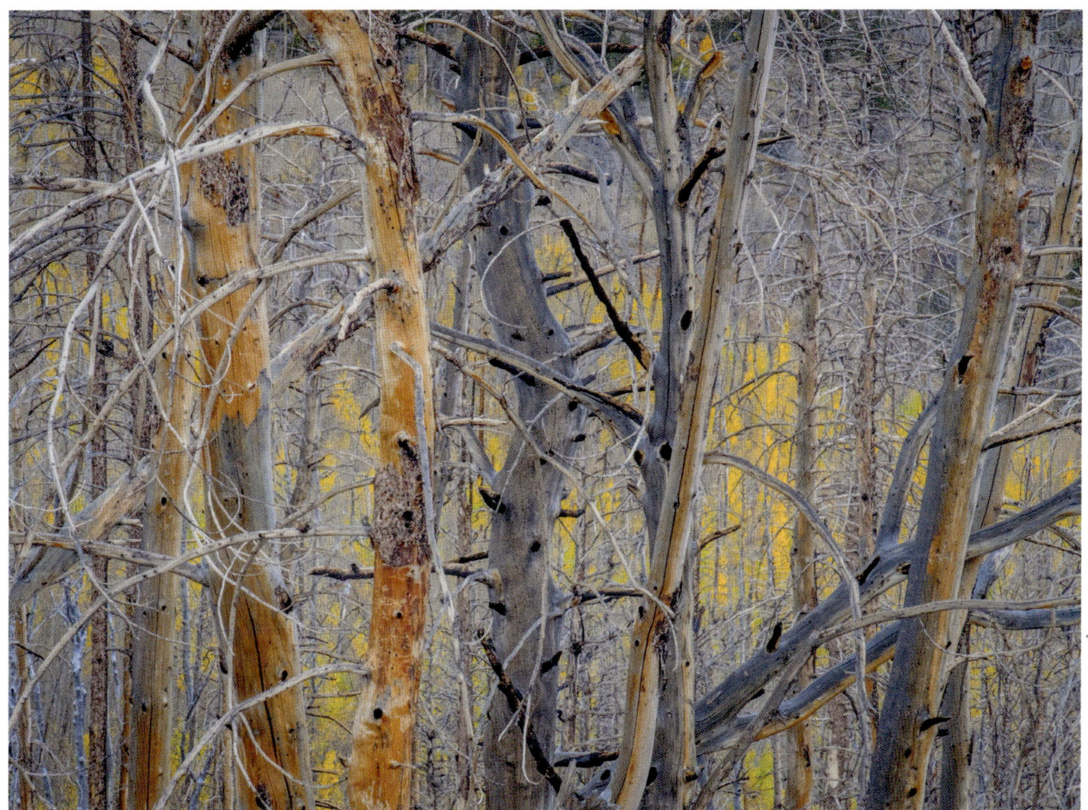

investigation—are now coming true. Much as I try, I find it hard to imagine these places without aspen trees, without pinyon and ponderosa pines, without junipers, without the communities of life that depend on these trees. But I may not need to imagine for much longer. I may experience such changes in my own lifetime.

It is easy when reading some scientific paper predicting environmental decline to accept that such transformation may happen in some far future, in some abstract characterization of Earth as a place where mountains constantly form and erode; climate patterns constantly change; oceans constantly freeze and thaw; continents collide, shift, and subduct. But to see it happening in real time, to notice these changes within the span of a human lifetime, is a different matter.

To see trees I have known—alive and thriving—better and longer than I've known some human friends, now dry, hollowed, broken, or fallen, is cause for mourning. To visit favorite places I have known to harbor grasses, mosses, mushrooms, and delicate flowers, and to find these things absent, is cause for worry and despair. To realize, standing by a sand-filled basin that was once a deep pool where I used to swim on hot summer days, that the air no longer smells of wet earth and the familiar emanations of living and decaying flora, is—in a visceral and undeniable way—jarring and uncomfortable.

Seeing these places as closely and as often as I do, year after year, I struggle to reconcile the glee that some feel about economic growth, about new construction and "development," about increased tourist visitation in once-lonesome places. I understand it. I do. But it also makes me sad. Because I know. I know that this new reality, just like the old reality, is by necessity ephemeral. I know that change is inevitable. I know it's more complicated than just "good" or "bad." I also know better than to tilt at windmills. I savor what there is, when it is, and am grateful to have it, and to have had so much of it, coincide with my own lifetime.

It is in acceptance that sadness turns to beauty—in the acknowledgment that I still have abundant wild spaces available to me to roam in; in the confidence I have that this will likely continue to be the case for what remains of my ever-diminishing lifespan; in the gratitude I feel when I consider that, despite overwhelming odds, I have somehow found a home in this place and got to see it, to know it, to experience it as I have, and as I still do. I now await the flowers. I look forward to another season of camping and hiking, to the mysteries and discoveries still awaiting me in the days and years ahead.

I may not be happy, but I am content and filled with anticipation. And this is really the point: if I had the choice to trade this gratitude, this reverence, this melancholy for some simple and carefree flavor of happiness, I wouldn't. I feel more alive and hopeful being a witness to change—even painful change—than I would feel by any reassuring platitude, no matter how sincere, that "everything" will be OK.

I am a realist. To be a realist is to be unable to set aside the knowledge that "everything" never is, never was, and never will be just OK. Only moments can be OK. Only ephemeral, transient, fleeting experiences can be OK. To be sure, they can also be a great deal more than just OK.

There can be no "new normal" because there was never an "old normal." Normal is not a fixed or lasting state. Normal is dialectic. Normal is change. Normal is transition, evolution, transformation, extinction, creation, flux. Normal is what it is, and "it"—for one who lives mindfully—is always astoundingly, tragically, and by nature, fleetingly beautiful.

Spring is here. The desert is here. I am here.

It is beautiful.

**To chart a course, one must have a direction. In reality, the eye
is no better than the philosophy behind it.**
—Berenice Abbott

As a child, I fell in love with everything wild and natural. Animals, landscapes,
trees, flowers, seashores, deserts, mountains—the more removed from the artifice
of humanity, the better. I spent much of my time in the fields around my home,
observing lizards and insects, learning to identify flowers and birds and the cycles
of nature. I read anything I could get my hands on, about natural places and things
and adventures. I watched with awed fascination the rare documentary film offered
on occasion on the single channel of public television available to me at the time.
With the naïve imagination of a child, I dreamed of growing up to live alone in some
remote jungle, feeding myself on exotic fruit from abundant trees, making friends
with birds and beasts, even learning their language. My childhood dream world was
as rich and vivid and beautiful as anything you can imagine, and I was the only
human being in it.

During my life so far, human population has doubled, and wildlife population
has been cut in half. The correlation is not a coincidence. The trend continues and
even accelerates. Numbers—empirical observations and statistical inferences—tell
us what so many public figures refuse to: there is no "fixing" such things as climate
change, mass extinction, urban sprawl, soil degradation, habitat loss, ocean acidifi-
cation, and so many other related threats.

I now look back across the decades at my childhood dreams with a mix of
agonizing sadness and profound gratitude—sadness for all the loss and suffering,
and for all the beauty never to be seen again; gratitude for what I got to see and

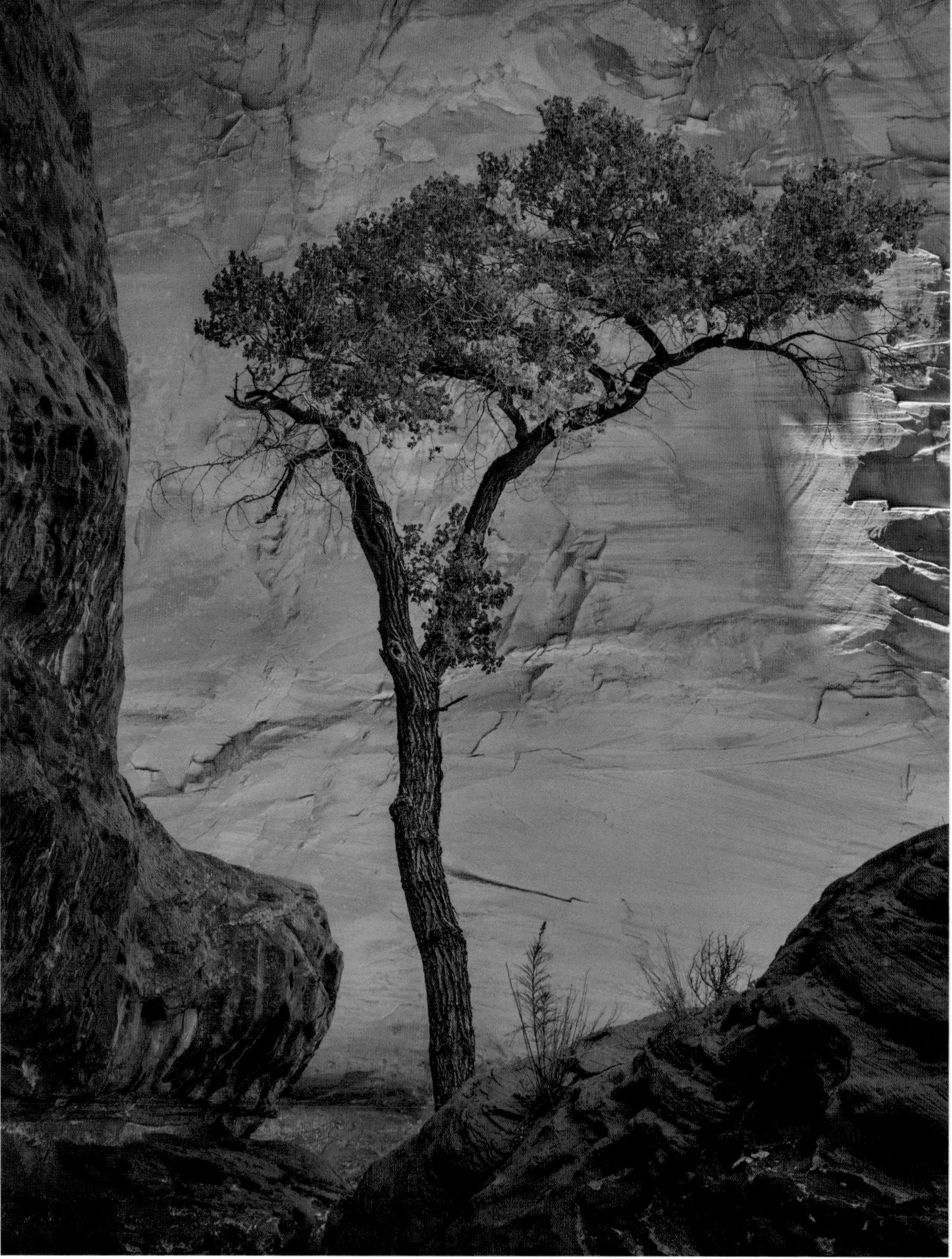

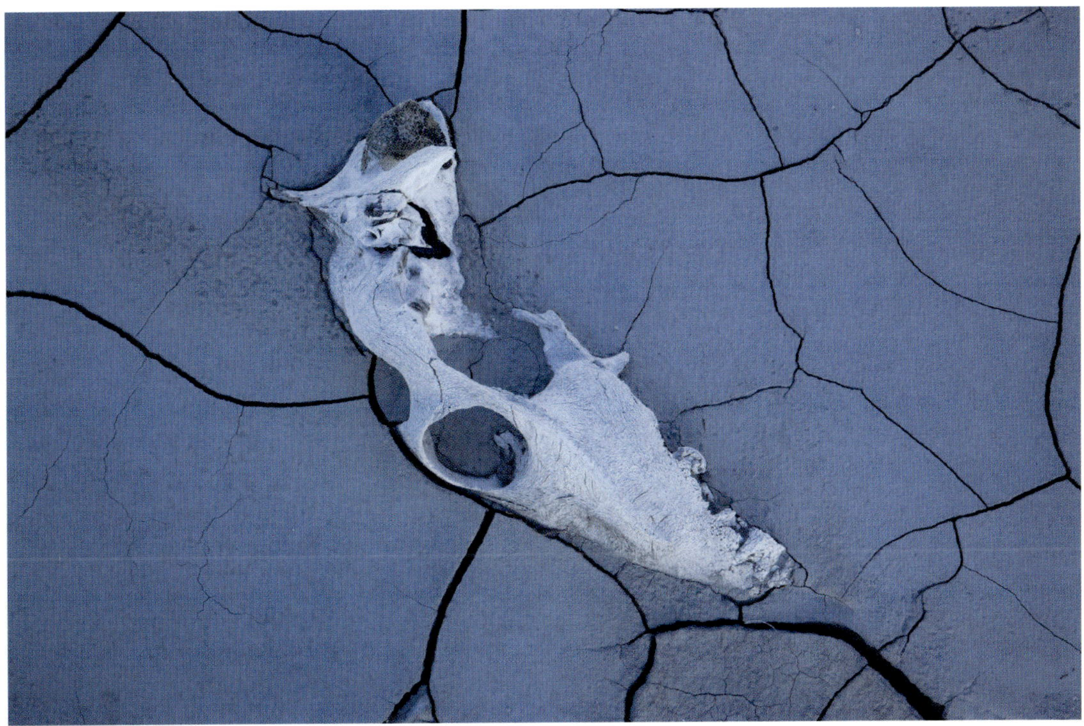

experience, and for the life I have made for myself. My journey was at times arduous and unpredictable, at times beautiful and gratifying, often uncertain, rarely easy, and yet profoundly satisfying. This is because, among so many mixed feelings I have today about the state of the world and the course of my life, one feeling is conspicuously absent: regret.

Unlike so many false prophets, I am not here to offer a message of blissful hope against odds. I have no tips or tricks to help you find some fabled, easily accomplished "next level." I am not rallying for any cause. I have no assurances that "everything" will be OK. Hope is a powerful thing, but like with all powerful things, one must engage in it with caution. This is because hope comes in many flavors, some beautiful and elevating, others seductive but harmful. Of the kinds of hope to be wary of, one that is found in great abundance is false hope—hope for the untenable, hope that cannot be sustained without ignoring one or more inconvenient truths, hope that is not hope at all but self-deception in disguise.

Another flavor of pernicious hope (that is understandably common) is hope as substitute for action: hope regarding things that, while perhaps difficult and risky to accomplish, may still be within reach, but only if pursued actively rather than just hoped-for. This kind of hope easily becomes false hope when detached from action—when people assume some desirable outcome will "just happen, somehow," perhaps by the efforts of other people. The reason to be cautious of this kind of hope is that, if sustained for too long while waiting for some circumstances that likely (or surely) will never come, it ultimately becomes regret.

But some hope is good hope—elevating and motivating hope. One such good hope, that is likely within your power to fulfill, is this: hope that a day will come when, after some years or decades of living, you will be able to look back at your life and know without doubt that you've made the most of whatever gifts and opportunities came your way, even if not always leading to outcomes you hoped for. Where false hope may lead to disappointment and lamentation, this kind of hope—the hope to someday reflect on your life without regret—often leads to a sense of dignity and pride in having proved, if only to yourself, that you have in you the courage and grit to remain true to who you are; to go about the world as you are; to persist through adversities; and to embrace beauty where you find it, without cynicism and jadedness, without need for rationalizations and self-deception.

*   *   *

If, like me, you find meaning and purpose in things wild and natural, and if you are resistant to such things as cognitive dissonance and motivated reasoning, the conclusion is difficult to avoid: your opportunities for wild experiences are diminishing rapidly. I don't wish to discourage you but to do the opposite: to encourage you to consider that, in matters having to do with wildness and natural beauty, certainly in matters having to do with making the most of your living moments, you should not let false hope blind you to real urgency. What you do, or fail to do now, will determine what you may someday look back on with either pride or regret. I encourage you to choose pride.

If you examine scientific evidence and prognostications, if you look beyond false hope, you too may realize that our species is, as United Nations Secretary-General António Guterres put it, "sleepwalking to climate catastrophe." In this light, if you wish to hope for the day of no regret to arrive, you will have to consider your attitude and your actions today. You may become discouraged and unmotivated; you may spend your coming days in jadedness and frustration, bemoaning your misfortune; you may find meaning in fighting for some untenable cause; or you may come to realize that, regardless of what the future may hold, you still have much opportunity for beautiful, meaningful living still available to you today. That is, if you are willing and courageous enough to pursue it.

If you hope that by raising awareness or by promoting some naïve, politically correct, but ultimately ineffective environmental platitudes, you may help humanity "wake" from its indifferent slumber, you will fail. There is simply not enough time, nor the political will, to do what needs to be done to avert catastrophe. But you may still wake yourself to the reality of the world and do what you can today to spare your future self the added catastrophe of regret—the terrifying thought that you have wasted your one and only chance at a meaningful life.

There is no purpose in decrying things being lost if you fail to appreciate these things while they still exist. Dare to hope for something that is neither about "winning" or "losing," nor about slogans or seductive impossibilities. Dare to hope for something that is as noble as any cause or struggle and that is almost certainly possible if you commit yourself to it: hope to someday take pride in having lived a fulfilling—even if difficult—life. Hope to spend as few of your conscious living moments feeling bored, uninspired, cynical, angry, desperate, discontented. But don't just hope—act!

*   *   *

I never believed in long-term plans and have often felt grateful to my younger self for not making them: for not locking me into some preconceived course, no matter how easy or tempting it may have seemed at the time, knowing that the person I will become in time will be wiser, more knowledgeable, and more experienced; and would appreciate as much freedom as I could leave for him to make his own choices.

Photography is among those choices that likely are as safe as any, and that have the capacity to enrich your life. But don't take for granted that photography of natural things will, by necessity, be your creative outlet, your contribution to conservation, your vocation, your therapy, something to "get you out of the house," or any other thing. Certainly, photography can be all those things and more, but in itself it is none of them. If these things are important to you beyond just being rationalizations for spending money on camera gear, you have to choose them decisively, to assimilate them into your life, and to work your hardest to accomplish them.

In proclaiming such things, people often ask: What's wrong with just taking pictures? What's wrong with photography being just a pleasant pastime? Just an entertaining distraction? Just something to do on vacation? Just a means of sharing experiences with others? What's wrong with doing the easy and obvious? These are unproductive and unnecessarily indignant questions. It's not about whether such things are right or wrong in the abstract; it's about whether they are right or wrong *for you*. It's not only about the value you get from practicing photography in certain ways but also about the opportunity cost you forfeit—what you may be giving up, perhaps without even knowing it—by *not* practicing photography in other ways.

*   *   *

Should you realize that limiting your photography to just taking pictures fails to satisfy, and should you decide to see what value there may be in pursuing photography in other, perhaps more difficult and more consequential, ways, you likely will find yourself at a loss for how to get there (if only because you cannot define what "there" is). Realize that your "there" may not be like anyone else's and that you may not learn what your "there" is until you find it. The only way forward requires not so much taking a "leap of faith," but recognizing that certainty is an illusion. In truth, anything you do is a leap of faith. Even if taking a seemingly safe route, you still risk losing much by denying yourself some opportunities. Get in the habit of examining your place, your aspirations, and your opportunities often. Each time you do this, decide what your next step will be, not necessarily where you expect to end up. Many people recite mindlessly that "the journey is the destination" without realizing that this holds true only if one treats the journey as a destination, not as a means to some other destination.

If you wish to become a commercial photographer, a photojournalist, a conservation photographer, a social media star, or anything else, pick a direction and make a step in this direction, not with the naïve belief that you will get exactly what you want, not by following your "bliss" or some other cliché, but with courage and intent, acknowledging you may discover worthier things along the way that you did not even know to aim for.

Of the many directions I explored in photography over the years, art was an accidental discovery for me. I'll give you the sales pitch for art, not because I believe that art is necessarily the best or only worthy direction in photography but because it happens to be a direction I know something about, and because it has transformed my life in ways more spectacular than I knew to hope for during most of my journey.

Of all the purposes that photography can serve, art is a peculiar one, different from the others in some important ways. Those of us committed to photography as a medium for artistic expression generally spend considerably more time and effort practicing our work and honing our knowledge and skills than bickering about it. This is because we don't photograph for the glory of the photographic medium, to justify our membership or ranking within some photographic community, or to "win" any arguments. We photograph primarily for the rewards of engaging in creative work, which are amplified in direct correlation with the amounts of time and effort we invest in our work. Certainly, these rewards are often not financially lucrative, but they are nonetheless extremely valuable. One such reward is freedom to pursue my work when and how I wish, not beholden to any daily routine or to anyone else's opinion about what I should do.

To some, an artist is simply one who makes art. Such a definition is perfectly suitable for those satisfied with artistic work during short-lived reprieves from otherwise less-satisfying pursuits. I tried it. For a long time, I made art on times off from "regular" jobs. While my times photographing were more enjoyable than times in the office, in meetings, or stuck in rush-hour traffic, I still needed a better reason than that to become a full-time professional artist. Convenience and aversion to risk did not seem like sufficient reasons to spend most of my limited supply of living

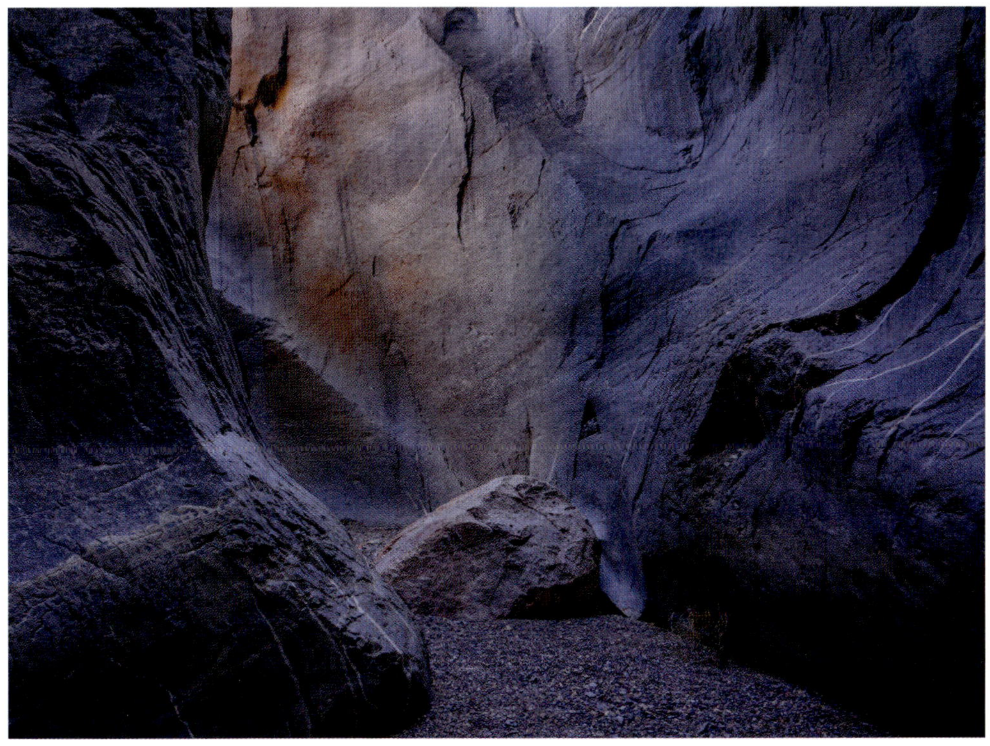

moments in meaningless ways. I didn't want art as a distraction from life; I wanted a life in which such distractions are unnecessary—a life expressed in, and elevated by, art—not a life I felt I needed to escape from by making art.

The kind of artist I aspire to be is not just a person whose purpose is to make beautiful art but a person for whom beautiful art is the byproduct of a beautiful life—a person free to experience powerful emotions and surrender to them without inhibition, who cares deeply and unapologetically about what I do, who doesn't need to tame passion or be concerned with the judgment of others, who is moved to seek and to discover new ways of assimilating and engaging with the world, who revels in gaining knowledge and skills, not in order to compete with others, but because it makes my life more satisfying and makes me a better artist.

My catalog of photographs is not a collection of neatly categorized records of places, things, or events; it is an expression of significant moments in my life story in all its dimensions and nuances, encoded and expressed in visual compositions. When I survey my past work, I don't see pictures of this or that; I relive experiences, reconstitute emotions and memories, see the path I've charted, one decision at a time, with no preconceived goal, through the intricate tapestry of all that a life can be. I'm reminded of times of metaphorical—not just literal—light and darkness. I recall sensations, thoughts, emotions, and doubts. I project myself into moments of joy among days of despair. I revisit hard-won lessons and random epiphanies. I sometimes re-examine my priorities, in life and in art. Usually, I don't remember what camera I used.

My life as an artist may not be easy, but it is beautiful to me. I get to say that with a straight face, not as a platitude but as a statement of fact. I can't say the same about any other life I've tried.

In a letter to his son, Sherwood Anderson wrote, "The object of art is not to make salable pictures. It is to save yourself." If you believe the life of an artist is for you, if your art is founded in things wild and natural, and if you are prepared for the challenges, make a step in this direction. You may realize some years from now that, even though you couldn't save the world, you may have saved yourself.

What do you wish to do next? Whatever it is, don't wait. Take your bearings, pick a direction, and take a step. Whatever step you take, it will put you in a better position to decide the next one, and the one after that. Unlike so many grandiose plans, taking just one step in the direction of your hopes, even if rife with fear and uncertainty, even at the risk of breaking with others' expectations or inherited allegiances, is within your power.

My Important Way 33

The most important step in emancipating oneself from social controls is the ability to find rewards in the events of each moment.
—Mihaly Csikszentmihalyi

I confess to feeling awkward these days, as I suspect many do, writing about photography, art, and qualities of experience as momentous events unfold in the world. These may seem petty considerations in a time when the very forces of nature are conspiring to threaten the existence of the human species. But there is also a sense in which celebrating beauty and inspiration may be even more important in such times than in others. Anxiety about the future may serve to remind one of the importance of considering the finite nature of life and the wisdom of not taking anything for granted. While such reminders may be prompted by worries and difficulties, their true value is in realizing that they remain every bit as important even without the difficulties that may force them to the surface.

I am writing again from a campsite in the desert. It is November, in the latter days of the autumn season, when much of the life in this desert usually falls dormant before winter sets in. Yet several species of plants that normally flower in the spring months are attempting to bloom. I am enough of a naturalist to recognize that this is not normal and that there is reason for alarm. But I am also not one to pass up an opportunity to stick my nose into a flowering sand verbena or cliffrose. To do otherwise seems not only to deny myself a moment of bliss but also to rudely decline a great gift.

Psychologist Mihaly Csikszentmihalyi passed away recently, which is perhaps as good a reason as any to mention his work on flow—his theory of optimal experience.

The basic premise of flow is that any activity having the power to consume a person's attention entirely, if approached with the right attitude, may become autotelic—rewarding in its own right. Csikszentmihalyi described the experience of flow, resulting from being immersed completely in an autotelic experience, as "the state in which people are so involved in an activity that nothing else seems to matter; the experience itself is so enjoyable that people will do it even at great cost, for the sheer sake of doing it."

There are some photographers for whom the process of making photographs is autotelic and some for whom it is not. This explains why some photographers find sufficient reward in just being out with a camera, immersed in creative thought and experimentation, whereas others may consider photography less rewarding, perhaps not even worth pursuing, without additional rewards like popularity, awards, sales, or being part of a community. Creativity researcher Teresa Amabile of Harvard Business School described the former group—those who find sufficient reward in engaging in an activity for its own sake—as driven primarily by *intrinsic* motivations and the latter group as driven primarily by *extrinsic* rewards. In a paper titled "Creativity and the Labor of Love," Amabile defined intrinsic motivation simply as "the drive to engage in a task because it is interesting," in contrast to extrinsic rewards, which she defined as "reward offered by someone else." Based on her research, Amabile believes there is a link between motivation and creativity, and concluded that "people will be more creative when they are motivated primarily by the interest, enjoyment, satisfaction, and challenge of the work itself—and not by extrinsic motivators or constraints."

The link between creativity and intrinsic motivation has to do, among other things, with the fact that creative work requires experimentation and may not yield an outcome that another person may relate to or offer reward for. Some may even criticize or be offended by creative work that departs too far from common norms. There are also cases in which successful creative ideas may not win any recognition from peers and contemporaries within the lifetime of the creator. In such cases, even if a person finds some initial intrinsic reward in creative work, this motivation may erode over time if that person works toward extrinsic recognition that fails to materialize. This perhaps explains why, in this era of social media, when so many become obsessed to the point of addiction with constant feedback, judgment, celebrity, and peer approval, creativity in developed countries is diminishing measurably.

The distinction between the primacy of intrinsic versus extrinsic rewards in driving a photographer's work occurred to me recently during an email exchange with a photographer who was preparing to travel to Yellowstone National Park. This

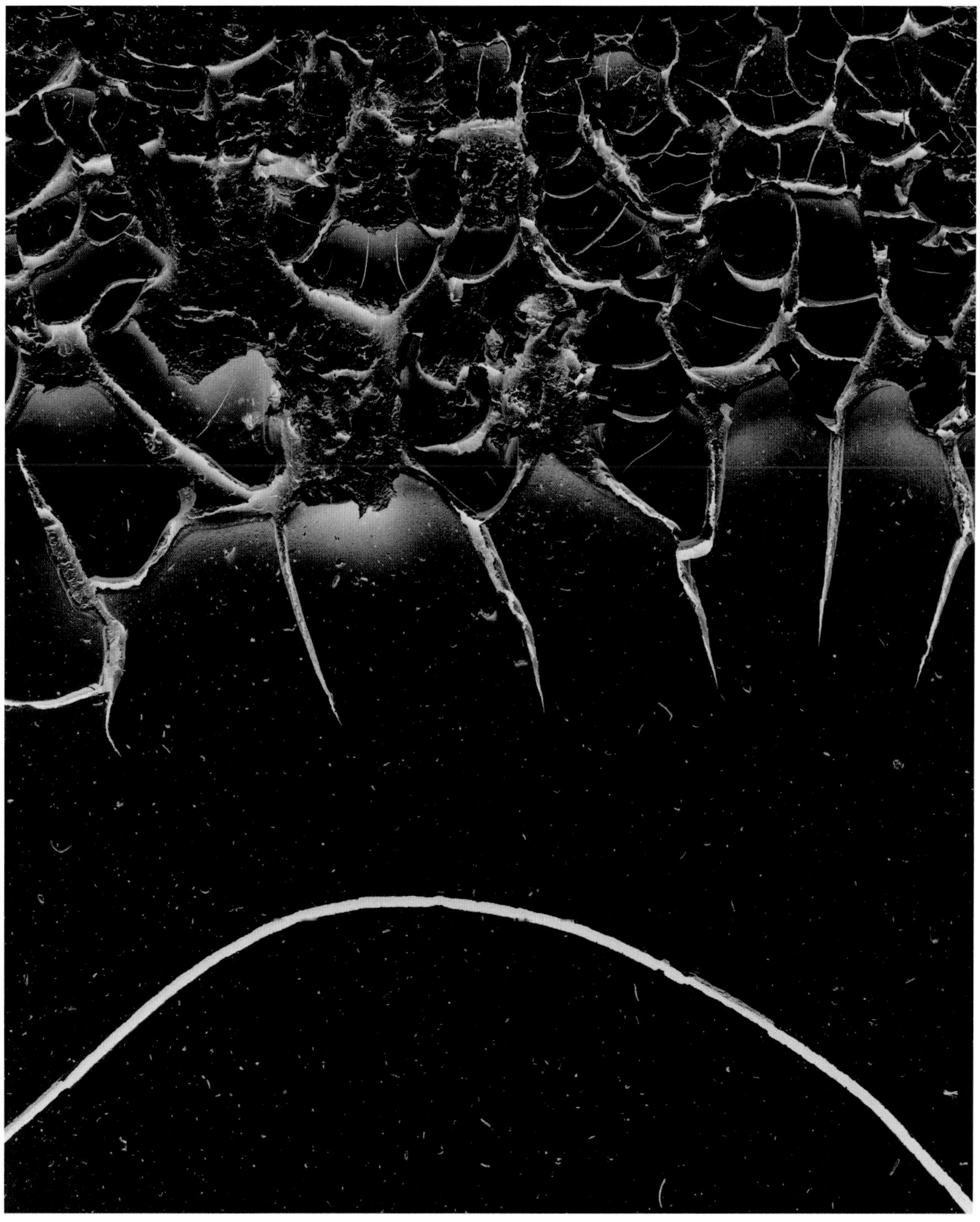

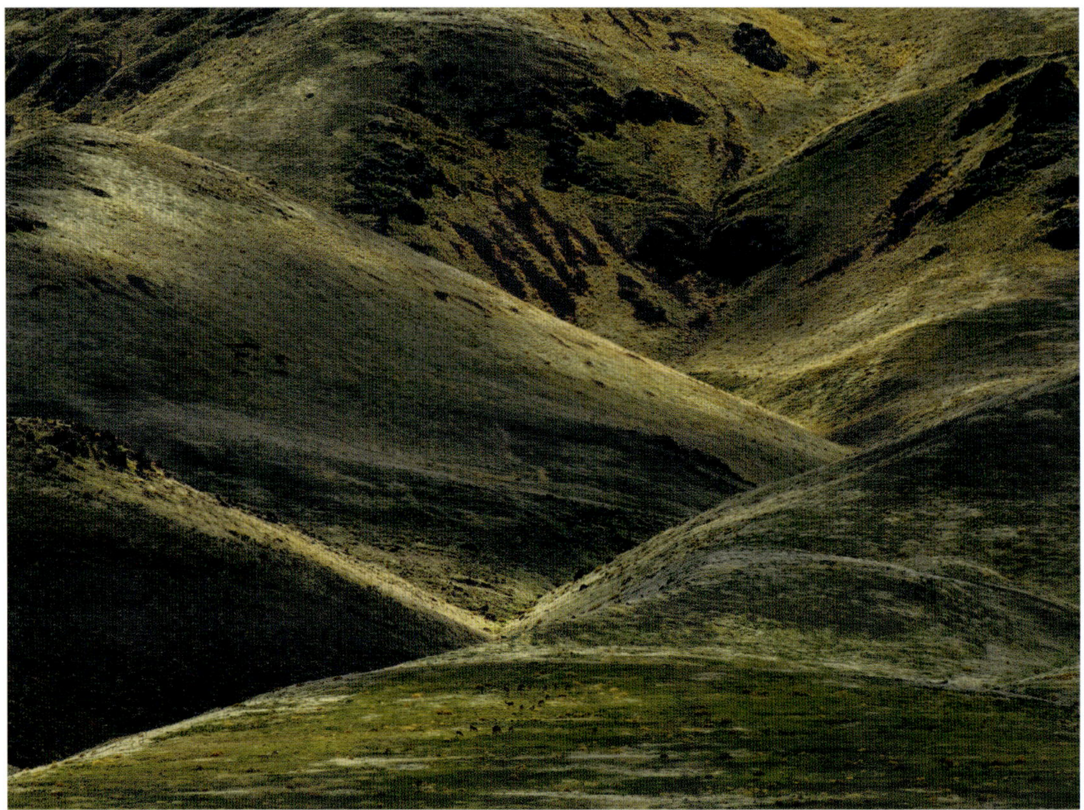

photographer expressed concern about the crowds in the park. I suggested to her some alternative destinations where crowds may not be a concern. She conceded that she may enjoy herself more in these places and then added in exasperation, "but I'm a wildlife photographer," as if referring to an incurable disability rather than to an ostensibly enjoyable and voluntary activity.

The self-defeating nature of relying primarily on extrinsic rewards in any endeavor extends beyond diminishing the value of pursuing creative work. Put bluntly, to rely on extrinsic rewards is to cede to other people control of one's happiness and sense of meaning in life. Why not choose instead to consider intrinsic rewards more important? Why not choose to free yourself creatively, and in so doing, also gain the benefits of becoming more confident, more self-sufficient, less anxious, and more creative?

The importance of artistic work may be considered objectively or subjectively. The subjective view of deciding for oneself what is important and meaningful,

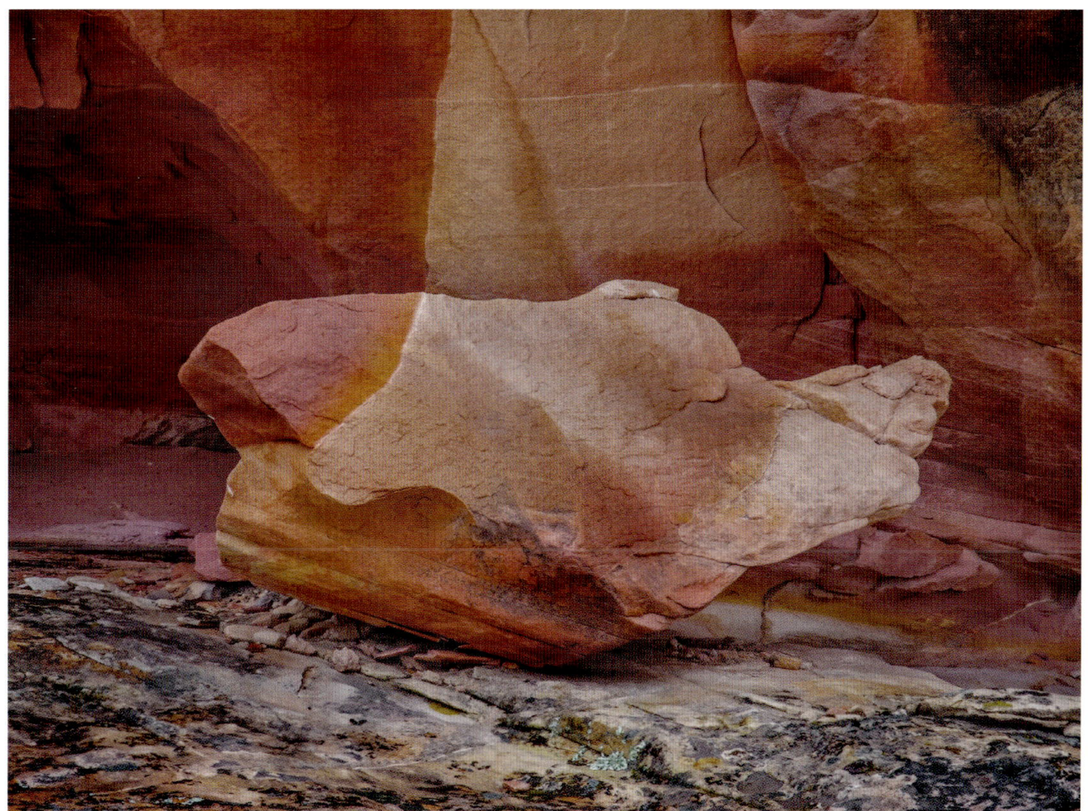

taking control of one's own sense of value in life and in artistic work, is obvious. The objective view may be less so. Describing the objective view of artistic importance, David Galenson wrote, "Important artists are innovators whose work changes the practices of their successors; important works of art are those that embody these innovations." Considering that innovation is the result of creativity and creativity is linked with intrinsic motivation, we may conclude that the objective view, like the subjective view, also suggests that an artist is more likely to produce important work when motivated intrinsically.

Suppose I've convinced you that intrinsic rewards are worth prioritizing above extrinsic ones. Now what? Driven purely by the desire to experience flow in creative work, one may become stymied in trying to decide what work may be most rewarding and important, and therefore worth investing one's time, effort, and creative energy in. The question occurred to Edward Weston, who worked with various

subjects and styles during his career and came to wonder which of them may ultimately be worthiest.

In *The Daybooks of Edward Weston*, the photographer pondered, "When I work
in the field with rocks, trees, what not, I think that this is my important way: then
comes a period of 'still-life' which excites me equally." He then concluded (correctly,
in my opinion) that "the best way is not to theorize, but do whatever I am impelled
to do at the moment." There is no telling at the outset whether a great creative
breakthrough may be possible in one subject that will later prove more important
than whatever progress one might achieve in a different subject. On the other hand,
any activity that is autotelic is always rewarding, sometimes to the point of flow—an
optimal experience—independent of any outcome or later judgment of importance.

Referring to my exchange with the photographer who felt implicitly entrapped
in her characterization of herself as a "wildlife photographer," I think that, by the
same token, such categories as "landscape photographer," "film photographer,"
"black-and-white photographer," or "documentary photographer" should not be
treated as incurable handicaps or as creative fetters. If the muse calls, in whatever
direction, it is best to heed it. Inspiration and creative energy are rare and valuable—and autotelic—enough in their own right, that one would be a fool to refuse
them, regardless of labels or personal styles or any other category one may try to fit
into. A moment of creative bliss, no matter what medium it manifests in, is always
worth experiencing, certainly more so than any experience that may seem tedious
or uninspired in comparison.

This is not to say that one should fall into the trap of hedonism. As many studies show, excessive hedonic behavior leads, ultimately, to misery and dissatisfaction
due to the effect known as hedonic adaptation. By comparison, hard work, when
applied to autotelic activities, as well as traits such as kindness, compassion, and
generosity, all pay dividends in happiness and sense of self-worth even if involving
considerable degrees of effort and discomfort.

When I read Weston's musings about his "important way," I felt compelled to
wonder what my important way is. Without intending any disrespect to Weston, I
think he was a bit myopic in his characterization of importance strictly in terms of
photographic work, or even in terms of photography itself. Photography is important
to me, but by itself it is at best just one means to "my important way," not the way
itself. When considering the effect of flow and the nature of experiences that may
lead to flow, in the context of the finite and diminishing count of living moments I
may yet have, I think that the only "important way" is to strive to experience flow

and meaning in as many of my remaining experiences as I can, whether or not they involve photography.

Wherever there is contention between work—artistic or other—and having a meaningful experience, to the degree that one has a say in the matter, I believe that work, not experience, must be the wild card. Experiences are the building blocks of life. If making a popular and lucrative photograph requires that one eschew more elevated and personally meaningful experiences, even if yielding no product, then I say: to hell with that photograph. As Nobel laureate Thomas Mann put it, "The important thing for me, then, is not the 'work,' but my life. Life is not the means for the achievement of an esthetic ideal of perfection; on the contrary, the work is an ethical symbol of life."

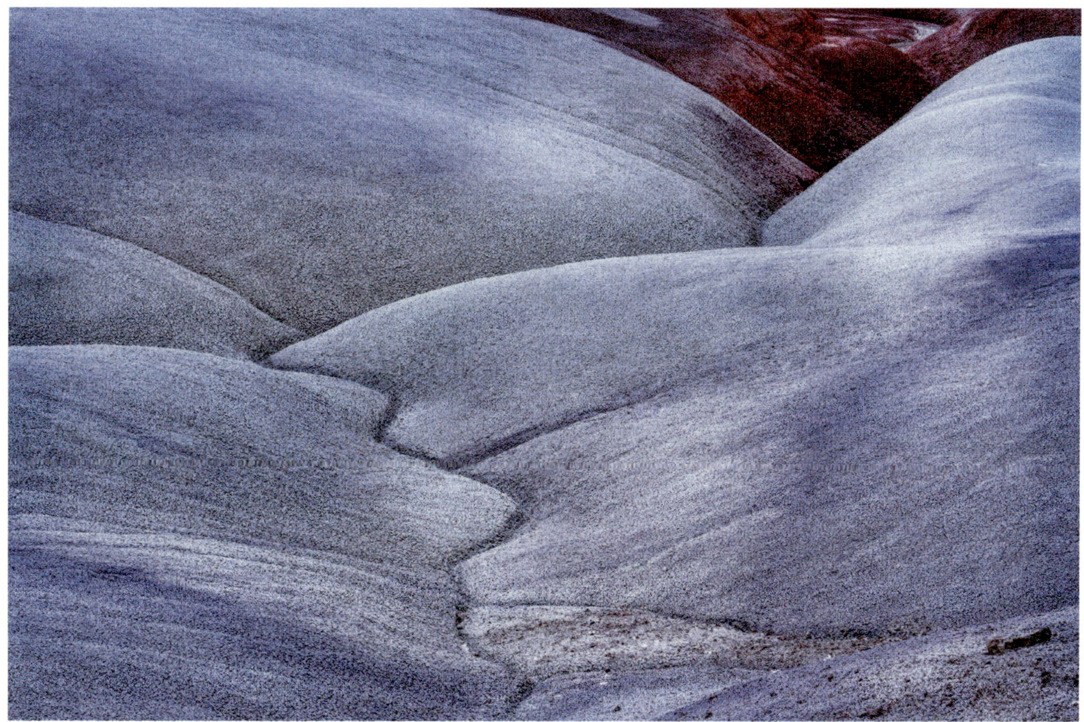

34 The Deed and the Glory

I don't photograph when teaching workshops. My temperament is such that I can't
produce meaningful work when other people are present, when I can't take prolonged time to become mindful, to contemplate the nuances of my surroundings
and my inner experience, to consider creative possibilities. Certainly, I can make
beautiful, successful photographs without these things, but such photographs would
be meaningless and unsatisfying to me. As such, my favorite times when leading
photography workshops are those spent in the classroom, especially when conversations drift beyond the scripted material to more philosophical topics related to
living and working as an artist. One such recent conversation centered on the topic
of success.

Discussions of success often revolve around how one defines the term. This
time, however, the conversation started when one of the participants asked a different question: How do you know you have achieved success? Thinking about success
in these terms—reflecting on past experiences rather than aiming for future accomplishments—proved revealing. My response (paraphrased from imperfect memory)
was this: some days, especially when out in a remote natural place, reveling in peace
and beauty, conscious of and grateful for my good fortune to be able to be where
I am, to do what I do, feeling inspired, even awed, recognizing that these are not
fortuitous anecdotes but the theme to my everyday life—or even just the memory of
such experiences—I feel I have succeeded.

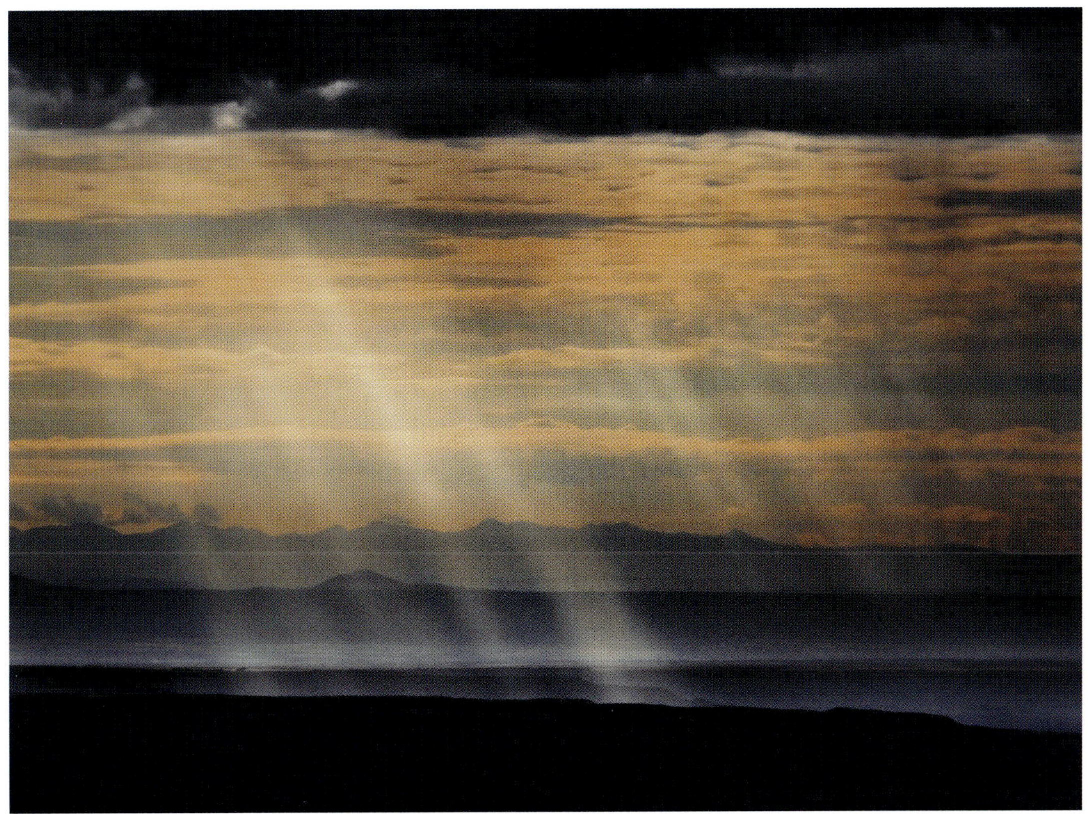

Most people think about achieving success as a forward-looking progression: first define what success is, then design a strategy to accomplish success, and finally, congratulate yourself if you have succeeded in what you set out to do (or wallow in self-recriminations and doubts about your self-worth if you haven't). This strategy has never worked for me. Even in times when I set grandiose goals for myself and managed to achieve them, I didn't experience the elation that most people expect to feel when achieving success. On the other hand, when reflecting on my life—the things I got to see and experience, the improbable and turbulent path I took to get where I am—I take pride not only in finding success but also in learning—by experimentation, by occasional failure, by coincidences and serendipity—what success means to me, which I could not have known until after I had found it.

Recalling some job interviews I've had in former lives, I remember my difficulty answering such trite questions as, "Where would you like to be in five years?" Of course, at the time I made up a contrived answer having to do with professional

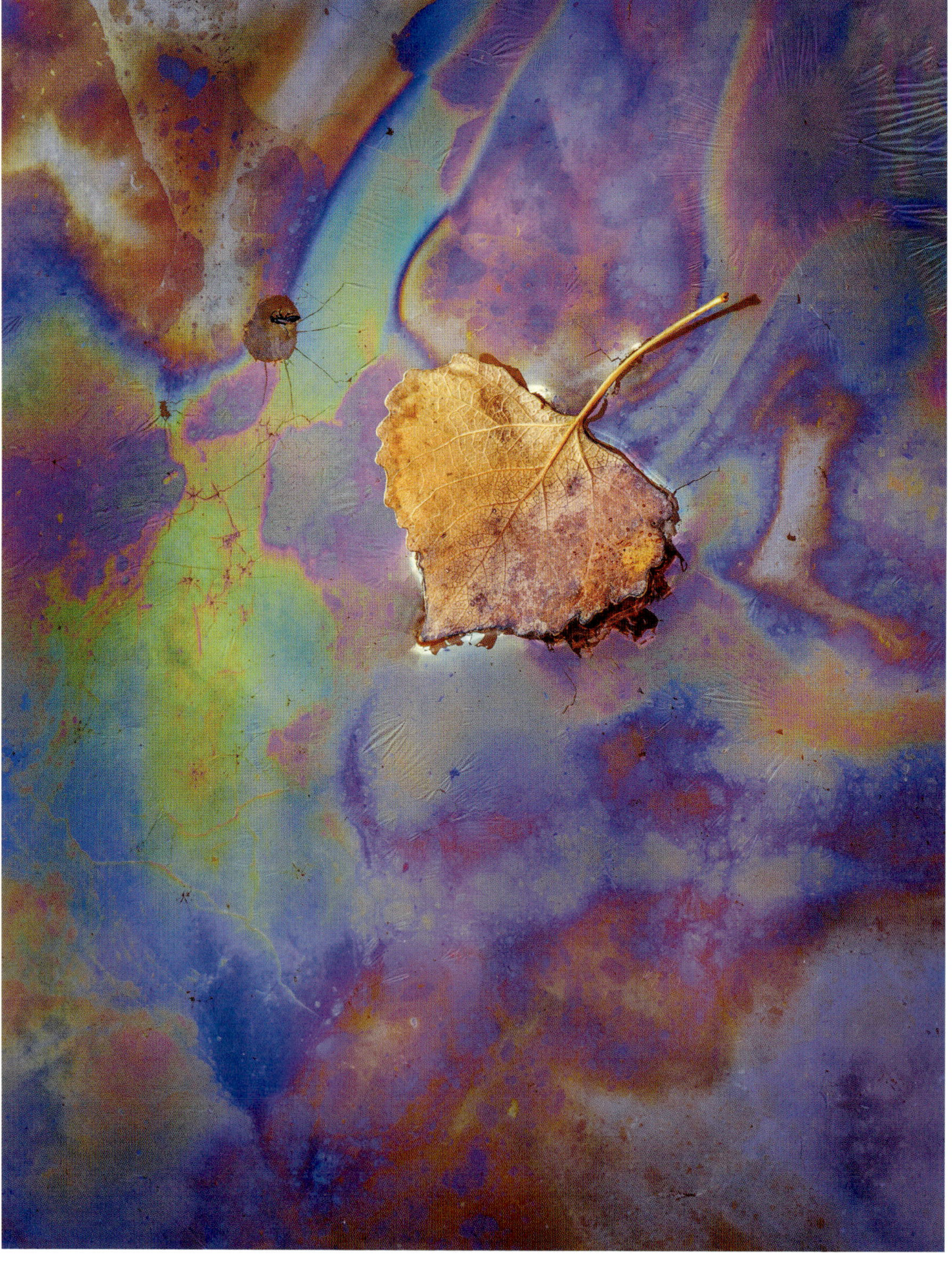

aspirations: a feigned desire for more senior titles, greater responsibilities, higher pay. Still, as my mind was attempting to formulate this answer, I would also hear a voice within me answering inaudibly but earnestly, "I would like to earn my living doing something more interesting than working here," "I would like to spend more time outdoors," "I would like to have more free time," "I would like to be my own boss," "I would like to decide each day how to best spend my time," "I would like to learn more about science, philosophy, and art," "I would like to live in a beautiful place, close to nature." Although I could not have predicted it at the time, I have, in fact, succeeded in all these things. It took considerably longer than five years. For much of that time, it never occurred to me that I may find this success by becoming an artist. For most of that time, I didn't know what being an artist meant, or would come to mean, for me.

Over the years, I have heard many accounts of professional photographers lamenting that the reality of their lives is different from what they thought being a professional would be like—that the need to make an income in photography has made it a less enjoyable and less creative pursuit. This has not been my experience. Before becoming a professional, I imagined it to mean being able to spend as much of my time outdoors as I wanted, photographing almost any time I wanted to, having more time to pursue personal interests, and learning to make do with less income than I had in my former corporate career. In my case, this is exactly what becoming a professional turned out to be. That may sound like a success story, but what I couldn't know in advance is that this was just the first chapter.

What I couldn't foresee when deciding to take the proverbial plunge into professional photography was that these accomplishments in themselves would turn out to be means, not ends—means for discovering greater ends than I knew, or could have known, are possible. What I couldn't know was how living as an artist, spending more time outdoors, investing more time in experiences and in pursuit of personal interests, and making do with less income would shape me as a person.

My true measure of success as I consider it today is not any goal I had set for myself in advance, nor any anecdotal accomplishment I might list on a professional CV. My true measure of success is to live, and to have lived, a considerable portion of my life as an artist, scholar, and explorer—the things I get to experience and to learn, the constant and oft-rewarded anticipation of greater knowledge and unforeseen discoveries, my joy in communing frequently with wild places and wild lives, my daily doses of inspiration, beauty, and creative challenges. All these things upon reflection have this in common: so long as I can sustain them, their value to me will not diminish one iota if nobody else even knows I have accomplished them. In the words of Johann Wolfgang von Goethe, "The deed is everything, the glory nothing."

I believe many people set themselves up for disappointment by pursuing some form of glory—fame, wealth, prizes. If I had tried to define success in such terms before embarking on my artistic journey years ago, I likely would have been much poorer today if all I had managed to achieve was exactly what I set out to do. It's no wonder that so many who achieve such preconceived notions of success find themselves unsatisfied, even if successful by their own prematurely decided definition.

Certainly, I find pride and satisfaction when learning that my work, writings, and experiences have been useful to others. I must concede that, although a wonderful bonus, this was never a goal I pursued explicitly. I mention this hoping it may allay whatever guilt or concern may plague those who feel it must be their priority to be of service, to fall in line with (or at least avoid upsetting) some tradition, or to bind themselves to other people's notions of propriety. Robert Henri was correct in observing, "Your only hope of satisfying others is in satisfying yourself." This, of course, is not inevitable, but it is a likely consequence of leading by example: doing your best according to your own sensibilities, in whatever way suits your unique talents and temperament, within the opportunities available to you, and in doing so, also helping others discover what may be satisfying to them and demonstrating that it is not impossible.

Rather than hoping for glory by aiming for known goals, I believe that art can be more satisfying as a means of discovering things about yourself—the kind of person you are, the kind of things that bring you joy and satisfaction in accordance with your own personality and philosophy, learning what success means to you, if only to you alone. As jazz pianist Bill Evans noted, "Through art you can be shown part of yourself you never knew existed."

You may learn, as I have, that success measured by some form of glory—trophies, milestones, riches, or some other forms of "notches on your belt"—is much less satisfying, and much more ephemeral, than the rewards of everyday living according to your nature: doing what is interesting and meaningful to you; pursuing experiences, sensations, and contemplations for their own sake and not for any measurable outcome.

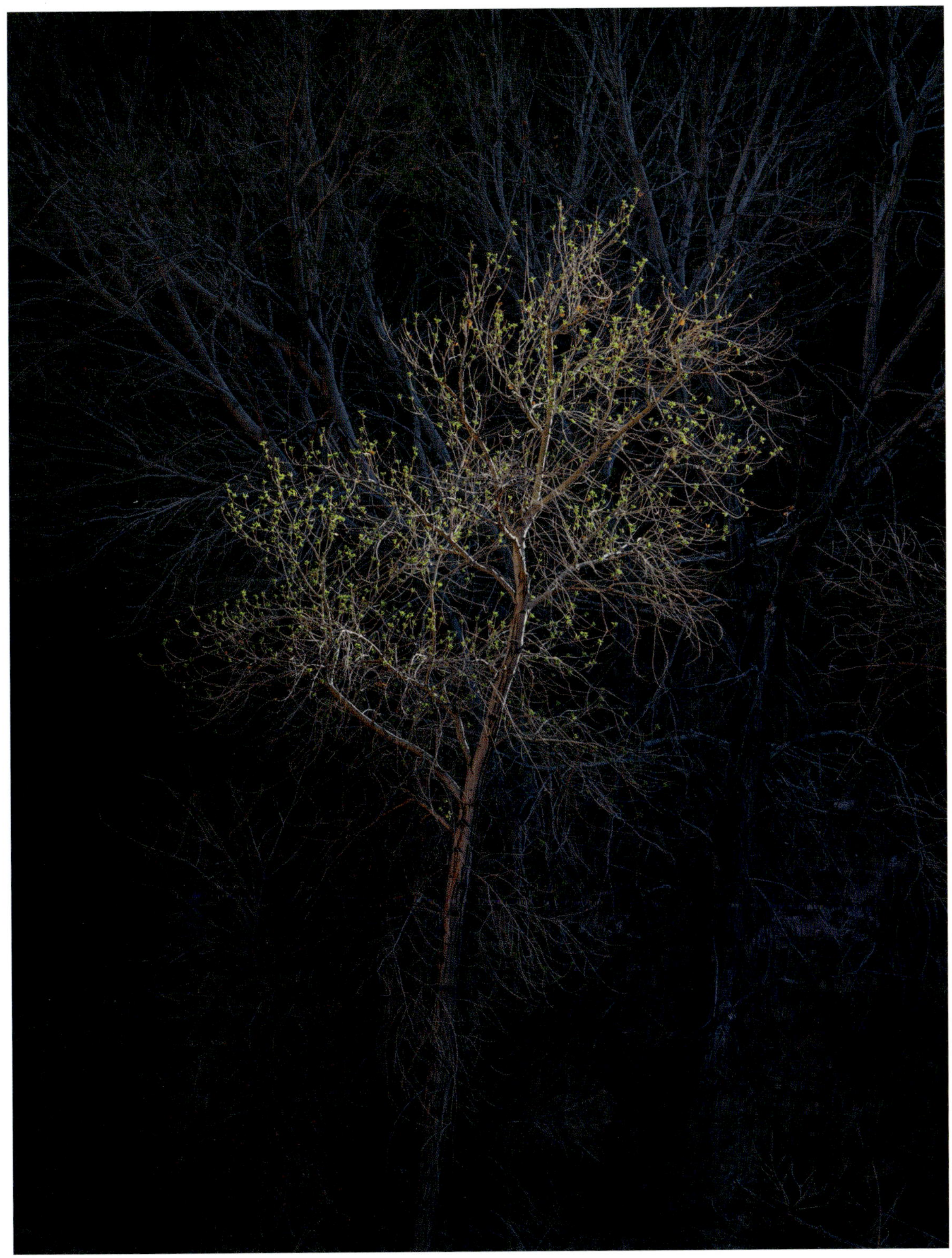

About the Author

As a professional artist and writer, I believe that the practice of creative pursuits not only manifests in the making of art, but also has the ability to enrich life, foster meaningful experiences and contentment, and bring healing through life-long discovery and adventure.

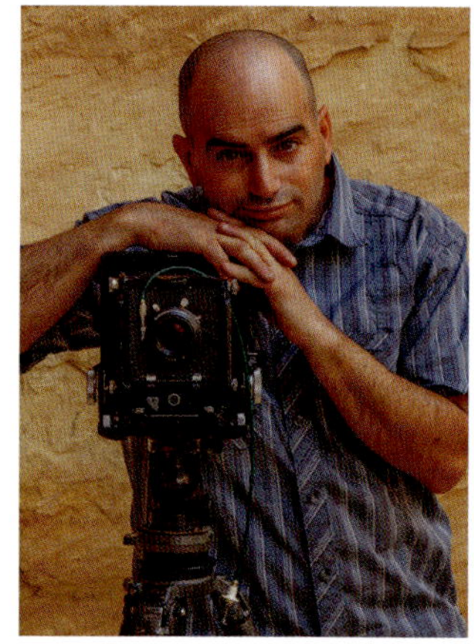

I wish to create images that convey my connection with the wild places of the American West. My images are the result of a complex relationship with these lands that has evolved over many years—through times of bliss and conflict, love and loss, and life changes. In my images, I seek to convey a reverence and gratitude for how these places have shaped my life. My subjects are not just attractive models to me, they are friends and sanctuaries and characters in my own story. I do not consider myself a photographer who creates art, but rather an artist working in the medium of photography.

My work has been featured in various publications, including *LensWork Magazine*, PHOTOGRAPH, *Outdoor Photographer*, *Popular Photography*, *Digital Photographer*, *Landscape Photography Magazine*, *PhotoLife*, and *On Landscape*, among others.

Guy Tal
www.guytal.com